Workers' Compensation in Ontario Handbook

Garth Dee
B. Math., LL.B.

Nick McCombie
Vice-Chair
Workplace Safety and Insurance Appeals Tribunal

Gary Newhouse
B.A., LL.B.

Toronto and Vancouver

Workers' Compensation in Ontario Handbook
© Butterworths Canada Ltd. 1999
October 1999

The Butterworth Group of Companies

Canada:

75 Clegg Road, MARKHAM, Ontario L6G 1A1
and
1732-808 Nelson St., Box 12148, VANCOUVER, B.C. V6Z 2H2

Australia:

Butterworths Pty Ltd., SYDNEY

Ireland:

Butterworth (Ireland) Ltd., DUBLIN

Malaysia:

Malayan Law Journal Sdn Bhd, KUALA LUMPUR

New Zealand:

Butterworths of New Zealand Ltd., WELLINGTON

Singapore:

Butterworths Asia, SINGAPORE

South Africa:

Butterworth Publishers (Pty.) Ltd., DURBAN

United Kingdom:

Butterworth & Co. (Publishers) Ltd., LONDON

United States:

Michie, CHARLOTTESVILLE, Virginia

Canadian Cataloguing in Publication Data

Dee, Garth
  Workers' compensation in Ontario handbook

Includes index.
ISBN 0-433-42204-1

1. Workers' compensation — Law and legislation — Ontario.   I. McCombie, Nick.   II. Newhouse, Gary.   III. Title.

KE0689.D44 1999	344.713'021	C99-932077-7
KF3615.D44 1999		

Printed and bound in Canada.

Preface

In November 1987, Butterworths first published *Workers' Compensation in Ontario*. At that time, it was the first work in Ontario to take an in-depth look at a subject that had a huge impact on the lives and fortunes of hundreds of thousands of Ontario workers and employers.

In 1993, rather than producing a second edition, hardcover book, it was determined that a looseleaf service, with periodic updates, was necessary to keep readers abreast of constantly changing policy and law. The result was the *Butterworths Workers' Compensation in Ontario Service* (looseleaf).

Since 1993, there have again been major changes to workers' compensation legislation. The number of decisions by the Workplace Safety and Insurance Appeals Tribunal (formerly the Workers' Compensation Appeals Tribunal) has more than doubled since 1993. There has been an increase in the importance of Board policy, since the coming into force of Bill 99 in January 1998. Benefits, entitlement, time limits, assessment policy; all these areas – and more – have undergone huge changes.

The current work is intended to give the lay reader as accurate and objective an overview as possible of the state of workers' compensation law, policy and procedure in Ontario at the end of the 20th century.

This work, like the previous ones, has made every attempt to present the material in an impartial fashion. However, the express or implied opinions, the inclusions and exclusions presented, and the emphasis given are those of the authors and do not necessarily represent the views of any organization. In particular, these opinions should not be taken to represent the official view of the Workplace Safety and Insurance Board or the Workplace Safety and Insurance Appeals Tribunal.

We would like to acknowledge the wealth of assistance provided by friends, co-workers and sometime adversaries who have turned workers' compensation into a legitimate and dynamic area of law and social policy.

Finally, we would like to dedicate this work to the late Nicole Godbout, who was one of those friends and colleagues whose inquiring mind, relentless pursuit of justice for injured workers and good humour provided us all with so much.

Garth Dee
Nick McCombie
Gary Newhouse

October 1999

Table of Contents

Chapter 8: Compensation for Occupational Disease

Chapter 9: Mental and Behavioural Disorders

Chapter 14: Permanent Disability Benefits

Chapter 15: Pension Supplements for Pre-January 2, 1990 Claims

Chapter 16: Future Economic Loss Benefits

Chapter 20: Survivors' Benefits

Chapter 21: Labour Market Re-Entry Services

Chapter 22: Re-Employment

Chapter 23: Employer Duties and Assessments

Appendices

CHAPTER 1

A Short History of Workers' Compensation

It is felt, and very properly, that in many cases the imperfect protection af-
forded to workmen is simply a question of money, and there is no reason why
the employer's profit should prevail against the employees' injury.

("Editorial", *Globe*, Toronto, February 25, 1886:4.)

1. ORIGINS

In modern times, the pressure to financially compensate workers who have received injury or disease by virtue of their employment has flowed from two
main sources: social insurance principles and a replacement for common law
right of action. In continental Europe, the source was more the former, while in
Great Britain, the United States and Canada, the latter was a far greater influence on the development of workers' compensation statutes.

Workers' compensation had its first modern incarnation in Imperial Germany
in the 1880s. In an attempt to undermine the influence of a growing socialist
movement, the German Reichstag, under Chancellor Otto von Bismarck, passed
a variety of measures designed to forestall the growing popularity of the political
program of the Social Democrats. Among these pieces of social legislation was
a compulsory, state-run accident fund. The money for this fund was to come
from workers and employers.

In Britain, the history of workers' compensation developed more as a response to the very real impediments that had arisen in attempts by workers to
recover damages from their employers in common law actions. A series of court
decisions in the early nineteenth century established potent defences for employers being sued by their workers. These decisions resulted in three doctrines
which were used to successfully thwart claims:

(a) Contributory Negligence: Under the doctrine of contributory negligence,
     established in the 1809 case of *Butterfield v. Forrester*, a defendant em-
     ployer could escape judgment if it could be established that the injured
     worker had contributed in any way at all to the mishap, even if such a
     contribution was minor.

(b) Fellow Servant/Common Employment: In 1837, the case of *Priestley v.
     Fowler* established that an employer was not responsible for accidents

caused by a co-worker. It was therefore necessary that the employer be found directly responsible for the accident. Needless to say, most employers were not directly involved in the work process and were therefore exempt from action.

(c)   Assumption of Risk: The final hook that employers could hang their hats on was the doctrine that held that when a worker accepted a job, he or she understood that there were certain inherent risks entailed therein. So, for example, a miner should assume that the job he was performing might well entail the risk of cave-ins. Having assumed that risk at the outset of the job, he should therefore have made his own financial arrangements for himself and his family in the event of an accident.

These three defences — designated as the "unholy trinity" — combined with the prohibitive costs of litigation for most nineteenth-century workers to ensure that very few work-related disabilities were compensated.

The first attempts to deal with these problems were undertaken in 1880 with the *Employers' Liability Act* of Britain and 1886 with the *Workmen's Compensation for Injuries Act* of Ontario. These laws attempted to ameliorate the worst aspects of the "unholy trinity" for plaintiffs bringing action. However, while these Acts did tend to lessen the burden of proof for injured workers, they maintained financial limits on employer liability, placed time limits on bringing actions and severely limited the amount of damages recoverable.

From the employers' point of view, these Acts opened the door for an increased chance of lawsuit, and those few suits that were successful often resulted in an unexpected expense which could result in bankruptcy. But more importantly, in the early years of the twentieth century, there was an increased public pressure to totally revamp the system by which injured workers could recover damages for work-related disabilities.

This pressure was no doubt enhanced by developments in Great Britain where the passage of the *Workmen's Compensation Act* occurred in 1897. The significance of this change in Britain was that it replaced a compensation law based on negligence principles with one based on no-fault insurance principles.

By 1912, an American observer, F.H. Bohlen, wrote:

> Within the last few years, particularly within the last two, there has been a complete change in the attitude of public opinion. There are now in force in no fewer than ten states acts by which the owner of a business is made to bear a part of the loss resulting to his workmen from injuries received by them in his service, whether due to a defect in the conditions or operations of the business or not, or to insure his workmen at least partially against such loss. Nor has this movement spent its force: on the contrary, the impulse towards such legislation seems stronger than ever.

2. THE MEREDITH REPORT

This wave of reform did not leave Ontario unscathed. In 1910, the Conservative Premier, J.P. Whitney, appointed the Chief Justice of Ontario, Sir William Ralph Meredith, to study workers' compensation schemes and make recommendations to his government. The rather wordy title of Meredith's study explains his mandate: *Laws Relating to the Liability of Employers to make Compensation to their Employees for Injuries Received in the Course of their Employment which are in Force in Other Countries.*

Meredith's study resulted in three reports: a preliminary one outlining the submissions made by labour and business groups; a draft bill; and a terse Final Report in 1913 which sets out many of the guiding principles of the current workers' compensation system.

The position of labour, was represented in particular by the Trades and Labour Congress (TLC), while that of employers by the Canadian Manufacturers' Association (CMA).

As might be imagined, the respective positions of labour and business concerning how a compensation system should be structured were considerably at odds. While Meredith was clearly a representative of the *status quo*, as might be expected of a former leader of the Conservative Party and a Chief Justice, his recommendations were far more sympathetic to labour's position than that of business. In his final two reports he laid out the groundwork for a system of workers' compensation which has remained virtually intact until today.

(a) No Fault

While Meredith is credited with establishing a "no fault" system, and while he rejected the CMA's proposal that an injury due "wholly or principally to intoxication" or "intentionally caused by the workman" not be compensated, he did suggest that an accident solely attributable to serious and wilful misconduct not be compensated unless such injury resulted in death or serious disablement.

(b) Administration

Despite the CMA's insistence that an agency set up by the state would be subject to partisan political pressure, Meredith declared that his system should be run by a Workmen's Compensation Board, appointed by the provincial government. Of more importance — given the subsequent developments in the United States — Meredith insisted that the appeal structure of the system should be removed entirely from the courts and remain internal to the Board. His rationale for this was that:

> A compensation law should, in my opinion, render it impossible for a wealthy employer to harass an employee by compelling him to litigate his claim in a court of law after he has established it to the satisfaction of a Board such as that which is to be constituted, and which will be probably quite as

competent to reach a proper conclusion as to the matters involved, whether of fact or law, as a court of law.

Perhaps more pragmatically, he also pointed out that, "the transfer from the courts to the Board of the determination of claims for compensation ... will lessen very much the cost of the administration of justice."

(c) Benefits

Meredith's recommendations on benefit levels and duration was a major victory for labour over the proposals of the CMA. Rejecting any time limitations he stated that compensation:

> ... should be paid as long as the disability lasts, and the amount of compensation should have relation to the earning power of the injured workman.
> To limit the period during which the compensation is to be paid, regardless of the duration of the disability, as is done by the laws of some countries, is, in my opinion, not only inconsistent with the principle upon which a true compensation law is based, but unjust to the injured workman for the reason that if the disability continues beyond the prescribed period he will be left with his impaired earning power or, if he is totally disabled without any earning power at a time when his need of receiving compensation will presumably be greater than at the time he was injured, to become a burden upon his relatives or friends or upon the community.

In most U.S. jurisdictions, by way of contrast, "permanent" disability is judged to be a set number of weeks, according to the relevant schedule. In addition to rejecting time limits, he also insisted that compensation payments be tied to the individual worker's pre-accident earnings, rejecting the CMA's position which would have set a flat rate for all injured workers, regardless of income. In so doing, Meredith envisioned that the wages of *all* wage earners would be covered by the Act.

The concept of workers' compensation covering virtually all wage-earners, earnings was, at some point, quietly abandoned so that Professor Weiler would write, in 1980, that, "In practice the ceiling has been set at about 125% to 130% of average wages in the province ... which will cover earnings through the 80th percentile of the provincial wage scale." With the changes in Bill 162 in 1989, the current level of coverage is set at 175 per cent of the provincial average industrial wage.

(d) Funding

The major battle between labour and business had been over who would fund the system. Once again, Meredith provided labour with a reason to be pleased with his report. The concept of contributory premiums paid by workers and/or financing from government revenues was rejected.

He recommended that the system be funded by way of a collective liability fund, by which employers would be placed in different rate groups, or classes, according to the nature of their business and all members of the class would pay the same assessment rates, based on a percentage of payroll, into the WCB accident fund.

This system of funding is now universal across Canada, as opposed to many U.S. jurisdictions which allow for privately run "self insurance".

(e) Removal of Litigation Rights

The major trade-off for labour was that any accident to which the Act applied removed the victim's rights to a common law action. It was also provided, however, that in occupational accidents which were not covered by the Act, the "unholy trinity" of employer defences would no longer apply.

Meredith's report was, by and large, an incredibly far-sighted document. Having investigated the laws in other jurisdictions and having heard from labour and business in Ontario, Meredith had no hesitation in stepping on the toes of some of the business community who had warned that his proposals would drive industry from the province. He did so, not because he was politically "radical" or "pro-worker", but rather it was his acute political awareness of the growing strength and resentment of the labour movement which seems to have motivated him. The concluding paragraph in his Final Report sums up this concern:

> In these days of social and industrial unrest it is, in my judgement, of the gravest importance to the community that every proved injustice to any section or class resulting from bad or unfair laws should be promptly removed by the enactment of remedial legislation and I do not doubt that the country whose Legislature is quick to discern and prompt to remove injustice will enjoy, and that deservedly, the blessing of industrial peace and freedom from social unrest. Half measures which mitigate but do not remove injustice are, in my judgement, to be avoided. That the existing law inflicts injustice on the working man is admitted by all. From that injustice he has long suffered, and it would, in my judgement, be the gravest mistake if questions as to the scope and character of the proposed remedial legislation were to be determined, not by a consideration of what is just to the working man, but of what is the least he can be put off with; or if the Legislature were to be deterred from passing a law designed to do full justice owing to groundless fears that disaster to the industries of the Province would follow from the enactment of it.

Having tabled his Final Report in October 1913, Meredith's enquiry was now at an end and the political process began. It was not an easy one, with both business interests lobbying against the bill and labour urging its adoption in equally strident language.

Caught between these strong lobbies and the pressure of his old mentor Meredith, Whitney continued to dither. Finally, in the spring of 1914, while Whitney was ill, acting Premier I.B. Lucas introduced the *Workmen's*

Compensation Act in the Ontario Legislature. On May 1, 1914, the Bill received royal assent, to come into force on January 1 of the following year.

Since that time, while there have been a number of Royal Commissions and Task Forces which have reviewed workers' compensation in Ontario, the basic structural framework and principles set out by Meredith have remained intact. It is for that reason that workers' compensation can be said to be a truly hybrid piece of legislation. As one which flowed from common law remedies and pre-dated other pieces of "social" legislation such as Unemployment [Employment] Insurance, Old Age Pensions and Medicare by several decades, it does not have the hallmarks of "welfare state"-type remedies. The concept of social responsi-bility for social problems was one which emerged much later. On the other hand, workers' compensation maintains an essentially private relationship between worker and employer, albeit one which is mediated and for all practical purposes administered by an agency of the state: the Workers' Compensation Board, now the Workplace Safety and Insurance Board.

3. RECENT DEVELOPMENTS

Space does not permit an exhaustive survey of the 65-year history of the Act between Meredith and the restructuring of the legislation and administration resulting from Professor Paul Weiler's study. Unfortunately, the definitive his-tory of workers' compensation is still to be written. For that matter, *any* full his-tory is still to be written.

By the late 1960s and early 1970s, the compensation system was perceived by injured workers to contain a number of fundamental flaws. In 1974, injured workers joined together to form the Union of Injured Workers (UIW) in an effort to bring pressure on the government and the WCB. Of critical importance to the Union was the question of permanent partial disability awards — pensions.

Throughout the mid-'70s the UIW staged a number of militant demonstra-tions in an attempt to bring their complaints to public attention. As the '70s waned, there was also a concern about pensions, and other matters, developing at the WCB itself. A 1978 actuarial report to the provincial government, pre-pared by the Wyatt Company, raised questions about the financial soundness of the workers' compensation system. As a result, on February 11, 1980, the Min-ister of Labour announced the appointment of Professor Paul C. Weiler to "make recommendations with respect to the workmen's compensation system in Ontario."

Weiler's report, *Reshaping Workers' Compensation for Ontario*, was tabled on November 18, 1980. It contained a blueprint for a major overhaul of the benefit and administrative structure of workers' compensation, although it left unchanged the basic principles set out by Meredith.

Since the Weiler report, successive provincial governments have tried to re-form workers' compensation. These changes have often been cumulative so that there are now a number of parallel schemes in place. The major changes since 1984 are discussed below.

4. MAJOR CHANGES IN BILL 101 (1985)

While Bill 101 was certainly the most extensive revision of workers' compensation law since Meredith, it left intact the fundamental principles of the system. Its changes can be summarized under two headings: benefits and administration. The lasting changes were administrative; the controversial dual award, wage loss system for permanent partial disability compensation was *not* included. The major benefit change was the change from 75 per cent of *gross* wages to 90 per cent of *net* wages as the basis for compensation benefits. In addition, the ceiling of covered earnings was raised considerably.

With respect to administration, the Workers' Compensation Appeals Tribunal (WCAT) was created as an independent body to serve as a final level of appeal from decisions of the WCB. Associated with the WCAT is a panel of Medical Assessors, which is responsible for providing independent medical evidence to the Tribunal in cases of medical dispute.

The Industrial Disease Standards Panel (IDSP) was also created as an independent agency to recommend on compensation criteria for occupational diseases. This body was later renamed the Occupational Disease Panel (ODP) and was disbanded in 1998 as part of the Bill 99 changes.

Finally, the Bill established the Office of the Worker Adviser and the Office of the Employer Adviser to provide information, advice and representation to injured workers and employers respectively.

All of these agencies, while independent of the Board, ultimately received their funding from it. The agencies receive funding from the Ministry of Labour which, in turn, bills the Board for the costs.

5. MAJOR CHANGES IN BILL 162 (1989)

The legislative passage of Bill 162 was a considerably rougher voyage than that taken by Bill 101. Both labour and management raised serious objections to the major provisions of the Bill.

The two most significant areas of change in Bill 162 involve compensation for permanent disabilities and vocational rehabilitation/re-employment provisions.

(a)　Permanent Disability Compensation: The Weiler dual award, wage loss system of compensating the permanently disabled had become no less controversial over the years. Yet, while it had not been included in the amendments in Bill 101, the dual award system was finally introduced in Bill 162. With the passage of time, and a further report from Professor Weiler on the subject, there were some modifications to Weiler's original proposals. However, many of the underlying principles remained.

(b)　Rehabilitation/Re-employment: The Bill enshrined a greater obligation on the Board to quickly identify an injured worker's need for vocational rehabilitation. In addition, it introduced legislative requirements that employers, in certain circumstances, re-employ workers who had suffered work-related disabilities.

(c) Other Changes: There were also a number of other changes of lesser significance. The earnings ceiling became indexed to 175 per cent of the provincial Average Industrial Wage. The Bill provides that injured workers' employment benefits will be maintained while they are unable to work. There are also provisions that require a percentage of benefit money be set aside for an injured worker's retirement pension.

After considerable opposition, from worker groups in particular, the Bill was passed and received royal assent on July 26, 1989. Most of its measures came into effect on January 2, 1990.

6. 1994 — A ROYAL COMMISSION AND BILL 165

The 1990 election in Ontario returned a majority New Democratic government. Employers' groups, highly vocal about budget deficits in general, stressed the growing unfunded liability at the Board and lobbied hard to prevent assessment rate increases. At the same time, there was an expectation of increased coverage and benefits among injured workers and labour from the traditional NDP constituencies. However, as the 1990 recession took hold and the government was under pressure from both these groups, immediate legislative action in the area of workers' compensation reform was delayed.

As a result of these conflicting pressures, in the spring of 1993, the responsibility to develop legislative proposals was turned over to the "Premier's Labour-Management Advisory Committee" (PLMAC) — a committee, as the name suggests, composed of trade union and business leaders. After a year of negotiations, the government announced that the PLMAC had negotiated a "framework agreement" and that the government intended to introduce legislation based on this agreement.

On May 18, 1994, the government introduced *An Act to amend the Workers' Compensation Act and the Occupational Health and Safety Act,* Bill 165. By the time that the Bill was introduced, the perceived harmony surrounding the PLMAC negotiations was out of tune and most employers announced that an agreement had not been reached.

Bill 165 provided for a number of administrative changes. Some of these were short-lived such as the "bipartite" corporate structure so that directors, representative of workers and employers, would be responsible for recommending other directors and the WCB Chair. Other administrative changes were adopted and later expanded upon in Bill 99. These changes included the introduction of the purpose clause, now found at s. 1 of the *Workplace Safety And Insurance Act, 1997.*

Bill 165 also provided two substantial benefit changes. First, the automatic, full cost-of-living provisions that were introduced in 1986 have been modified by the adoption of the so-called "Friedland formula", which provides for partial indexation only for a large number of injured workers. It was this change which most upset injured workers, as the indexation of benefits had been a key demand in the inflationary 1970s. Secondly, there was a $200 per month increase to some permanently disabled workers who were injured prior to 1990.

In addition to Bill 165, the NDP government established a Royal Commission to look into systemic problems in workers' compensation. However, in the June 8, 1995 general election, the Progressive Conservatives replaced the NDP in government. With respect to workers' compensation, the new government scrapped the Royal Commission and appointed C. Jackson as Minister without portfolio, responsible for workers' compensation. That minister was mandated to investigate structural changes in the system and to provide recommendations for change by April 1996.

In late 1995, Minister of Labour, E. Witmer, tabled Bill 15, which provided short term amendments to the Act while awaiting more comprehensive legislation. There had been an earlier indication by the Minister that she would be proposing substantive amendments which would lower benefits' levels to 85 per cent of net wages, introduce a three-day waiting period, prohibit the compensability of chronic stress claims, and amend the entitlement provisions to provide for a predominant cause test to replace the significant contributing factor test.

7. MAJOR CHANGES IN BILL 99 (1998)

In his report dated July 3, 1996, Minister Jackson made a number of recommendations for extensive changes to the workers' compensation system. These recommendations formed the basis for the introduction of Bill 99 by the Minister of Labour on November 26, 1996. Bill 99 provides for the most comprehensive revision to the compensation system since 1914. Worker and injured worker groups responded to its changes with strenuous disapproval. Employer groups provided generally favourable reviews. The Bill was given royal assent on October 10, 1997 and most of its provisions came into effect as of January 1, 1998.

(a) Benefit Changes

Bill 99 provides that benefits will be reduced from 90 per cent to 85 per cent of net average earnings. The concept of "temporary disability/impairment" leading to possible "permanent disability" or "permanent impairment" has been dispensed with in exchange for a "loss of earnings" ("LOE") benefit that is payable from the point at which the LOE begins until such a loss is deemed to have ceased.

Generally, the LOE benefits will be reviewed annually (as opposed to the current two-year and five-year review) or if there is a "material change in circumstances", although there will be no review after six years, again, unless there has been a material change in circumstances.

Chronic stress is explicitly exempted as a compensable condition and there are potential limitations on entitlement for chronic pain conditions arising from compensable accidents. The cost-of-living formula for benefits is further reduced.

Finally, entitlement to Board-provided vocational rehabilitation for injured workers was removed from the Act.

(b) Structural Changes

Bill 99 contains a number of highly visible cosmetic changes. The name "workers' compensation" will no longer appear as an operative term. Workers' Compensation Board became Workplace Safety and Insurance Board ("WSIB") and Workers' Compensation Appeals Tribunal became Workplace Safety and Insurance Appeals Tribunal ("WSIAT"). Workers' compensation, as a general concept, along with the term "accident fund", have been replaced by the term "insurance plan". Vocational rehabilitation has been replaced by "labour market re-entry", or "LMR".

For reasons that are not immediately apparent, ss. 101 and 102 note that the regime prior to January 1, 1998, is governed by the "pre-1997 Act" as it applies to "pre-1998 injuries". The Act is the *Workers' Compensation Act* "as it read on December 31, 1997", and an injury is "a personal injury by accident or an occupational disease that occurs before January 1, 1998."

Several of the terminology changes are made retrospectively. So, for example, while the previous Act is continued for pre-1998 injuries, the pre-1997 Act is amended by substituting, for example, "labour market re-entry" for "vocational rehabilitation". Also changed in this fashion is "maximum medical rehabilitation", which now becomes "maximum medical recovery".

More substantively, Bill 99 introduces a number of important time limits for the first time in workers' compensation legislation. There is, generally speaking, a six-month time limit for a worker to file a claim, a six-month limit for objecting to a decision within the Board, and a six-month limit in filing an appeal with the Appeals Tribunal. Similarly, the Appeals Tribunal has a time limit of 120 days to decide an appeal.

The Appeals Tribunal also changed in that there is no longer a requirement for a tripartite hearing panel to hear appeals. The Tribunal must also now apply "an applicable Board policy" when making a decision, whether such decision arise under the new Act or the pre-1997 Act.

CHAPTER 2

Resources

1. INTRODUCTION

Since the advent of the legislated changes that came into effect in 1985, two factors in particular have influenced the growth of new resource materials in the workers' compensation area: the decision of the Workplace Safety and Insurance Appeals Tribunal (WSIAT, formerly WCAT) to publish its decisions, and the vastly increased involvement of the employer community in the workers' compensation process.

2. THE ACTS

As is outlined in Chapter 1, there have been several major revisions to the *Workers' Compensation Act* since 1984, including the *Workplace Safety And Insurance Act, 1997.* Further complicating the work of a practitioner, the Revised Statutes of Ontario 1990, were issued in November 1991. As the amendments to the *Workers' Compensation Act* had been spliced into it during the 1980s, the result in the 1990 R.S.O.s was that virtually all the sections of the Act were renumbered.

While much of the language remained the same, the changes in section numbers are confusing. More problematic are the substantive changes brought about by Bill 101, Bill 162, Bill 165 and Bill 99. The legislature has defined the pre-Bill 101 *Workers' Compensation Act* as the "pre-1985 Act" and pre-Bill 162 as the "pre-1989 Act" (s. 144). In addition there is the pre-1997 Act, both the R.S.O. 1980 version, as amended, and the R.S.O. 1990 version. It should be noted that there are no substantive changes between these two, only the section numbers have been changed. Finally, there is Bill 99.

In essence then, there may be as many as four Acts governing a workers' compensation claim. In almost all instances, the date of injury is the determining factor which Act applies. There are instances, however, in which the dates during which benefits are being sought become important. Table L-1 indicates some of the more common section number changes for the sections among the Acts.

For example, if a worker sustained an injury in 1983 he or she might be eligible for a pension supplement under subs. 43(5) of the pre-1985 Act, as continued by s. 136 of the pre-1989 Act, during a period in 1986 when she or he was looking for work. Subsequent to July 26, 1989, the worker's claim for a further supplement would be adjudicated under subs. 147(2) or (4) of the pre-1997 Act.

The legislative criteria are considerably different under subs. 147(2). Finally, the worker might now be eligible for the $200 pension increase under subs. 147(14). And, if that worker wanted to appeal a denial of these benefits to the WSIAT, Bill 99 requires that he or she do so within six months of a final decision from the Board.

3. ONTARIO WORKERS' COMPENSATION DECISIONS

The WSIAT publishes all its decisions. In addition, the WSIAT publishes a Reporter series of decisions which are selected on the basis of various criteria. These decisions do not necessarily represent the "leading cases" concerning the various topics, but are selected by an editorial board which attempts to publish decisions which deal with a broad range of issues. This editorial board consists of WSIAT staff, but not adjudicators. The WSIAT Reporter series is available in various libraries and may also be purchased from the WSIAT Publications Department.

A hard copy of any individual decision is available in the WSIAT library and may also be ordered through the WSIAT's publication department. WSIAT decisions are summarized by the Tribunal's publication department and a subscription to this weekly summary of WSIAT decisions is available. Full text WSIAT decisions are also available through the Quicklaw database service known as OWCA. This service may be subscribed to by computer users with modem facilities.

At the WSIAT library there is a standalone database facility which provides searchers with various data on WSIAT decisions. Library staff are available for assistance in conducting these searches. The Tribunal web site also contains a representative sample of summaries, updated weekly. The WSIB never has, and does not now, publish its decisions.

4. OTHER DECISIONS

A number of other Canadian jurisdictions now publish workers' compensation decisions. In Nova Scotia, there are court decisions dealing with questions of law in a workers' compensation context. There are also some significant court decisions in which various aspects of workers' compensation law have been addressed. Probably the most significant of these was the Supreme Court of Canada's 1989 endorsement of the Newfoundland Court of Appeal's decision on the constitutionality of the provision in the Newfoundland Act — one which is also found in the Ontario and other Canadian legislation — which restricts a worker's right to sue.

5. LIBRARIES

Prior to 1985, there were no libraries in Ontario dedicated to making available to the public material specific to workers' compensation. When the WSIAT began operation in 1985, one of its goals was to provide a full library of workers' compensation materials which would serve, in particular, representatives of workers and employers in the preparation of appeals. The Tribunal library, now combined with the library holdings from the Ontario Labour Relations Board and Pay Equity Hearings Tribunal, is open to the public during regular office hours.

6. PUBLICATIONS

(a) Books

Prior to 1987 there were no books published on Ontario workers' compensation. Since then there have been a number of books published.

In addition to these publications, which deal exclusively with the provincial scene, there is the second edition of Professor T.G. Ison's seminal review of all Canadian jurisdictions, *Workers' Compensation in Canada* (Toronto: Butterworths, 1989).

(b) Newsletters and Videos

There are also a variety of newsletters which range in frequency and cost between the weekly *Canadian Occupational Health and Safety News* at a yearly subscription rate of $399 in 1999, to the *I.A.V.G.O. Reporting Service*, published three times a year. The WSIB itself also has a variety of publications.

In the video age there are also a number of video resources available. The WSIB library has a broad selection of videos concerning workers' compensation issues. The WSIAT has produced a video entitled "Final Appeal", dealing with its operation.

(c) WCB Manuals

Until recently the Board — and users of the system — had to rely on a variety of manuals, which first became available to the public in 1979. Some of the practices and procedures varied, depending on which manual was being consulted. It was therefore necessary to maintain up to seven binders, with periodic updates.

In 1989 the Board amalgamated these various policy and procedure manuals into one — the *Operational Policy Manual (O.P.M.)*. This is available from the WSIB for a total cost of $200 (in 1993). This price includes $125 for the manual itself and $75 annually for an update service. The update fee is payable annually.

In late 1997, the Board issue a new manual for Bill 99 policies, with a promise that it would issue a consolidated manual soon. As of September 1999 this manual has yet to appear.

(d) Miscellaneous

The Board and WSIAT are also accessible on the Internet. The addresses are <http://www.wsib.on.ca> and <http://www.wsiat.on.ca>.

CHAPTER 3

General Principles

1. INTRODUCTION

In this chapter, the interpretation of workers' compensation legislation, the use of Board policies, the burden and standard of proof in workers' compensation, retroactivity, and limitation periods are discussed.

2. INTERPRETATION OF WORKERS' COMPENSATION LEGISLATION

Questions of statutory interpretation frequently arise when individual sections in the Act are in issue. Broadly speaking there are two legislative schemes in place: the pre-1997 Act which applies to pre-1998 injuries, and the current Act. The considerable change in focus from the pre-1997 Act to the current Act can be seen when the "purposes" provisions of the two Acts are compared.

Section 0.1 of the pre-1997 Act reads as follows:

> The purposes of this Act are,
>
> (a) to provide fair compensation to workers who sustain personal injury arising out of and in the course of their employment or who suffer from occupational disease and to their survivors and dependants;
>
> (b) to provide health care benefits to those workers;
>
> (c) to provide for rehabilitation services and programs to facilitate the workers' return to work;
>
> (d) to provide for rehabilitation programs for their survivors; and
>
> (e) to require the board of directors of the Workers' Compensation Board to act in a financially responsible and accountable manner in governing the Board.

Section 1 of the current Act reads as follows:

> The purpose of this Act is to accomplish the following in a financially responsible and accountable manner:
>
> 1. To promote health and safety in workplaces and to prevent and reduce the occurrence of workplace injuries and occupational diseases.

2. To facilitate the return to work and recovery of workers who sustain personal injury arising out of and in the course of employment or who suffer from an occupational disease.

3. To facilitate the re-entry into the labour market of workers and spouses of deceased workers.

4. To provide compensation and other benefits to workers and to the survivors of deceased workers.

Section 163(1) of the current Act provides that:

> The board of directors shall act in a financially responsible and accountable manner in exercising its powers and performing its duties.

In the *Pension Assessment Appeals Leading Case Interim Report* the Appeals Tribunal stated:

> There is ample judicial authority for the proposition that workers' compensation legislation is to be regarded as remedial legislation and interpreted broadly and non-technically from the point of view of facilitating the expeditious and fair treatment of injured workers' claims.

In another decision the Appeals Tribunal stated:

> The Worker's Compensation Act reflects a balancing of the legitimate interests of workers and employers. With respect to the application and implementation of the purpose of the Act, it necessarily involves continued trade-offs and bargains between the interests of workers and employers. Many of the provisions of the Ontario *Workers' Compensation Act* as it now reads do not make sense when read alone. They must be read within the context of the entire piece of legislation.

3. USE OF BOARD POLICY AND PRINCIPLES OF DECISION-MAKING

Section 73(1) of the pre-1997 Act provides that any decision of the Board shall be upon the real merits and justice of the case, and the Board is not bound to follow strict legal precedent but shall give full opportunity for a hearing. A similar provision in s. 92 of the pre-1997 Act applies to the Appeals Tribunal. Sections 119(1) and (3) of the current Act carry forward these concepts into the new scheme, but the Board is now only obliged to give an opportunity (rather than a full opportunity) for a hearing. A similar provision in s. 124(1) applies to the Appeals Tribunal.

Board policy provides that Appeals Resolution Officers may, at their discretion, admit other relevant Board decisions into evidence, although these decisions would not be binding. The policy also notes that Appeals Tribunal decisions and the arguments which support them should also be considered, although they are not to be treated as precedents. The Board is also willing to consider arbitration decisions, Ontario Labour Relations Board decisions, Ontario Human Rights Commission decisions, *etc.*

Both the Board and the Appeals Tribunal have acknowledged that as the body of workers' compensation law has developed (largely since 1986), consistency of decision-making is important (and indeed has become possible).

The Board has developed policy on a wide variety of topics, much of which is published. Most policies now being written (or when being revised) contain a statement to the effect that a claim is to be decided on its individual merit and circumstances if it does not fit within a general policy guideline. Both the Board and the Appeals Tribunal accept that the statutory provision regarding real merits and justice applies whether or not a statement along those lines appears in a policy document. The lower adjudicative levels of the Board in particular have been criticized for failing to be aware of, or have an understanding of, policies; for applying policies in a manner which is inconsistent with the wording of the Act; or failing to take individual circumstances into account when applying policy.

The Appeals Tribunal is directed by s. 126(1) of the Act to apply an applicable Board policy with respect to the subject-matter of an appeal when making its decision. The Board is obliged to state in writing which policy, if any, applies, and if it fails to do so, the Appeals Tribunal may ask the Board to notify it of an applicable policy. In practice, panels of the Tribunal have been prepared to apply relevant Board policies which have not been included in a "policy package" forwarded in any particular case, without requesting notification from the Board. Section 126(4) provides that if the Appeals Tribunal concludes in a particular case that a Board policy of which it is notified is inconsistent with, or not authorized by, the Act or does not apply to the case, it shall not make a decision until it refers the policy to the Board for its review and the Board issues a written direction that determines the issue raised. This provision is proving to be cumbersome to apply.

At all levels of decision-making, it may be possible to argue that a policy is illustrative but not applicable. It may also be that a decision can be reached which, while not fitting squarely within a policy, nonetheless is not contrary to it.

4. BURDEN OF PROOF AND STANDARD OF PROOF

In its policy on "decision-making" the Board acknowledges that it is involved in an inquiry system and its duty is to gather relevant information, weigh evidence, and make a decision. As such, there is no burden of proof for a claimant or an employer. However, at all levels of decision-making in the workers' compensation system there are limits in adhering to the information gathering duty. The *de facto* onus may be upon the party to bring forward information of both a medical and non-medical nature. One WCAT Interim decision stated:

The balance-of-probabilities standard of proof is applicable to findings of fact in civil court cases and is the standard which both the Board and the Appeals Tribunal apply, although this is not stated in the Act or Board policy.

Pre-1998 injury claimants are assisted by s. 4(4) of the pre-1997 Act which reads:

In determining any claim under this Act, the decision shall be made in accordance with the real merits and justice of the case and where it is not practicable to determine an issue because the evidence for or against the issue is approximately equal in weight, the issue shall be resolved in favour of the claimant.

A policy to this effect has been on the books with the Board for years, but this statutory provision was first enacted as of April 1, 1985. The Board's view is that this provision is applied when the facts of a case are so evenly balanced that a clear decision is impossible. The Appeals Tribunal has not been reluctant to apply this "benefit of the doubt" principle using an approach similar to the Board's.

Current Act claimants are assisted by s. 119(2) of the Act which reads:

If, in connection with a claim for benefits under the insurance plan, it is not practicable to decide an issue because the evidence for or against it is approximately equal in weight, the issue shall be resolved in favour of the person claiming benefits.

This provision re-appears in s. 124(2) as a principle of decision-making at the Appeals Tribunal.

Another aspect of the burden of proof is whether an objective or subjective standard is to be used. Must a decision be based on how an "ordinary worker" would be affected or respond in a similar situation (objective standard) or does one look at the effect on the individual worker whose claim is under scrutiny? The standard is subjective (*i.e.*, look at the effect on the individual worker), although in some chronic stress cases the Appeals Tribunal has used a "reasonable person" test. The thin-skull doctrine applies. This is of particular significance in occupational disease, disablement situations and psychiatric disability claims where many other workers with a comparable employment history to the disabled individual do not suffer from any disability.

5. RETROACTIVITY OF POLICIES AND DECISIONS

The Board takes the position that with regard to new policies or policy changes, the effective retroactivity date is based upon the individual circumstances surrounding the policy change. With respect to policy "overrulings", the Board will choose a retroactivity date considering factors such as the Board's statutory obligations, social and equitable implications, numbers of stakeholders affected, implementation considerations, legitimacy of previous policy or interpretation, and whether the new policy is more restrictive or less restrictive than the old policy.

Generally (with the exception of entitlement policies regarding occupational diseases), the Board will not review denied claims which might be affected by a policy change although it will be willing to re-open cases that are brought forward.

In the past (when not obliged to apply stated Board policy), the Appeals Tribunal did not necessarily accept the retroactivity date set out in Board policy, although it gave due consideration to the rationale behind the Board's choice of a date.

Where a decision is reversed and a previously denied claim is allowed, full arrears of payments will normally be paid. However, full retroactivity will be in issue where the decision results from a change in policy involving questions of developing medical knowledge or a change in the interpretation of the law.

If a policy changes, claimants seeking to benefit from the change will likely have to bring their claims forward to whatever level in the decision-making process is appropriate (see Chapter 25, The Appeals Procedure).

6. LIMITATION PERIODS

There are limitation periods in the Act. These are set out in Table 3-1, below. In general, claims for compensation or health care must be made within six months from the happening of the accident, or in the case of death, within six months from the time of death. In both Acts, the relevant provision is s. 22(1).

There is a saving provision in subs. 22(5) of the pre-1997 Act. Failure to make a timely claim does not bar the right to compensation if, in the opinion of the Board, the employer was not prejudiced thereby, or, where compensation is payable out of the accident fund (*i.e.*, a Sch. 1 employer), if the Board is of the opinion that the claim is a just one and ought to be allowed. The saving provision in the current Act, found in s. 22(3), states that the Board may permit a claim to be filed after the six-month period expires if, in the opinion of the Board, it is just to do so.

Historically this limitation period was of no significance, but it has been used by the Appeals Tribunal to deny a claim. In another Appeals Tribunal decision, the Panel ascertained from the Board that in practice it is unlikely that a claim would ever be denied solely on the basis that a s. 22 notice was not provided in a timely fashion. The real problem with "untimely" cases relates to the evidence, which generally is more problematic the older the claim.

The time limit for objections is set out in s. 120. Return to work and labour market re-entry decisions have a 30-day appeal time limit, while other decisions at the Board have a six-month time limit. These deadlines also apply to pre-January 1998 decisions giving deadlines of January 30, 1998 and June 30, 1998, respectively (see s. 112(3)). By virtue of s. 125(2), all appeals to the Appeals Tribunal must be made within six months of the Board decision, or by June 30,

1998, in the case of decisions rendered prior to January 1998 (see s. 112(3)). Both bodies have the power to extend these time limits.

Until Bill 99, there had never been any time limits on objections or appeals. The Board did send out notification letters regarding the new time limits, but these were only sent out in active claims (and many injured workers with active claims did not receive these letters). There was also limited media attention given to this change. It is therefore quite likely that many affected claimants were and still are unaware of the June 30, 1998 deadline for appealing old decisions. Both the Board and the Appeals Tribunal have demonstrated flexibility with respect to time limits for old decisions, but the standard for fresh decisions appears to be more strict.

7. MATERIAL CHANGE IN CIRCUMSTANCES

There has always been an implied obligation on the part of injured workers and employers to inform the Board of changes relevant to their claims (in the case of workers) or assessment obligations (in the case of employers). With the passage of Bill 15 in 1995, there became an explicit obligation to do so.

Section 22.1 of the pre-1997 Act provides that a person receiving benefits or who may be entitled to receive benefits shall notify the Board of a material change in circumstances in connection with his or her entitlement to benefits within ten days after the material change occurs. Wilful failure to do so is an offence and conviction carries the penalty of liability for a fine not exceeding $25,000 or up to six months' imprisonment, or both. For post-1998 injury claimants, the relevant (and identical) provision is s. 23(3). The offence provision is s. 149(2). Section 158(1) sets out similar penalties to those in the pre-1997 Act. The Board defines a "material change in circumstances" as any change which affects a person's entitlement to benefits and services, and lists as examples these types of changes:

- Changes in a person's medical condition (for example, the worker becomes capable of modified work);
- Changes in a person's earnings or other income (for example, a worker receiving temporary benefits returns to some form of work or a worker begins to receive C.P.P./Q.P.P. benefits for the work-related impairment);
- Changes that affect a person's availability for work or ability to participate fully in a medical or vocational rehabilitation program (*e.g.*, a worker changes place of residence or is imprisoned, or has a non-work-related medical condition that begins to affect availability); and/or
- Changes that affect a dependant's entitlement to benefits under the Act.

Section 109.1 of the pre-1997 Act provides that an employer shall notify the Board of a material change in circumstances in connection with the employer's obligations under the Act within ten days after the material change occurs. Wilful failure to so inform the Board is an offence and conviction carries the penalty of liability for a fine not exceeding $25,000 or up to six months' imprisonment, or both, for a person, or a fine of up to $100,000 if the person is not an individual (*i.e.*, is a corporation). In the current Act, s. 77 sets out the obligation, while the offence provision is s. 149(3) and the penalty provision is s. 158(1). Board policy is that, for employers, a material change is any change that may affect their obligations under the Act, and lists as examples these types of changes:

- Classification of business activity;
- Assessable payroll;
- Business name and/or address;
- Ownership;
- Legal affiliations with other companies;
- Ongoing operations (*e.g.*, dissolutions, bankruptcy); and/or
- Personal coverage earnings.

The Board's position is that a failure to inform the Board of a material change in circumstances is presumed to be intentional or deliberate and thus "wilful", unless the "person" or the employer can demonstrate having had no knowledge of the change. Board decision-makers determine whether or not the party reasonably ought to have been aware of the change. Since a failure to report may have very serious consequences, one would be well advised to provide written rather than oral notice and to keep a dated copy in case the copy forwarded to the Board goes astray.

Board policy is that notice of material changes should be provided as soon as the change occurs, but no later than ten calendar days (including the day the change occurs) after the change. Notification of a change *before* it occurs is acceptable. Where possible, the notice is to be provided to the relevant decision-maker and must be communicated by telephone, personal delivery, mail, courier, or fax. In many cases it may be difficult to determine who should be notified at the Board.

Table 3-1
Limitation Periods

Topic	Reference Pre-1997 Act	Current Act	Comment
Worker's Notice of Accident	s. 22	s. 22; see also s. 31(4) and (5)	Six-month limitation period which can be waived at the discretion of the Board.
Employer's Notice of Accident	s. 133(1)	s. 21	Written notice to be provided within three days after employer learns of accident which is disabling or requires health care. Financial penalty for breach.
Worker's Notice of Election to Claim Benefits vs. To Bring Civil Action or Claim Benefits From Another Jurisdiction	s. 10(6), s. 9	s. 30(4), s. 20	Three-month limitation period which can be waived at the discretion of the Board. See Chapter 10.
Employer Requested Medical Examination of Worker	s. 23	s. 36	For pre-1998 injuries where worker objects, worker or employer may apply, within 14 days of the objection having been made, to the Appeals Tribunal to hear and determine the matter. See Chapter 24.
			For current Act injuries where worker objects, employer may request within 14 days after receiving the objection, the Board to make a "final" decision on the objection. See Chapter 24.

Table 3-1 (cont'd)
Limitation Periods

Topic	Reference Pre-1997 Act	Current Act	Comment
Access to Worker's File	s. 71	s. 58	Under the pre-1997 Act, worker, employer, or party of record may appeal a decision of the Board regarding release of material in a worker's file to the Appeals Tribunal within 21 days of the mailing of the Board's decision. See Chapter 25. Under the current Act, worker can object to disclosure to employer of medical information and worker or employer can object to the Appeals Tribunal within 21 days of the Board's disclosure decision.
Board's Determination Re Employer's Compliance With Non-termination Provisions of Act	s. 54(12)	s. 41(12)	Re-employed worker who has been terminated within six months of re-employment must apply within three months of termination to the Board for determination re employer's failure to fulfill reemployment obligation. See Chapter 22.
Older Worker Directing Board Not to Review Loss of Earnings Payments	n/a	s. 44(4)	Older worker must give the "no review" direction within 30 days after later of MMR date or date on which labour market re-entry plan is fully implemented. See Chapter 17.
Worker's Choice of Doctor for Non-Economic Loss Medical Assessment	s. 42(4)	s. 47(4)	Worker must select doctor from list within 30 days after provision of list, or else the Board will choose. See Chapter 18.

Table 3-1 (cont'd)
Limitation Periods

Topic	Reference Pre-1997 Act	Current Act	Comment
Provision of a Labour Market Re-Entry Assessment to Surviving Spouse	s. 35(2)	s. 48(9)	Request must be made within 1 year after the death of the worker. See Chapter 20.
Provision of Bereavement Counselling for Surviving Spouse or Children	s. 35(3.4)	s. 48(12)	Request must be received within 1 year after the worker's death. See Chapter 20.
Payment of Non-Economic Loss Award as a Lump Sum	s. 42(3.1)	s. 46(4)	Where worker has a choice between lump sum or monthly payments, request (election) for lump sum must be made within 30 days of worker's notification of non-economic loss award.
Objection to a Return to Work or Labour Market Re-Entry Plan Decision	See s. 112 of Current Act	s. 120(1)(a)	Any party objecting to this type of decision must do so within 30 days. Time limit may be extended at Board's discretion. Retroactive for pre-January 1998 decisions.
Objection to Other Board Decisions	See s. 112 of Current Act	s. 120(1)(b)	Six-month time limit. Retroactive for pre-January 1998 decisions thereby establishing deadline of June 30, 1998. Limit may be extended at Board's discretion.
Appeals to Appeals Tribunal	See s. 112 of Current Act	s. 125(2)	Six-month time limit. Retroactive for pre-January 1998 decisions thereby establishing deadline of June 30, 1998. Limit may be extended at Tribunal's discretion.

CHAPTER 4

Administration

1. INTRODUCTION

Workers' compensation in Ontario is administered by a centralized government agency called the Workplace Safety and Insurance Board (WSIB). Prior to January 1, 1998, the Board was previously referred to as the Workers' Compensation Board.

Since 1985, changes of government have had a profound impact on the manner in which the Board has been administered and by whom. The Board has experienced successive waves of reform to the legislation is administers, to its own senior executive ranks, and to its internal administrative structures. These changes have been motivated by worker, employer, and government dissatisfaction with the operation of the workers' compensation system.

2. CORPORATE STRUCTURE

The WSIB is created by the *Workplace Safety and Insurance Act, 1997* (the Act). The Act also defines the responsibilities of the WSIB and provides the authority to manage the WSIB to a Board of Directors who are appointed by the Lieutenant Governor in Council (*i.e.*, cabinet). The Board of Directors includes a person designated as Chair of the Board and a person designated as the President.

The authority of the Board of Directors to manage the WSIB as it sees fit may be limited by the terms of a memorandum of understanding that the Board is required to enter into with the Minister of Labour every five years. The authority of the Board of Directors may also be limited by policy directives issued by the Minister of Labour and approved by the Lieutenant Governor in Council.

The Board of Directors may delegate its powers or duties to a member of the Board of Directors or to an officer or employee of the Board. Such delegation must be made in writing.

3. ADMINISTRATIVE STRUCTURE

An overview of the Board's most recent administrative structure as of the time of writing is provided in Table 4-1, below.

By far the largest division of the WSIB is its Operations Division. The Operations Division is where individual claims are adjudicated. It also houses the Board's Appeals Branch. An overview of the manner in which the Operations Division is organized is provided in Table 4-2, below.

Initial claims registration for all claims takes place in the Toronto head office. The WSIB attempts to make the initial decision to allow or deny a claim from this centralized location as well, although some claims may be referred on to "industry sectors" where an investigation is required before reaching a decision.

Once a claim is recognized, assuming that is not a no lost time injury, an occupational disease claim, or a serious injury, the claim is passed on to an adjudicator working within an industry sector. Industry managers are responsible for the management of all claims occurring within their specified industry sector. These sectors include the industry categories of agriculture, automotive, construction, education, electrical, food, forestry, health, manufacturing, municipal, pulp and paper, process/chemicals, schedule 2 employers, services, steel, and transportation.

These industry sectors are further broken down into "dedicated sector teams". Only some industry sectors will have teams in any particular regional office. The existence of a dedicated sector team from a particular industry will depend on the volume of claims from that industry in that region.

Where the office dealing with the claim does not have a dedicated sector team to administer a claim, the claim is managed by one of the Board's small business units that are present in the Board's regional offices and in the Toronto office. In the regional offices, it is the small business unit manager that manages the office for the Board although individual dedicated sector teams in those office report to their sector manager.

Most of the work on a claim will be handled by an adjudicator. However, the adjudicator may arrange for labour market re-entry services to be arranged from an external supplier. As well, there are a number of other individuals at the Board who may become involved in the claim including the nurse case manager.

Appeals of decisions reached by adjudicators are appealable first internally to the Appeals Branch of the Operations Division and then externally to the Workplace Safety and Insurance Appeals Tribunal.

Table 4-1. Organizational Chart

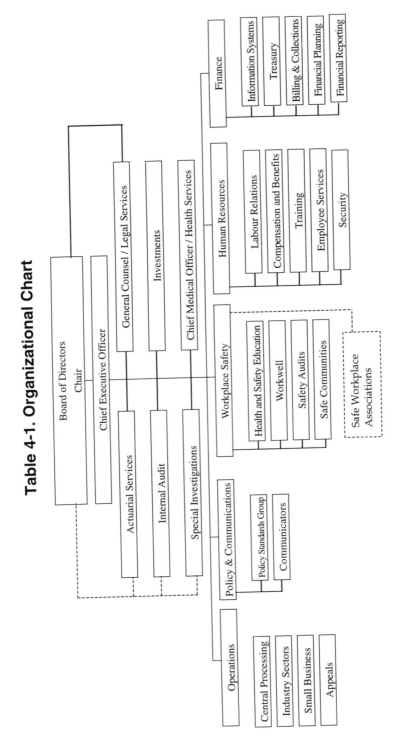

(*Source:* W.S.I.B.)

Table 4-2. Operations Organizational Chart

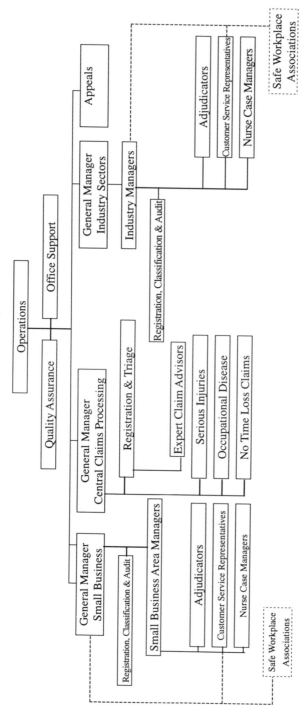

(*Source:* W.S.I.B.)

CHAPTER 5

Coverage

1. INTRODUCTION

This chapter deals with coverage for injuries occurring on or after January 1, 1998. The actual requirements of coverage before January 1, 1998 were not radically different than after January 1, 1998. However, there are some substantive differences and the legislative references have been completely changed.

Individuals or their dependents are entitled to compensation from the Ontario Board for personal injuries by accident arising out of and in the course of employment if three conditions are met:

(1)   The individual's employer has coverage;
(2)   The individual is considered to be a worker; and
(3)   The injury occurs within the geographic limitations specified under the Act.

2. WHICH EMPLOYERS HAVE COVERAGE?

Workers' compensation coverage is defined in inclusionary rather than exclusionary terms. Therefore, the assumption is that unless the law includes an employer under workers' compensation coverage, the employer is not covered.

For the purposes of the Act, an "employer" means every person having in his, her or its service under a contract of service or apprenticeship another person engaged in work in or about an industry and includes a trustee, receiver, liquidator, executor or administrator who carries on an industry; a person who authorizes or permits a learner to be in or about an industry for the purpose of undergoing training or probationary work; or a deemed employer.

(a) Mandatory Coverage

The failure of a mandatorily included employer to register with the Board will not result in the denial of compensation to workers of the employer suffering accidents.

The vast majority of employers mandatorily included under workers' compensation coverage are covered by being:

- Included under Sch. 1 or 2 under the Act;
- Covered under the *Government Employees' Compensation Act*;
- The deemed employer of an emergency worker; and/or
- The deemed employer of a municipal volunteer fire or ambulance brigade.

The Act's provisions regarding coverage apply to the provincial Crown. Coverage under Sch. 1 or 2 also applies to such bodies as municipal corporations, public utilities commissions, public library boards, and school boards.

Most employers are included in coverage under Sch. 1 or 2. These schedules are created by regulation and list the categories and classifications of industries mandatorily covered under the Act. Employers included under Sch. 1 operate under a joint liability scheme for the costs of injuries whereas employers included under Sch. 2 self-insure. The industry classifications contained in the schedules are in some instances quite archaic. Specific questions about the inclusions of particular industries may be addressed to the Board.

An employer of a worker or workers doing work that would usually be considered to fall within Sch. 1 is excluded from coverage under the Act if the work is not being done as a business or a trade or for profit or gain. For example, hiring someone to work on a car or a house that is intended for personal use does not make the car or house owner a Sch. 1 employer.

The *Government Employees' Compensation Act* (GECA) is federal legislation that affects hundreds of thousands of federal government workers including those workers in federal Crown corporations. Under this legislation, the federal government has entered into an agreement with the Ontario Board that allows the Board to provide benefits and services to federal government employees in Ontario in the same manner as they are provided to the employees of other Sch. 2 employers. Due to the fact that coverage for these employees arises under the GECA rather than under the WSIA, the application of particular provisions of the WSIA to these claims is sometimes questioned. However, for the most part, few differences exists between WSIA claims and GECA claims.

The deemed employer of an emergency worker is as follows:

- An authority who summons a person to assist in controlling or extinguishing a fire;
- The Crown where a person assists in a search and rescue operation at the request of and under the direction of a member of the Ontario Provincial Police;
- The Crown where a person assists in connection with an emergency declared by the Premier of Ontario to exist; or
- The municipality where a person assists in connection with an emergency declared by the head of the municipal council to exist.

The deemed employer of a volunteer fire or ambulance brigade is either a municipal corporation, a public utilities commission or any other commission or any board (other than a hospital board) that manages the brigade for a municipal corporation, or the board of trustees of a police village.

(b) Application Coverage

An employer not mandatorily covered under the WSIA is almost always permitted to apply for coverage but the WSIB may apply conditions. Workers of employers who are only included by application will not have entitlement to compensation unless the employer has requested coverage and is paying assessments.

Examples of industries that would only be included by application are banks, insurance companies, trust companies, other financial institutions, recreational and social clubs and associations, churches, theatres with live performances, broadcasting stations, trade unions, motion picture productions, educational and recreational camps and law offices.

By regulation the industries of barbering, shoe-shining, educational work, veterinary work, dentistry, funeral directing and embalming, photography and taxidermy are excluded from the application of the Act. However, even employers in these industries may apply for coverage.

Training agencies that place trainees with a placement host may also elect to have the trainees considered to be workers of the training agency so long as specified conditions are met.

3. INDIVIDUALS WHICH ARE CONSIDERED TO BE WORKERS

The word "worker" is defined in s. 2 of the Act as follows:

> "worker" means a person who has entered into or is employed under a contract of service or apprenticeship and includes the following:

1. A learner (defined by the Act).

2. A student (defined by the Act).

3. An auxiliary member of a police force.

4. A member of a municipal volunteer ambulance brigade.

5. A member of a municipal volunteer fire brigade whose membership has been approved by the chief of the fire department or by a person authorized to do so by the entity responsible for the brigade.

6. A person summonsed to assist in controlling or extinguishing a fire by an authority empowered to do so.

7. A person who assists in a search and rescue operation at the request of and under the direction of a member of the Ontario Provincial Police.

8. A person who assists in connection with an emergency that has been declared to exist by the Premier of Ontario or the head of a municipal council.

9. A person deemed to be a worker of an employer by a direction or order of the Board.

10. A person deemed to be a worker under section 12.

11. A pupil deemed to be a worker under the Education Act.

A worker does not include:

- A person whose employment is of a casual nature and who is employed otherwise than for the purpose of the employer's industry; and/or
- Persons to whom articles or materials are given out to be made up, cleaned, washed, altered, ornamented, finished, repaired or adapted for sale in the person's own home or other premises not under the control or management of the person who gave out the articles or materials.

The Act does not extend coverage to sole proprietors, independent operators, partners or executive officers, unless a specific application for coverage is received from such a person under s. 12 of the Act.

An independent operator is a person who carries on an industry included in Sch. 1 or Sch. 2 who does not employ any workers for that purpose.

In determining whether an individual is an independent operator or a worker, both the Board and the Appeals Tribunal use what is known as the organizational test that focuses on the alleged employer's control of the individual and the opportunity of the individual to experience profit or loss. The Board uses standard questionnaires to assist in its decision making and has some industry-specific policies. The specific wording of a contract that purports to create an independent operator status may not be determinative of the relationship.

Board policy indicates that an executive officer is anyone holding the position of chair or vice-chair of a board of directors; the president, vice-president, secretary, treasurer, or director of a limited liability company; or the general manager, or other designated position as an officer through by-law or resolution of the directors, or appointment by the Crown. Board policy indicates further that appointment of an officer by by-law or resolution of the directors must be recorded in the minute book of the company. The Board does not regard the above guidelines as always being determinative and when in doubt the Board considers the nature of the company's business, the manner in which the work of the company is distributed among the officers, and whether the individual has a voice in the policies of the company.

Appeals Tribunal decisions have indicated that a person's status as an executive officer will usually be determined by objective evidence such as government or corporate documents. However, it also appears to be clear that the Appeals Tribunal will closely examine the actual duties of the person to determine whether or not the person is an executive officer.

4. GEOGRAPHIC LIMITATIONS ON THE OCCURRENCE OF INJURIES

Workers who live and work in Ontario and who suffer their injuries in Ontario will not have any problems with the geographic limitations on entitlement. The problems arise where the injury arises outside of Ontario or where there is some question whether the worker is employed in Ontario.

The general rule set out in subs. 13(3) of the Act is that a worker is not entitled to benefits in Ontario if the accident occurs while the worker is employed outside of Ontario. However, exceptions to this general rule are outlined in ss. 18 and 19 of the Act.

For workers who travel to work within Canada, the Ontario Board is a party to an interjurisdictional agreement with all other Canadian jurisdictions except Prince Edward Island and Nova Scotia. This agreement provides that an Ontario-based worker may claim benefits from either the Ontario Board or in the jurisdiction where the worker is injured. Under this agreement employers are only required to report their worker's earnings in the jurisdiction where the worker is working.

Where a worker is entitled to claim compensation in Ontario and is also entitled to claim compensation under the laws of another jurisdiction in respect of the same accident, the worker shall elect whether to receive benefits from the Ontario Board or under the laws of the other jurisdiction. The Board must be notified of the election. So must the employer if the employer is a Sch. 2 employer. The deadline for electing is three months after the accident occurs, or, if the accident results in death, within three months after the date of death. The Board may extend this time limit. Failure to elect leads to a presumption that the worker has elected not to receive benefits from the Ontario Board unless the contrary is shown.

Non-resident workers who are employed in another jurisdiction and who are working temporarily in Ontario may or may not be covered by the Act. A "substantial connection" test is used to determine whether or not the worker will have coverage.

CHAPTER 6

Entitlement: Personal Injury by Accident

1. INTRODUCTION

Simply put, in light of s. 4(1) of the pre-1997 Act, and s. 13(1) of the current Act, the source of a compensable disability must be "personal injury by accident". It is sufficient if this personal injury by accident is the probable cause of the disability.

2. MULTIPLE CAUSES

If there are multiple causes of the disability it must be established that the "personal injury by accident" contributed in a significant or material way to the disability, and it need not be the major contributor to the disability. Pre-existing conditions or disabilities will not bar entitlement unless they account totally for any disability to the exclusion of any material contribution from the personal injury or accident.

If the disability is a "natural consequence" of the "personal injury by accident", it is compensable even if triggered or aggravated by a non-work related incident. This issue frequently arises with recurrences, which are discussed in more detail below.

3. PERSONAL INJURY

The term "personal injury" is not defined in any version of the Act, but the Board uses the following definition:

> Personal injury is the physical damage to the body, with medical support for the injury. It includes damage to the extensions of the body (enhancing bodily functions) which are worn and damaged at the time of injury; *e.g.* braces, glasses, prostheses and hearing aids. Personal injury does not include damage to personal effects; *e.g.* clothing and jewellery.

By virtue of s. 50(3) of the pre-1997 Act and s. 39(2) of the current Act, personal injury includes:

• Damage by accident to a worker's artificial member or apparatus sufficient to render the worker unable to work pending its repair;

- Nervous disorders or conditions (non-organic or psychological injuries); *e.g.*, aphonia — loss of voice, psychologically based — has been accepted in one Appeals Tribunal decision as personal injury); and
- A harmful physiological change within a worker (*e.g.*, a ruptured aneurysm) — the entitlement issue here entails relating the injury to work activities rather than natural processes.

The test regarding personal injury and the individual worker is subjective, not objective. Individual reactions (physical or mental) to work, or a work event, may vary. It is accepted that a frightening incident might cause one worker to suffer a heart attack, while another suffers aphonia and a third, more phlegmatic individual, barely reacts at all. However, with stress claims the Appeals Tribunal has started to apply a "reasonable person" test. (See Chapter 9, Mental and Behavioural Disorders).

Increasingly, the phrase "personal injury by accident" is being applied as if it reads "accident". The Appeals Tribunal has held that "injury by accident" means "accidental injury" or "unexpected injury", and that it is not necessary to have both an accident and an injury. Thus, a sudden unexpected injury is both the injury and the accident.

4. ACCIDENT

In s. 1(1) of the pre-1997 Act, and s. 2(1) of the current Act, it is stated that "accident" includes:

(a) a wilful and intentional act, not being the act of the worker,

(b) a chance event occasioned by a physical or natural cause, and

(c) disablement arising out of and in the course of employment.

This definition is broader than most dictionary definitions of the word "accident". Further, since the word "includes" is used in the statutory definition (as opposed to "is") the definition is open-ended. It has also been observed that the term "accident" is sufficiently broad to include a gradual onset of a disabling condition.

Do the words "by accident" mean only accidental causes, or do they include accidental results? Historically this has been a controversial issue. This distinction is important since work injuries frequently arise when the event giving rise to the personal injury was part of the normal work routine, *i.e.*, lifting an object, pushing or pulling something, *etc.*, and it is the result (sprain, strain, hernia, *etc.*) which was unexpected. The Appeals Tribunal has accepted that accidental results are included, while the Board deals with accidental results as disablements.

(a) Wilful and Intentional Act

This branch of the definition of accident covers the worker as the victim of a designed event as opposed to a chance event. The "act" may be that of a complete stranger (*e.g.*, an armed robber), or it could be the act of a co-worker or a supervisor. A deliberate act by the worker to intentionally cause the worker's own death at work would not be considered a compensable accident, although a worker's suicide following (and related to) a compensable accident may be compensable. A victim of horseplay could be covered under this definition of "accident". In one decision the Appeals Tribunal held that incidents of sexual harassment could be construed as accidents (it may also be appropriate to characterize this situation as falling within the disablement branch of the definition of accident). In another decision the Appeals Tribunal found that the escape of an inmate was a wilful and intentional act causing the worker (a correctional officer) to suffer a psychological injury.

The victim of a wilful and intentional act may wish to consider a lawsuit against the perpetrator or compensation under the *Compensation for Victims of Crime Act*. While the Board does not offset against any criminal injuries award, the Criminal Injuries Compensation Board does have the authority to do so.

Simply because the injured worker is a victim of a "wilful and intentional act" it does not follow that the "personal injury by accident" will be compensable. The work-related nature of personal injury by accident must also be established. To illustrate, a personal enemy of a worker chooses the workplace as opposed to anywhere else, to murder the worker. The enemy simply walks into the factory, shoots the worker dead, and then leaves. In this case it is clear that the "personal injury by accident" did not arise out of the employment; rather, it arose out of personal differences between the aggressor and the worker. The concept of "work-relatedness" is dealt with in Chapter 7.

(b) Chance Event

Both the courts and the Appeals Tribunal have articulated that the key aspect of a chance event is its unexpected nature in the eyes of the victim. Historically the Board has believed that "chance event" must be an external chance event, such as unusual exertion or something happening in the work environment such as a machine malfunction. In Board policy "chance event" is still defined as "an identifiable unintended event which causes an injury", and "an injury itself is not a chance event".

The Board has policies dealing with some chance event situations such as premature termination of pregnancy, blood poisoning, heart attacks and so on.

There are secondary chance events which can be classified as "second accidents". There may be new accidents resulting from the initial compensable injury, or new accidents arising out of treatment. Where a second accident is shown to be caused by a compensable disability, injuries sustained will themselves be considered compensable.

In one case a worker with a compensable knee problem suffered a hand injury at home when his knee gave out while he was operating a table saw. It was accepted that the bad knee contributed to the hand injury and it was acknowledged that workers' compensation is a no-fault system. However, it was felt that the worker's conduct (breach of safety rules, failure to take reasonable precautions) broke the chain of causation and entitlement for the hand injury was denied.

The Board policy covering second accidents arising out of treatment can be summarized as follows. If an accident happens en route to or from a treating agency, for the treatment of a compensable condition, there is no entitlement. However, if an accident happens while travelling, at the direction of the Board, there may be entitlement. There is no entitlement for an accident on the treating agency's premises, but there may be entitlement when disability arises out of treatment. There is entitlement for accidents occurring at the Board's Rehabilitation Centre (the Centre no longer operates). In some cases there may be a right of action against the treating agent (including the Board). The Board treats injuries arising out of treatment as part of the original claim, while injuries arising out of vocational rehabilitation or labour market re-entry activities are treated as a new claim, and this distinction may have benefits implications.

If an unrelated second accident aggravates the compensable disability, benefits under the claim may be terminated if the compensable disability was at or near the stage of full recovery. If it was not, ongoing entitlement should not be affected. Benefits may become payable again in this situation if they had stopped prior to the second accident. In one case the worker was found to be entitled to benefits following a slip at home, which involved twisting. Twisting had been identified by the Board doctors as exactly the type of injury that would aggravate the compensable condition. The Board will closely monitor any legal proceedings arising out of the second accident, especially if the claimant/litigant is alleging a significant disability related to the second accident.

There may also be secondary physical or psychological complications of the original injury, or arising out of treatment. These complications are compensable if they are a consequence of the injury or treatment. The issue is whether or not it can be concluded that the original accident made a significant contribution to the development of the secondary condition.

In one case a worker exposed to sodium hydrochloride fumes developed speech and throat problems, psychological problems and allergies. Approximately three years after the accident the Board terminated all benefits and two months later the worker committed suicide. The Appeals Tribunal found that the psychiatric disability was compensable and there were various symptoms including anxiety and depression. The suicide was also found to be compensable.

(c) Disablement Arising out of and in the Course of Employment (Gradual Injury)

The disablement branch of the definition of accident was added to the Act in 1963. In fact, the Board had compensated on a limited basis for disablement-type injuries prior to 1963. Until 1986, when the Appeals Tribunal first began releasing decisions dealing with the disablement definition of accident the Board had taken a very restrictive view of the provision. Essentially there had to be an unusual incident in the course of normal work activities (perhaps less dramatic or definitive than a typical "chance event"), or some significant change in work activities over a fairly short period of time, for a "disablement" claim to be accepted. The position established by the Appeals Tribunal was that if an injury occurs over time and there is something about the employment that causes the injury, the injury is compensable. Another way of expressing this is that there must be an injuring process which is part of the employment.

If the disability is caused in a significant or material way by work activity, a triggering incident need not occur at work for the disability to be compensable. In one case the Appeals Tribunal reasoned it out as follows:

> The origin of the worker's disabling injury in this case is founded in his employment as a radiator repairman. The time bomb, in the form of the worker's back condition, was constructed during his employment as a radiator repairman. It happened to go off because of a non-occupational incident outside of the worker's employment. However, it was not the incident at the worker's sister-in-law's place that caused the lost time disabling injury. The origin of the disabling injury was the back condition caused by the worker's years of employment as a radiator repairman.

In 1988 the Board developed a policy which provides that the definition of disablement includes a condition that emerges gradually over time, or an unexpected result of working duties. Thus while the Appeals Tribunal has treated unexpected results as "chance events," the Board has been willing to compensate them as "disablements". The statutory presumption regarding work-relatedness (see Chapter 7, Arising Out of and In the Course of Employment) is therefore more widely available at the Appeals Tribunal level than at the Board level because it applies in the case of chance events but not in the case of disablements.

5. RECURRENCE OF DISABILITY

A recurrence of a compensable disability will be compensable if it can be established (on a balance of probabilities) that the original compensable disability has made a significant contribution to the current disability. The situation may be complicated by the presence of a pre-existing disabling condition or a non-work related incident.

Key factors in determining the compensability of a recurrence are:

(1)   Continuity of complaint and/or medical treatment following the original disability;
(2)   The severity of any pre-existing condition and the likelihood of its deterioration over time in the absence of the compensable event;
(3)   The severity of the "personal injury by accident";
(4)   The severity of any non-employment accidents subsequent to the compensable personal injury by accident, including any triggering aggravation;
(5)   The nature of any work undertaken subsequent to the compensable disability with a view to assessing its effects on the compensable disability; and
(6)   Medical compatibility between the current problem and the original disability.

If there is a pre-existing compensable condition which has been somewhat disabling and then a work-related flare-up under circumstances which arguably amount to a new accident, the relative contributions will have to be evaluated to determine whether the flare-up is a recurrence or a new claim. The distinction has cost consequences for employers and payment consequences for workers. These payment consequences are very complex, especially if the worker has had a claim (or claims) for similar injuries covered by different versions of the Act. There may be recurrences of post-January 2, 1990 claims for which no compensation is payable.

6. OCCUPATIONAL DISEASE
(INDUSTRIAL DISEASE)

This topic is dealt with in more detail in Chapter 8. The diagnosis of disease does not preclude an argument for entitlement pursuant to the disablement definition of accident. Generally it is difficult to gather evidence on a case by case basis to support the conclusion that a worker's medical condition amounts to an occupational disease. It may be easier to establish that work has made a significant contribution to the worker's disabling condition (or disease). In one case where entitlement on both bases was argued, the Appeals Tribunal found in the worker's favour with respect to "disablement" and observed that there was insufficient evidence to suggest that the worker was suffering from an occupational disease. It felt that an assessment of the effects of the particular work process on more than one worker would be required before any occupational disease determination could be made.

7. ADJUDICATING THE ACCIDENT (CLAIMS RECOGNITION)

(a) General

The Board uses a "five point check system" to evaluate information on file to determine if entitlement is in order. This policy is intended to encourage a uniform approach when applying the principles of adjudication to any given claims situation. An allowable claim must have these five points: an employer, a worker, personal work-related injury, proof of accident, and compatibility of diagnosis to accident or disablement history. The last two points are usually the most contentious.

Regarding proof of accident, the Board is concerned about accident vs. disablement, witnesses, discrepancies between date of accident and date of lay-off, and delays in onset of symptoms or the seeking of medical attention.

Regarding compatibility of diagnosis to accident history the policy provides that where it is not clear that the resulting disability is the consequence of the history described (and usually it is quite clear) the opinion of the medical adviser (a Board doctor) is to be obtained. The absence of a clear diagnosis is not necessarily fatal to a claim as long as it can be determined that a symptom-complex or some sort of condition exists.

(b) Onset of Symptoms

While in work accident situations there is usually an immediate onset of symptoms, this is not invariably the case. Quite often a minor bump or strain may be barely noticed at work for any number of reasons (stoic worker, fast pace of work, *etc.*), and will only become disabling later in the day during a rest period, or after work. In disablement cases the worker may have great difficulty pinpointing the exact date of onset in what was really a gradual onset situation.

If there is a good explanation given by the worker regarding the onset of symptoms and some evidence of compatibility of the disability to what was identified as a work incident, or to the work environment in general, the lack of immediate onset of symptoms should not preclude entitlement.

(c) Delays in Reporting/Seeking Medical Attention

Delays in a worker's reporting an accident or seeking medical attention require clarification because such delays create doubt that the accident occurred, and doubt regarding the relationship of the disability to the accident. Further, the more discomfort any injury creates, the more important the need for clarification of the reason for delays.

There are often reasonable explanations for delay. Indeed, there may be dispute as to whether or not there was a delay. Typical explanations include:

- Fairly minor injury at the end of a shift or on a Friday and an expectation on the part of the worker that the problem will disappear with rest;
- High frequency of minor injuries which are never reported and never seriously disabling;
- Underestimation on the worker's part of the severity of the injury;
- Stoical worker with high pain threshold;
- No realistic means of obtaining medical treatment for a relatively minor injury (*i.e.,* doctor's offices closed, medical situation not severe enough to warrant a trip to the emergency ward of the hospital);
- Language difficulties;
- Unfamiliarity with workers' compensation or misconception of what an "accident" is; and
- Fear of being fired or laid off.

(d) No Witnesses

Since workers frequently work alone, or are busy with their own tasks while on the job, very often there are no witnesses to a work incident. This probably troubles employers more than it troubles the Board. Certainly, if injuries are clearly visible, there will not usually be any concern about the absence of witnesses.

If an onset of pain is promptly reported and the worker seems to be in pain, albeit with no cuts or bruises, the absence of witnesses to the accident will not be a problem. On the other hand, the Board will expect that there are witnesses to "immediate" complaints following the onset of pain, either on the job site or once the worker encounters someone to whom one might reasonably expect the worker would complain (for example, a spouse upon the worker's arrival home). Explanations for a lack of witnesses regarding complaints are often similar to those regarding delay.

(e) Inconsistencies in the Worker's Evidence

A worker who is not accurate, reliable and credible will encounter difficulties in a disputed claims recognition case. There are many opportunities for the worker to be inconsistent. An accident report will probably have been completed and it may have been followed by a number of letters describing the accident. The worker may have telephoned or may have been interviewed by Board personnel. The worker may have said something to someone who in turn passed this information along to the Board. Inconsistencies will either have to be reconciled or discounted before entitlement will be allowed. Relevant considerations are that:

- There may be language problems or literacy problems;
- Doctors are often taking second- or third-hand histories;
- Board employees frequently record what they think they hear and this may not bear much resemblance to what was said. These people are not required to give *viva voce* evidence;

- Board employees below the Appeals level are under tremendous time pressures and rarely have the opportunity of giving workers a chance to explain or elaborate; and/or
- The worker's "accident report" (if on file at all) is often completed by someone other than the worker and may therefore be inaccurate.

8. ADJUDICATING ONGOING ENTITLEMENT/RECURRENCES

A worker may be seeking ongoing entitlement where no permanent impairment award was ever made and/or claiming a recurrence of an old disability which may or may not carry a permanent impairment award. The Board will carry out essentially similar enquiries in any of these situations.

Board policy (which focuses more on the recurrence versus new accident issue rather than the ongoing entitlement issue) is that a recurrence will be accepted when there is obvious medical compatibility and continuity, and an absence of a new accident. The same approach is taken regarding general ongoing entitlement.

If there is a need to obtain information regarding continuity, the Board will look for ongoing:

- Complaints to supervisors/co-workers;
- Symptoms;
- Work restrictions/modifications;
- Medical treatment; and/or
- Changes in lifestyle consistent with the alleged disability that establish a connection between the original condition and subsequent problems.

Especially with continuity, the situation must be taken as a whole. The question of what is "good continuity" (as opposed to "no continuity") is always open to debate. Lack of continuity of treatment may be explained by the fact that there was no specific beneficial treatment for the condition.

CHAPTER 7

Arising Out Of and In the Course Of Employment

1. INTRODUCTION

The cornerstone of entitlement in a workers' compensation scheme is the concept of personal injury by accident arising out of and in the course of employment. This chapter will deal with the phrase "arising out of and in course of employment" which is, in essence, a test of work-relatedness.

As a general rule, both aspects of the work-relatedness test must be met. The personal injury by accident must both arise out of the employment and arise in the course of the employment.

2. THE SECTION 4(3) PRESUMPTION

The requirement that both aspects of the test must be separately met, before compensation is payable, is considerably modified by two factors. First, as can be seen from the discussion below, the interpretation of "course of employment" has grown to include some situations not normally considered to be included in the course of employment where the hazard the worker is exposed to results from the employment situation or where the worker is under the control or supervision of the employer. Second, is the "presumption" in s. 13(2) of the current Act and s. 4(3) of the pre-1997 Act, which reads:

> **13.** (2) If the accident arises out of the worker's employment, it is presumed to have occurred in the course of the employment unless the contrary is shown. It if occurs in the course of the worker's employment, it is presumed to have arisen out of the employment unless the contrary is shown.
>
> **4.** (3) Where the accident arose out of the employment, unless the contrary is shown, it shall be presumed that it occurred in the course of the employment and, where the accident occurred in the course of the employment unless the contrary is shown, it shall be presumed that it arose out of the employment.

There is no Board policy on the work-relatedness presumption. The Board's practice has been to apply it only when the injury occurred in the course of employment and it was impossible to know whether the injury arose out of the employment. The presumption was almost always only invoked in cases of death or injury-induced amnesia on the job.

A number of Appeals Tribunal decisions have considered when the presumption should be applied and the standard of proof required to rebut the presumption (*i.e.*, how the contrary is "shown"). There seems to be consistency on the issue of when the presumption should be applied, but disagreement on the standard of proof issue.

Regarding the application of the presumption, the accepted position is that the presumption applies to factual issues, not legal issues, and that it is available with respect to every personal injury by accident except those which fall within the disablement part of the definition of "accident".

Regarding the standard of proof required to rebut the presumption of work-relatedness, it was held in one decision that the contrary had to be shown *beyond a reasonable doubt*. This position has not been followed in subsequent Appeals Tribunal decisions. The "current consensus" in these decisions is that "clear and convincing evidence" (or "sufficiently convincing evidence") showing the contrary is required to rebut the presumption of work-relatedness. The problem remains, however, that what may appear "clear and convincing" to one decision-maker, may strike another decision-maker differently.

There is still a great reluctance amongst many decision-makers at the Board to apply the work-relatedness presumption and the safest approach for workers or their representatives is to bring forward arguments and evidence intended to establish *both* aspects of work-relatedness on a balance of probabilities. Arguments about the work-relatedness presumption will be more useful at the Appeals Tribunal hearing if one is required.

3. ARISING OUT OF THE EMPLOYMENT

(a) General

In essence, the "arising out of" test involves establishing a causal relationship between the work activity and the injury. Although Board policy documents deal with some particular problems in the "arising out of" context (these are discussed below), the Board has not established any general policy statement on how the issue of "cause" will be determined.

The late Professor Larson suggested that there are three alternative approaches to this question being followed in the United States. The first approach is to require that it be shown that the injury was caused by an increased risk to which the claimant was subjected, as compared to the general public ("increased risk"). The second approach is to require only that the risk, even if common to the public, was actually a risk of the employment ("actual risk"). The third approach is a test whereby it must be shown that the employment put the worker in a position where there was exposure to a risk of injury which would not otherwise have been the case ("positional risk").

Although the theory underlying Board policy is not clearly articulated, for the most part, in practice, the Board has adopted an "actual risk" or "positional risk" approach to "arising out of" areas of controversy. Typically, the significant "arising out of" issue is medical causation, *i.e.*, establishing that the work activity contributed to the risk of personal injury by accident.

(b) Lightning, Tempest, Sunstroke, Heat Prostration, Frostbite, Insect Bite

Historically these have been "arising out of" problem areas because members of the public were usually exposed to the identical risks which were seldom, in the narrowest sense, caused by the employment. The problem disappears if an "actual risk" or "positional risk" analysis is adopted, and the Board in practice has done so with the following policy laid out in the *WCB Operational Policy Manual*:

> Where disability is caused due to lightning, tempest, sunstroke, heat prostration, frostbite or insect bite, the criteria to be used in determining entitlement shall be that, if the worker is in the course of employment at the time of exposure, and if there is no serious or wilful misconduct on the part of the worker, the disability will be considered to be one rising out of and in the course of employment.

(c) Food Poisoning

The Board has adopted an "actual risk" or "positional risk" policy here as well. The "arising out of" factor will be satisfied if the food was obtained through facilities authorized by the employer or the food was obtained in a food outlet while on company business. The "company business" may raise a "course of employment" issue.

(d) Blood Poisoning

In this potentially mixed-risk situation, Board policy is that the point of entry (lesion) must result from a work-related accident, and when and where the actual germ of infection entered the wound is unimportant. Where the point of entry was not incurred at work, or the condition appears incompatible, a medical opinion will be sought regarding compatibility of the disability to the history of onset.

(e) Infected Blisters/Calluses (Feet)

The current policy is that if injury to the feet (including infected blisters) is sustained and traceable to work, it is compensable, regardless of the actual footwear worn or the specific contribution of the footwear. This amounts to an "actual risk" analysis. The logic of this policy can be extended to apply to infected blisters or calluses on the hands; *i.e.*, compensation would follow if the blister or infection is traceable to work.

(f) Seizures

Historically, this was also an "arising out of" problem because there may have been no work contribution at all to a seizure resulting in an injury on the job. In a policy which dealt with epileptic seizures it was established that even though the seizure itself may not be compensable, injuries secondary to a seizure at work are compensable. The policy, in effect, compensates for a work-related result and also is an application of the "actual" or "positional" risk approach.

(g) Other Situations

The Board has policies covering a variety of other situations. These policies reflect an "actual risk" analysis. The logic of all of these policies could presumably be extended by decision-makers at the Board to cover situations not covered by policy. The absence of a specific policy should not be fatal to a claim, and it certainly has not been at the Appeals Tribunal.

(h) The Approach of the Appeals Tribunal

The analysis of "arising out of employment" has proceeded along fairly simple lines at the Appeals Tribunal. The focus is on the accident (or disablement) and its causation, using the significant contribution test. Essentially, work, or some reasonably incidental work activity, must be found to be a significant contributing factor in the onset of disability. In the disablement cases the "arising out of" issue is generally a medical one. Sometimes the analysis of the "arising out of" element is blurred with the analysis of the "course of employment factor", most often if the "arising out of" issue is non-medical, and if the "in the course of" circumstances are more marginal. In cases where the medical connection between the injuring event and the injury is obvious, but the *employment* connection is not, a risk analysis has been used by some Appeals Tribunal panels to determine the employment connection.

4. COURSE OF EMPLOYMENT

(a) General

This part of the formula deals with questions of place, time and activity. Generally, personal injury by accident can be seen as arising (or occurring) in the course of employment if it takes place in, or had definite origins in, the period of employment, at a place where the worker reasonably may be while the worker is carrying out work-related tasks or something reasonably incidental to them (for example, going to the washroom).

The Board has put it this way:

A personal injury by accident occurs in the course of employment if the surrounding circumstances relating to *place*, *time*, and *activity* indicate that the accident was work-related.

. . .

The importance of the three criteria varies depending on the circumstances of each case. In most cases, the decision-maker focuses primarily on the activity of the worker at the time the personal injury by accident occurred to determine whether it occurred in the course of employment.

Also, the Board has another policy which provides that:

Compensation benefits are not payable to workers who voluntarily take themselves out of the employment. Such situations may include:

— doing something outside their allotted duties, such as transacting personal business, or

— going places having nothing to do with their employment or doing something not reasonably expected of them.

(b) Going To and From Work

Injuries sustained going to and from work, off the premises of the employer are generally considered to have arisen outside the course of employment. There are a number of exceptions. Also, there may be some latitude in the definition of "premises".

There are three basic exceptions outlined in Board policy and also addressed in various Appeals Tribunal decisions.

A worker is considered to be "in the course of employment" when the conditions of the employment require a worker to drive a vehicle to and from work for the purpose of that employment, except when a distinct departure on a personal errand occurs. Various Appeals Tribunal decisions have given some definition to this concept.

The second exception is that a worker is considered to be "in the course of employment" when going to and from work in a conveyance under the control and supervision of, or chartered by, the employer. A related concept is that where an employer hires a worker from a distant place and offers travel time or travelling expenses to induce the worker to leave and travel, the journey may become part of the employment. The mere payment of travel expenses may not be determinative.

With both of the above exceptions a decision regarding "in the course of employment" may involve a careful weighing and balancing of the employment features and the personal features of the situation.

The third exception is for workers travelling to answer an emergency call from the employer, requiring immediate action on the worker's part. Coverage starts from the time the telephone call is received, and while travelling by a reasonable and direct route to work. There will also be coverage for the return trip. Board policy does not define an emergency, but this has come up in an Appeals Tribunal decision.

(c) Defining "Premises"

(i) General

Board policy is that:

> If a worker has a fixed workplace, a personal injury by accident occurring on the premises of the workplace generally will have occurred in the course of employment. A personal injury by accident occurring off the premises generally will not have occurred in the course of employment.

The Board defines the employer's premises as:

> [T]he building, plant or location in which the worker is entitled to be, including entrances, exits, stairs, elevators, lobbies, parking lots, passageways and roads controlled by the employer for the use of the workers as access to and egress from the work site.

While wording in the definition is broad, on the whole, the definition lacks clarity. The words "location" and "work site" connote premises which may have somewhat imprecise boundaries (even given an entry gate or clocking-in point) such as a construction work site, a complex of residential or office buildings, a university campus, *etc*. Lack of access to the general public may not be a feature of the entire "work site" and it may not be appropriate to give much weight to this factor when adjudicating "course of employment". The realistic boundaries of a worksite may vary with the type of employment. The Appeals Tribunal has demonstrated a flexible approach on the boundary issue. In effect, the concept of employer control of an area or the worker will be more important than a precise property line.

(ii) Access Roads

Board policy on accidents occurring on access roads is as follows:

> If part of the worker's journey to or from work takes place on a road that is completely controlled by means such as posted notices, warning signs, or opening or closing of gates, maintenance work or snow clearing, the worker is in the course of employment while using the roadway.
>
> The worker is not in the course of employment while using a road open to the general public.
>
> The condition of the employer's private roads must cause the accident.

The policy also deals with "arising out of employment" in the following terms:

> Accidents on employer's premises arise out of employment, unless
>
>> —— for personal reasons, the worker used an instrument of added peril, for example, an automobile, motorcycle or bicycle.
>>
>> —— the act causing the injury does not relate to work or employment obligations.

Generally, the Appeals Tribunal has adopted a flexible approach in access road cases, frequently commenting that the Board policy is not in keeping with the Act.

(iii) Parking Lots

Board policy dealing with "course of employment" and parking lots provides that:

> The employer must own or lease the parking lot. If driving, the condition of the employer's lot must cause the accident. If walking, the condition of the lot need not be a contributing factor. Workers are not entitled to compensation if injured by their own vehicle.
>
> Workers are not in the course of employment in public parking areas not under the employer's control.
>
> Workers injured in parking spaces regulated and allocated by the employer may be entitled to compensation.
>
> Workers are members of the general public once they leave the allocated areas and remain so until they arrive on the employer's premises.
>
> Workers have no entitlement if their injuries occur on indoor streets and walkways open to the general public and not under the employer's control.
>
> Entitlement is allowed if accidents occur on the actual premises of the employer within the mall or plaza.

The Appeals Tribunal has tended toward a broader (or more inclusive) interpretation of "premises" than that reflected in the above policy. For example an accident will generally be found to have occurred in the course of employment if it occurs in a public area which represents the most direct route to the employer's parking lot. This would include indoor streets and walkways (or stairwells). However, if an accident occurs in a non-employer controlled or owned parking lot in a "going and coming" situation where the worker is a "fixed premises" worker, it will likely be considered not to have occurred in the course of employment.

One current view is that there is a presumption that a personal injury by accident sustained on the employer's premises occurs in the course of employment unless the worker's activity is sufficiently remote from normal employment functions that the activity and resulting injury could not be characterized as reasonably incidental to employment.

(iv) Boundaries in a Multi-Storey/Occupancy Building

Board policy on this topic is as follows:

> The employer's premises are:
>
> —— all areas occupied solely by the employer
>
> —— all common areas for entering or exiting the building at street level, including outside stairs to public property
>
> —— escalators, elevators, stairs to areas occupied by the employer or common areas from a public concourse to the main floor lobby and from the lobby to the floor occupied by the employer.
>
> When the employer occupies a portion of a floor, workers are on the employer's premises in areas designated as common to the tenants on that floor. Workers must take the most direct route from the elevators/stairs to the employer's premises.
>
> Workers are members of the general public after leaving the allocated parking area and before reaching the areas designated above.
>
> Workers entering the building on any but the main floor or the floor occupied by the employer, are not in the course of employment until entering the elevator/stairs leading to the floor of the employer's premises.

The Board and the Appeals Tribunal make a distinction between horizontal workplaces (*e.g.*, plazas) and vertical workplaces (*e.g.*, office buildings) in terms of where premises boundary lines are drawn. There has been some inconsistency in decisions on this topic.

(d) Errands or Travel on the Employer's Business

This is not similar to going to and from work, because the journey or errand is clearly part of the work. The Board's general policy on errands or travel on the employer's business is as follows:

> If a worker with a fixed workplace was injured while absent from the workplace on behalf of the employer or if a worker is normally expected to work away from a fixed workplace, a personal injury by accident generally will have occurred in the course of employment if it occurred in a place where the worker might reasonably have been expected to be while engaged in work-related activities.

A more particular policy on "travelling" provides that:

> When the conditions of the employment require the worker to travel away from the employer's premises, the worker is considered to be in the course of employment continuously except when a distinct departure on a personal errand is shown. The mode of travel may be public transportation or by employer or worker vehicle if the employment requires the use of such a vehicle. However, the employment must obligate the worker to be travelling at the place and time the accident occurred.

A worker travelling to or from a convention (and/or participating in convention activities other than social activities or other personal business) is also considered by the Board to be in the course of employment.

The Board's policies on this topic are relatively straightforward and results consistent with them have been reached in many Appeals Tribunal decisions. Typically, two issues have to be addressed in a "course of employment" ruling: can the errand or travel be considered a reasonable employment activity; and, if so, has some personal activity of the worker (*e.g.*, a deviation or what the Board calls a "distinct departure on a personal errand" or dual purpose trip) taken the worker outside of the course of employment at the time of the accident? Usually the more troublesome cases involve the second issue.

Strictly speaking, travelling workers engage in a variety of activities while travelling, and unless there is a concept of universal coverage for all activities from departure until return, a course of employment issue may arise depending upon the worker's activity when injured while travelling. As a starting point, there is Board policy:

> Entitlement under the Act extends to persons travelling in the course of their employment to and from various places. Coverage also extends to accidents occurring in places such as hotels when the employer is paying the worker's expenses. The worker is covered should he suffer injury by accident at any time while in the hotel engaged in reasonable acts such as dining in the restaurant and using washroom facilities. If the worker chooses to dine in a restaurant other than in the hotel but within a reasonable distance of it, coverage is extended during this activity. There is no entitlement if the worker is injured while visiting a movie theatre or cocktail lounge or engaging in some other personal activity.

The Appeals Tribunal, in dealing with the activities of travelling workers has focussed on the purpose of the worker's activity. If it has a significant employment-related purpose, or is reasonably incidental to employment, then the worker will be in the course of employment. This analysis is consistent with other Appeals Tribunal decisions dealing with "activity".

(e) Dual Purpose Trips

A trip may serve a personal purpose as well as an employment purpose, and this may raise a course of employment issue. There is no Board policy on dual purpose trips, but Board policy as outlined above does refer to distinct departures on personal errands. Decisions from the Appeals Tribunal have adopted the American concurrent cause principle:

> Injury during a trip which serves both a business and a personal purpose is within the course of employment if the trip involves the performance of a service for the employer which would have caused the trip to be taken even if it had not coincided with the personal purpose.

Workers who carry out part of their job duties at home may be faced with the dual purpose problem. There should be little difficulty if the worker was travelling home to complete a specific work assignment. In more general cases the following factors may be relevant:

(1)   Whether the home (in part) is considered as an expense deductible for Income Tax purposes;
(2)   Whether there is a specific worksite (*i.e.*, a study or shop) within the home;
(3)   The presence of work equipment at home; and/or
(4)   Special features of the work conducive to, or necessitating, performance at home.

The worker would also have to demonstrate that the particular trip home would have been made even if there had not been a coinciding personal purpose (assuming that the worker is arguing that he/she was in the course of employment during the trip).

(f) Deviations During Trips

As stated above, Board policy on trips envisions coverage while the worker is on the most direct route. At the other extreme, an identifiable deviation for personal reasons takes the worker out of the course of employment until the direct route is regained. Small deviations (especially if for a reasonable personal comfort function) can probably be disregarded. Cases falling between the two extremes are the difficult ones.

The analysis in Appeals Tribunal decisions recognizes that during a deviation employment features may predominate (or the activity itself may be reasonably incidental to employment), or the deviation may represent a distinct departure for personal reasons (where, in effect, the employment features are merely coincidental). Factors to be assessed in determining the issue include:

*   The acceptability to the employer of the worker's conduct;
*   Whether the activity represents a direct or indirect discharge of the worker's duties and/or benefits the employer;
*   Whether the worker is entitled to be paid;
*   The amount of geographic deviation represented by the departure (if any) from the most direct route;
*   The ownership of any vehicle being used; and/or
*   Whether the deviation is for an act of reasonable personal comfort.

Conclusions in these cases often turn on very subtle factual distinctions.

(g) Time

The Board's general position about "time" and the course of employment is:

> If a worker has fixed working hours, a personal injury by accident generally will have occurred in the course of employment if it occurred during those hours or during a reasonable period before starting or after finishing work.
>
> If a worker does not have fixed working hours or if the accident occurred outside the worker's fixed working hours, the criteria of place and activity are applied to determine whether the personal injury by accident occurred in the course of employment.

More specifically, the Board "will consider entitlement" where a worker is injured when:

—— obtaining pay or depositing tools, etc., on the employer's premises after actual work hours,

—— on a lunch, break, or other non-work period (period of leisure) [and when injured] by ordinary hazards of the employer's premises.

The Appeals Tribunal has followed the general thrust of Board policy regarding time. In one case it was held that in construction work reasonable anticipation of remuneration was an appropriate indicator of work-relatedness. Thus a roofer who was injured while waiting close to a job site (to see if the weather would clear sufficiently to permit work) was found to be in the course of employment when injured. The Appeals Tribunal has also found workers repairing their own equipment after work hours to be in the course of employment because the activity is reasonably incidental to employment. In British Columbia the Board adopted the principle that:

> Compensation coverage is not automatically and instantaneously terminated by the firing or quitting of an employee. He is deemed to be within the course of employment for a reasonable period while he winds up his affairs and leaves the premises.

A similar principle has been articulated in Appeals Tribunal decisions.

When dealing with lunch or break cases the distinction between whether the injury occurred on or off the employer's premises will be of extreme importance for "fixed premises" workers. Generally, off-premises injuries are not compensable. However, even with on-premises injuries there is not automatic coverage.

(h) Activity

(i) General

The concept of "reasonably incidental" activities has been adopted by the Board (as well as the Appeals Tribunal) as reflected in the following policy statements:

> If a personal injury by accident occurred while the worker was engaged in the performance of a work-related duty or in an activity reasonably incidental to (related to) the employment, the personal injury by accident generally will have occurred in the course of employment.
> ... [E]ngaging in a brief interlude of personal activity does not always mean that the worker was not in the course of employment. In determining whether a personal activity occurred in the course of employment, the decision-maker should consider factors such as:
>
> —— the duration of the activity
>
> —— the nature of the activity, and
>
> —— the extent to which it deviated from the worker's regular employment activities.
>
> In determining whether an activity was incidental to the employment, the decision-maker should take into consideration
>
> —— the nature of the work
>
> —— the nature of the work environment
>
> —— the customs and practices of the particular workplace.

In one Appeals Tribunal decision it was noted that a routine part of daily living could be incidental to employment if it were essential to employment (the activity in question was removing safety shoes).

(ii) Acts of Personal Comfort

It is Board policy that a worker engaged in an activity to satisfy a personal need may have been engaged in an activity that was incidental to employment. In one case compensation was denied when a construction worker was hit by a car while crossing the street to take his coffee break in his car parked in a non-employer controlled parking lot. The Appeals Tribunal had little difficulty in concluding on the facts that the risk of being hit by a car was not an ordinary hazard of the employer's premises. In another case the Appeals Tribunal concluded that using the washroom facilities was reasonably incidental to employment and that the only factors contributing to the accident (a hand injury) were employment related.

(iii) Recreational, Social and Educational Activities

In addition to the general Board policy on "activity" discussed above, there are also some specific policy provisions. In the "On/Off Employers' Premises" policy the following appears:

> *Without limitation to the following*, the Board will consider entitlement in claims where a worker is injured when:
>
> ...
>
> —— participating in a work related sports activity, for example, school teachers and camp counsellors, when the employer condones these activities by making the premises available and/or exercising a form of supervision and control,
>
> —— attending compulsory evening courses,
>
> ...
>
> —— travelling to or from a convention and/or participating in convention activities.

[Emphasis added.]

A number of fact situations have come up before the Appeals Tribunal and the decisions reached in general are in keeping with the policies and principles already discussed.

The problem with conventions is that it may be difficult to distinguish between "convention activities" and "social activities" or non-work-related personal activities. At issue will be how closely the social activity is connected to or a valuable aspect of the convention.

(i) Residential Workers

The Board does not have any general policies on residential workers. Claims involving residential workers may raise both "arising out of" and "course of" employment issues. The distinctions between these two aspects of work-relatedness may be blurred.

The general "arising out of" test applies, *viz.* is work or a reasonably incidental work activity a significant contributing factor to the accident? In one case the Appeals Tribunal used this test: "has the worker in choosing a particular activity chosen to introduce a personal element which would not ordinarily be considered a reasonable by-product of the employment environment?" Using the washroom on board a ship while off duty was identified as reasonably incidental to employment.

It has been consistently held that a residential worker is not disqualified from workers' compensation benefits merely because she or he is off duty at the time of the injury. In effect, for these workers, there is generally no problem making a positive "course of employment" finding. There could, however, be a dispute over whether or not residency is a requirement, or at least reasonably incidental to employment given the nature of the worksite.

The use of alcohol or drugs in a residential setting could be characterized as the introduction by the worker of a personal element of major significance. The Appeals Tribunal has held that intoxication does not in itself bar entitlement, but compensation will be denied if the degree of intoxication is so severe that it can be said that the injury does not arise out of employment. The outcome of any case involving alcohol or drug ingestion will depend on such factors as the degree of intoxication of the worker, the employer's tolerance of this conduct, and any possible contributing conditions of the workplace to the accident. Although a residential worker is effectively in the course of employment on a continuous basis as long as he or she is present on the employer's premises, it could be argued that the worker's conduct or activity has removed the worker from the course of employment.

5. ASSAULTS, FIGHTING AND HORSEPLAY

These situations may raise "course of employment" and/or serious and wilful misconduct issues, since under certain conditions an instigator or participant may by virtue of his or her conduct remove himself or herself from the course of employment, or be guilty of serious and wilful misconduct. There are also "arising out of" considerations.

Assaults are compensable if the normal work entails a risk of assault given its nature and setting (for example, psychiatric nursing). The more difficult cases are where assaults would not be considered a normal risk of work. The factual analysis will be extremely important in a determination of the work-relatedness of an incident.

The Appeals Tribunal has found that the sexual or racial nature of an incident does not necessarily take the incident out of the scope of the Act.

Board policy (reflective of an actual or positional risk approach) is that if a fight results solely over work, the claim may be accepted if the injured worker was not the aggressor and did not provoke the fight or was an innocent bystander. Similarly, if a worker is an innocent victim of horseplay or larking and did not participate or retaliate, an injury claim will be accepted by the Board. The Appeals Tribunal has in some decisions rejected the "solely over work" aspect of the Board policy as too restrictive, noting that it was more in keeping with the usual "arising out of" test to ask if the fight was substantially related to work. Another way of putting it is to ask if work was a significant contributing factor to the incident.

Board policy regarding the instigators of, or participants (aside from innocent victims) in horseplay, larking, or fighting is that these individuals are generally not compensated for any injuries sustained, on the basis that they have removed themselves from the course of employment. This strict position has not been followed by the Appeals Tribunal. Indeed, it has been held that to begin a factual analysis of a "fight case" with the presumption that participation in a fight takes a worker out of the course of employment is not consistent with the wording or intent of the Act.

The Appeals Tribunal has looked beyond the Board policy on fighting, horseplay and larking to the Board's general course of employment policy and noted its similarity to factors which Larson has listed as helpful in determining whether initiation of horseplay amounts to a significant deviation from the course of employment. These factors are:

- The extent and seriousness of the deviation;
- The completeness of the deviation;
- The extent to which horseplay had become an accepted part of employment; and
- The extent to which the nature of the employment may be expected to include some such horseplay.

In one Appeals Tribunal case one of the issues was whether two workers who were involved in a horseplay incident lasting about five seconds had taken themselves out of the course of employment by their actions. In deciding that they had not, the Panel (in effect) applied the substantial deviation test and considered a number of factors consistent with the Board's serious and wilful misconduct policy (see below). Although the issue of serious and wilful misconduct has been discussed in many of the Appeals Tribunal decisions dealing with fighting or horseplay, it has not been an explicit factor in the outcome of these decisions, even where entitlement has been denied.

6. SERIOUS AND WILFUL MISCONDUCT

Subsection 17 of the current Act provides:

> **17.** If an injury is attributable solely to the serious and wilful misconduct of the worker, no benefits shall be provided under the insurance plan unless the injury results in the worker's death or serious impairment.

A similar provision is found in s. 4(7) of the pre-1997 Act.

This provision has rarely been applied by the Board because serious and wilful misconduct has historically been difficult to prove, and most impairments found to result from serious and wilful misconduct are also found to be "serious impairments".

The *Operational Policy Manual* contains nothing on this topic. Previously published Board policy provides:

> A worker injured by an accident due solely to his serious and wilful misconduct will not be compensated unless the injury results in death or serious

disablement (more than six weeks temporary total disability or permanent disability).

The misconduct must be deliberate or intentional and not merely a thoughtless act or one done on impulse or on the spur of the moment. Inattention will not constitute serious and wilful misconduct nor, as a rule, will mere imprudence, negligence, lack of care or caution, or error of judgment on the part of the worker. The danger to himself or others involved in the act, the worker's appreciation of probable consequence, and his age and experience are considered.

Disobedience to an express order or a deliberate breach of law or rule, well known to the worker and designed for his safety and enforced, will generally be held to be serious and wilful misconduct. Each case must be determined upon its own particular circumstances.

It seems well established that a finding of serious and wilful misconduct does not take the worker out of the course of his or her employment. Rather, it only potentially affects entitlement to "benefits or compensation". Thus if there is no finding of work-relatedness, the issue of the effect of a finding of serious and wilful misconduct would not arise. For example, in one case the Appeals Tribunal found that the worker was so intoxicated at the time of his accident that the injury did not arise out of employment (although it had occurred in the course of employment). There was no discussion of serious and wilful misconduct. In another case the Appeals Tribunal found that the worker had been drinking at the time of the accident, but the accident had occurred in the course of employment and the worker's drinking had not been so extreme as to break the causal nexus between employment and the accident (*i.e.*, the accident still arose out of employment). The Panel then went on to consider subs. 4(7) of the pre-1997 Act and held that the worker's drinking was not of a nature and extent sufficient to be considered serious and wilful misconduct that would deny the worker entitlement to benefits.

The Appeals Tribunal has articulated a three-question approach to serious and wilful misconduct cases:

(1)   Was the accident solely attributable to the serious and wilful misconduct of the employee?
(2)   Was the action of the worker serious and wilful misconduct?
(3)   Did the injury caused by the accident result in serious disablement?

In light of Appeals Tribunal decisions to date, it seems clear that by the time these three questions have been canvassed, very few workers will be disentitled to benefits by virtue of serious and wilful misconduct.

7. SUBSTANCE ABUSE

There are no provisions regarding substance abuse in the Act.

It could be argued that a worker who is so drunk or "high" that he or she is incapable of performing work activities, has abandoned the employment and therefore although nominally at work, is acting outside the course of the employment. It could also be argued that in this situation any injury did not arise out of employment. On the other hand, drunkenness could also be characterized as a species of serious and wilful misconduct.

The Appeals Tribunal has not been prepared to deal with intoxication or drug abuse strictly as a species of serious and wilful misconduct. In one decision the Panel stated:

> There is a general proposition in compensation law that intoxication in and of itself does not bar entitlement to compensation. It is only if the degree of intoxication is so severe that it can be said the injury does not arise out of the employment that compensation will be denied ...

In other decisions the Appeals Tribunal has considered intoxication or drug abuse as relevant in the first instance to employment-relatedness and then (if the injury has been found to have arisen out of and in the course of the employment), as a potential species of serious and wilful misconduct. Further, intoxication or drug abuse has been characterized as raising "arising out of" concerns rather than "course of employment" concerns.

8. FALLING ASLEEP

What are the course of employment implications of falling asleep on the job? In one Appeals Tribunal decision, the facts were that a deceased truck driver may have fallen asleep while still driving. The Panel was not satisfied on the evidence that this had happened, but commented that a finding that a worker had fallen asleep would not necessarily result in the conclusion that he removed himself from the course of employment. In this regard the Panel stressed the no-fault, remedial nature of workers' compensation legislation.

CHAPTER 8

Compensation for Occupational Disease

1. BACKGROUND

While occupational diseases have come increasingly into the public limelight over the last 20 years, Ontario had an historical head start over many jurisdictions in recognizing — in theory, at least — that diseases arising from the workplace were just as worthy of compensation as traumatic injuries. Sir William Ralph Meredith, the founder of workers' compensation in Ontario, in 1912 wrote in his *Final Report*:

> It would, in my opinion, be a blot on the act if a workman who suffers from an industrial disease contracted in the course of his employment is not to be entitled to compensation. The risk of contracting disease is inherent in the occupation he follows and he is practically powerless to guard against it. A workman may to some extent guard against accidents, and it would seem not only illogical but unreasonable to compensate him in the one case and to deny him the right to compensation in the other.

Yet, in contemporary studies carried out in Great Britain (1906) and New York State (1909), disease compensation was not recommended on the ironic grounds that the study commissions, having discovered a disease problem, felt confident that government and industry would hastily proceed to eliminate it.

Perhaps because of this early start, Ontario is ahead of many other jurisdictions in compensating for occupational disease. However, while in *relative* terms Ontario may compensate for disease more readily than other jurisdictions, in *absolute* terms most observers have noticed a considerable gap between the actual number of occupational disease victims and those who receive WCB benefits. In his 1983 report on occupational disease compensation, Professor Paul Weiler noted that only one out of 17 occupational cancer deaths was currently being compensated. Indeed, there is a large number of occupational disease victims who do not even bother to file claims, whether from ignorance that their condition may be compensable, or from a perception that a hopeless bureaucratic fight will ensue.

Sadly, despite this considerable attention paid to the problems of the underreporting of occupational disease during the 1980s, there does not seem to have been any significant change. A study published in late 1992 noted that, while physicians are required to report occupational diseases in three provinces — Alberta, Saskatchewan and Newfoundland — there continued to be significant underreporting of occupational cancer claims to the provincial WCBs. The authors estimated that, in the three provinces that were able to provide the data sought (British Columbia, Saskatchewan and Ontario) less than ten per cent of occupational cancers were compensated. The authors noted that "underreporting to the WCBs rather than rejection of claims was responsible for most of this deficit".

Another problem stems from misunderstandings about simple definitions. A report done for the World Health Organization, for example, divided diseases related to work as follows:

(1) *Occupational* disease, in which there is a direct cause and effect relationship between an occupational hazard and a disease — occupational exposure to asbestos and the onset of mesothelioma, for example;

(2) *Work-related* disease, in which "the work environment and the performance of work contribute significantly" to the development of a disease. In these cases, the disease may well be multifactorial with other, non-work factors playing a part — for example, a long-time coke oven worker who has smoked for many years and develops lung cancer; and

(3) Underlying disease processes which may be *aggravated* or *exacerbated* by the work environment — asthma, for example.

While all of these conditions may be compensated in Ontario, the second and third categories create problems in underreporting and often extreme complexities in adjudication.

There are also problems in determining whether a disease process can be accelerated by an accident. In one Tribunal decision, for example, it was determined that a compensable blow to a worker's shin resulted in the return of a bladder cancer that had been in remission and the spread to the site of the blow, the worker's fibula. It was held that the cancer of the fibula was thus compensable.

There is no area of workers' compensation more difficult to adjudicate than occupational disease claims. Traumatic injuries, even those of gradual onset, generally either do or do not stand the scrutiny of a workplace origin. Working conditions which may have led to traumatic injury can be fairly well reconstructed, even years after the fact. Workers claiming "repetitive strain" type injuries do not usually engage in non-work activity which can produce a similar ailment.

Occupational diseases, on the other hand, fall into two major categories. A small number are generally acknowledged to be occupation-specific. The fibrosing lung diseases (asbestosis, byssinosis, silicosis, *etc.*), mesothelioma and vibration-induced white finger disease are examples. These diseases are known as "marker" diseases because of the usually clear signature made by the "author" of the problem.

Then there are those diseases — the vast majority — which have any number of possible causes, including the workplace. These diseases are common to the population at large and are therefore the toughest to both prove and adjudicate. The evidentiary problems are often compounded by the fact that many of these conditions take years to develop. Determining exactly what exposures, and at what levels, took place 15 or 20 years previously can obviously be a daunting task.

Even if such exposures can be determined, there is still the question of whether the claimant was exposed to a non-occupational agent which could have brought about the problem. Then there is the problem of "synergism", by which it is possible that two or more agents may be completely benign by themselves, but when combined prove to be toxic.

Next, there is often uncertainty about causation within the medical and scientific community. It is not unusual in occupational disease claims, to see medical reports indicating the doctor's opinion that the problem has an "idiopathic origin". This is a euphemism meaning "I've got no idea what caused this".

Finally, most doctors are primarily concerned with the treatment of the disease itself, rather than its etiology.

These facts, added to the lack of general knowledge about, and training in, occupational health that most doctors have, result in less than perfect fact situations upon which to demonstrate, one way or the other, that a particular disease arose out of a particular workplace.

2. ADJUDICATION OF DISEASE CLAIMS

"Occupational disease" is defined in s. 2(1) Schedule A of the Act as including:

(a) a disease resulting from exposure to a substance relating to a particular process, trade or occupation in an industry,

(b) a disease peculiar to or characteristic of a particular industrial process, trade or occupation,

(c) a medical condition that in the opinion of the Board requires a worker to be removed either temporarily or permanently from exposure to a substance because the condition may be a precursor to an occupational disease, or

(d) a disease mentioned in Schedule 3 or 4.

Currently the Board, with respect to clause (c), has one specific policy of removal from exposure with respect to workers exposed to radiation as uranium miners and mill workers.

In one decision, the Panel found that the worker had a dust-induced pneumoconiosis, related to occupational exposure to silica dust. Such a condition might have warranted removal from exposure, but the Panel accepted that the worker was not impaired by this condition. However, the Panel noted that various doctors felt "that it was inadvisable for the worker to continue to be exposed to dust from mining" and awarded benefits.

The decision noted that it was not clear whether such benefits should be temporary or permanent. It might well be, the Panel concluded, that the worker had reached "maximal medical rehabilitation" and was therefore only entitled to a permanent partial disability. And it might be that the clinical rating in such a case might be zero per cent, but the Panel concluded that the worker would "*prima facie* have a strong claim for supplementary benefits".

In another decision, however, the Panel found that the worker's symptoms of shortness of breath were unrelated to his occupational exposure. One of the doctors treating the worker had noted findings of pleural plaques which, while not disabling in themselves, prompted the doctor to recommend that the worker be placed in different employment, although the same report stated that the worker could return to work. The Panel found, however, that this recommendation was "caused more by an abundance of caution than any positive finding of disease or disability." The Panel concluded that the worker was not entitled to benefits.

There are also workers, such as miners and loggers, who tend to travel to various work sites. Often these work sites are in different provinces. Subsections 159(10) and (11) of the *Act* provide that the Ontario Board may enter into agreements with other Canadian jurisdictions to provide for the apportionment of costs among Boards for hearing loss (subs. 11) and other occupational disease claims (subs. 10). A history of the negotiation of these interjurisdictional agreements reviewed in one Tribunal decision found that the worker's occupational noise exposure in all jurisdictions, not just within Ontario, should be considered in assessing his compensable hearing loss. The WCB responded by challenging the reasoning in this decision, and asking that Tribunal Panels rule otherwise in future decisions.

The Panels in two other cases took a different approach by finding that taking into account out-of-province exposure could be seen as consistent with the "thin-skull doctrine" accordingly:

> The worker's out-of-province exposure is not an irrelevant consideration. In certain cases, it could be that out-of-province exposure was the only significant contributing factor. On the other hand, the out-of-province exposure could be seen as something that made the worker more susceptible to develop lung cancer as a result of his exposure to radiation in his employment in Ontario.

It should also be noted that several regulations under the *Occupational Health and Safety Act* (OHSA) provide for the removal of workers from unsafe levels of exposure. For example, subs. 13(4) of the regulation proclaiming that lead is a designated substance under the OHSA, provides for blood lead level monitoring under a *Code for Medical Surveillance for Lead* published by the Ontario Ministry of Labour. The *Code* stipulates the level at which workers must be removed from exposure to lead, and levels at which they can return to work. Added to the *Code* is the caveat that "If symptoms or signs of lead intoxication are present the worker must be removed from lead exposure regardless of blood lead level." Subsection 16(2) of the regulation then provides that if a worker is removed because of a test result showing the worker "may have or has" a lead-related condition, and as a result suffers an earnings loss, the worker "is entitled to compensation for the loss in the manner and to the extent provided by the *Workers' Compensation Act*". It is not clear exactly what compensation the worker would be entitled to. Board policy only notes that "If exposure creates a situation of physical danger to a worker, requiring removal from employment, and the employer cannot provide alternate work, the worker may be entitled to compensation."

In one decision, the Panel noted that there was a similar but unpromulgated draft regulation relating to cadmium exposure. It also noted the inclusion of cadmium poisoning in Sch. 3. In that case it was found that the family doctor's recommendation to remove the worker from exposure may have been unfounded based on later evidence, but there was reasonable evidence to suggest that this was a prudent decision at the time.

Clause 2(1) (*a*) of the definition represents a greatly expanded definition for all the non-schedule diseases and presents a means for compensating diseases of the general population where an occupational link can be shown to a "substance". This would include, for example, lung cancers which might not be seen to be "peculiar to or characteristic of" any particular occupation, yet which may well have an occupational origin.

Once a disease meets one of these definitions, subs. 15(2) of the Act directs that the claim shall be treated "as if the disease was a personal injury by accident and the impairment was the happening of the accident".

The general approach to occupational disease claims has been to assume that the question to be answered is: Did the workplace exposure make a significant contribution to the development of the disease? This is the question that is asked in trauma and other disablement claims.

(a) The Scheduled Diseases

Sections 15(3) and (4) (ss. 134(9) and (10) of the pre-1997 Act) authorize the scheduling of diseases in which there is a presumption of entitlement. Subsection (3) provides for a *rebuttable* presumption for claimants with diseases listed in Sch. 3 of the Act, while subs. (4) provides an *irrebuttable* presumption for claimants with diseases listed in Sch. 4. Neither schedule is a creation of the Legislature, or even the Cabinet. Rather, they are drafted by the WCB, subject to the approval of the Lieutenant Governor in Council.

The Occupational Disease Panel recommended that "Schedule 3 should be updated and kept current on an ongoing basis". A two-phase process for updating the form and content of Sch. 3 was proposed.

(i) Schedule 3

As indicated earlier, the original Ontario Act from its inception contemplated compensation for occupational disease. One of the features of the 1914 Act was a schedule of diseases which carried a rebuttable presumption of occupational origin. Over the years, this has been added to, but certainly not at the same frequency as the discovery of new links between disease and occupation.

There are currently 16 diseases listed in Sch. 3. The 1914 Act listed six. The schedule has not, therefore, been a major vehicle for updating occupational disease data. Of the current 16, there are:

- Archaic diseases such as anthrax (a check at the Board reveals that no one can remember a claim for anthrax ever having been submitted);
- Diseases which are listed with no "process" in the adjoining column, so that the WCB has interpreted these claims to be essentially exempt from the benefit of the presumption clause;
- Diseases which are quite general in nature, such as poisoning by various substances — arsenic, chrome, lead, etc. — in which the process column lists "any process involving ..."; and
- Diseases which are fairly well recognized by the medical/scientific community as being marker diseases, or those whose very name denotes their cause, such as silicosis.

It has not always been enough, however, merely to demonstrate the existence of a scheduled disease arising from a scheduled process. The WCB has written policies on a number of the 16 scheduled diseases which may tend to limit the presumption. For example, item 14 of the schedule lists entitlement for "Tuberculosis contracted by an employee employed by and in" a number of workplaces with risk of infection. However, the presumption in favour of a hospital worker, for example, with tuberculosis, is tempered by the *Operational Policy Manual*, which adds the provisos that any previous history of the disease will be taken into account and, if it has not been "arrested for a period of at least three years", it "will be considered a re-activation of the original condition." This policy also states that "[c]laims for other than *pulmonary* tuberculosis must be considered on their individual merit." [Emphasis added.]

In British Columbia, where a similar presumption section and schedule of diseases exists, the B.C. Board, in a claim for silicosis, decided that the claimant had not been exposed long enough to silica dust to meet their criteria regarding entitlement, notwithstanding the lack of time limits in the schedule. On judicial review, the B.C. Court of Appeal ruled that the Board's ignoring of the presumption clause was "clearly in error", and ordered the Board to re-hear the claim.

Once a claim has been made for a Sch. 3 disease, the Board will still be responsible for determining whether the worker worked in the necessary "process", whether the diagnosis is, in fact, that claimed and whether there is a *disability* or *impairment* resulting from the condition.

The Tribunal, in deciding Sch. 3 cases, has demonstrated a reluctance to aggressively apply the presumptions.

In one Tribunal decision, the worker was claiming entitlement for a condition diagnosed as bursitis, a condition listed in Sch. 3. The Panel noted that there was nothing listed in the "process" column and relied on the "preponderance of medical opinions on file ... against any causal relationship". Therefore, the Panel ruled that "we cannot conclude that the requisite causal relationship has been shown between the worker's shoulder condition and his work, either as a disablement or as an industrial disease."

Another Sch. 3 disease, poisoning by beryllium, was addressed extensively in one case, where it was noted that, while the worker was entitled to the benefit of the presumption, it was still necessary to establish a correct diagnosis. The question became: Was the worker's disability caused by exposure to beryllium? The Panel answered in the affirmative, but relied on the benefit of doubt clause in s. 4(4). In other words, the presumption was of no assistance to the worker.

In another Tribunal decision, it was found that the worker was suffering from a condition known as "primary biliary cirrhosis" and that he had occupational exposure to chlorinated hydrocarbons. Paragraph 7(*ix*) of the schedule lists "poisoning and its sequelae" by reason of exposure to chlorinated hydrocarbons. The Panel found, however, that this particular cirrhosis was of unknown etiology and that it could have been caused by any number of factors. Because of that, it was reasoned, it could not be said that the worker was "poisoned" by workplace exposure. To get the benefit of the presumption, "there must be at least some evidence indicating that the disease could have been caused by such exposure". The appeal was denied.

In a different case, on the other hand, a worker was diagnosed as having lead poisoning. In that case, the Panel noted the words "poisoning *and its sequelae*" [Emphasis in the decision.] in the words of the schedule. It was found that the worker was disabled by lead poisoning and its sequelae, that the suggestions of a psychological component to the worker's disability would be compatible with lead poisoning and that, as the contrary had not been shown, the worker was entitled to benefits.

(ii) Schedule 4

Section 15(4) (s. 134(10) of the pre-1997 Act) provides an irrebuttable presumption for workers who contract diseases listed in Sch. 4. The pre-1997 Act provides that such diseases "shall be conclusively deemed to have been due to the nature of the employment." There is a slight wording change under Bill 99 and such diseases are now "deemed to have occurred due to the nature of the worker's employment." The significance of the removal of the adverb "conclusively" is not clear.

The provision for Sch. 4 was enacted in 1985, but it remained empty until May 28, 1992, when a regulation regarding occupational asbestos exposure and the conditions of asbestosis and mesothelioma (cancer of the lining of the lung) was filed. These entries to the schedule arose as the result of recommendations made by the Industrial Disease Standards Panel (IDSP) — later known as the Occupational Disease Panel (ODP) — in September 1988. In December, 1993, nasal cancer among Inco workers at the Copper Cliff sintering plant and at the Port Colborne leaching, calcining and sintering plant was added to Sch. 4.

The apparent help given by the schedules is somewhat illusory. The fact that Sch. 3 has been amended only once since 1961 and that Sch. 4 has only four entries would indicate a reluctance to provide this kind of blanket coverage, despite attempts to have the schedules updated. For example, the ODP recommended that a number of cancers attributable to asbestos exposure be included. In fact, the 1961 amendment merely revised the description of tuberculosis. Prior to December 1993, the last addition to Sch. 3 was in November 1955, when beryllium poisoning was added.

(b) "Guideline" Diseases

Most occupational disease claims dealt with by the Board fall under this category; in particular, the vast majority of claims which are not "diseases" in the classic sense. In 1980, three varieties of these claims — burns, toxic fumes and hearing loss — made up 73 per cent of the total number of occupational disease claims. In 1991, three similar conditions — inflammation of joints, chemical burns and hearing loss — accounted for 68 per cent of "disease" claims.

As of this writing the Board has policy guidelines on 33 diseases. In these cases, the Board has responded to claims filed, and developed policy guidelines by which claims are judged. Lung cancer in asbestos workers, for example, requires that the claimant have a "clear and adequate history of at least 10 years occupational exposure to asbestos, and, there is a minimum interval of 10 years between first exposure to asbestos and the appearance of lung cancer."

These guidelines are not necessarily absolute, as they are tempered by the caveat that claims not meeting them should be judged on their own merit and the benefit of doubt should apply. However, in these types of claims, the onus is more clearly on the claimant to establish entitlement.

Tribunal decisions have generally tended to take a broader view of the guidelines than the Board. There are a number of examples of Tribunal decisions allowing claims in which the letter of the guidelines has not been met, or in which it was found that the guidelines themselves were too restrictive. In the latter category, one case considered the history of the development of the Board guidelines on gastrointestinal cancer and asbestos exposure and determined that some of the guideline requirements were "contrary to the opinions from specialists commissioned to provide reports". The decision noted:

> The Panel is concerned that using the duration [of exposure] part of the guideline to deny compensation to a worker who meets the exposure intensity requirement and the other requirements would be placing an unduly restric-

tive interpretation on the guidelines and would unfairly restrict compensation to workers who meet the other guideline requirements. We note this especially in light of the statement in the guideline that claims which do not meet all the requirements should be individually judged on their own merits.

Board guidelines on cancer among gold miners is a more recent and carefully developed policy, yet another Tribunal decision, again warned against a rigid adherence to that guideline:

> ... But regardless of the advantages the guidelines may have, or the liberality of the standards applied, compensation cannot be denied simply because an individual worker does not meet the requirements set out in the guidelines. The Act requires that a decision about causation be made on the merits of the individual case. In making this decision, it is important to understand why the particular guideline requirements exist and what their significance is when one assesses the question of cause in an individual case.

(c) The Occupational Disease Panel

As part of the administrative changes introduced in 1985, s. 95 created the Industrial Disease Standards Panel (IDSP) — later known as the Occupational Disease Panel (ODP). The ODP was a body independent of the WCB, with a mandate set out in s. 95(8) of the pre-1997 Act:

(*a*) to investigate possible occupational diseases;

(*b*) to make findings as to whether a probable connection exists between a disease and an industrial process, trade or occupation in Ontario;

(*c*) to create, develop and revise criteria for the evaluation of claims respecting occupational diseases; and

(*d*) to advise on eligibility rules regarding compensation for claims respecting occupational diseases.

Given the other administrative changes wrought by Bill 101, the ODP was rather slow in getting established, its members not being appointed until June 1986. The membership reflected the Act's direction that the Panel be composed of "persons representative of the public and of the scientific community and technical and professional persons." The ODP could also appoint *ad hoc* members to investigate specific matters.

During its 12 years of operation, the ODP/IDSP published some 20 reports to the Workers' Compensation Board concerning various areas of occupational disease. In addition to these formal reports, the ODP/IDSP published a number of other research, discussion and "occasional" papers.

The ODP was not involved in individual claims. Rather, it served as a research body whose findings were reported to the Board. The ODP did, however, provide access, by appointment, to its literature reviews and other research material and therefore was an important resource for a representative handling an occupational disease claim. The response from the Board was co-ordinated by the Medical and Occupational Disease Policy Branch. This group also generated its own policy discussion papers on occupational disease topics. As of the middle of 1997, only two of these reports — on scleroderma and aluminum — had been addressed by the Board. In February 1999, the Board adopted five more reports.

As of January 1, 1998, the ODP, which had garnered an international reputation, ceased to exist. The government has indicated that the functions of the ODP will be assumed by an internal division of the WSIB. Subsection 4(1) provides the Board with a general authority to "promote health and safety in workplaces and to prevent and reduce the occurrence of workplace injuries and occupational diseases". The work done by the ODP/IDSP is still available through the website of the Canadian Centre for Occupational Health and Safety in Hamilton, Ontario (<www.ccohs.ca>). The Centre has also archived most of the papers and report produced by the ODP/IDSP in its 12 years of existence, and made them available on one CD-ROM.

In its final report, the ODP indicated that it had a number of items on its agenda and recommended projects for further research.

(d) Other Diseases

Undoubtedly the most difficult occupational disease claims are those which are not covered by either the schedules or the guidelines. As these two categories only deal with a handful of diseases, it can be seen that many occupational disease claims will fall under the "miscellaneous" heading. Included in this group there may well be some marker diseases which, due to occupational conditions in Ontario, have never been brought forward; for example, angiosarcoma — a rare liver cancer often associated with vinyl chloride exposure. And, in two Tribunal decisions, entitlement was granted for bladder cancer arising out of the tire industry.

The adjudication of these types of claims is done on a case by case basis. While the WCB investigates all these claims, the practical onus is often on the claimant to provide the scientific and medical data in support of the occupational relationship. These data should include:

(1)   As comprehensive a work history as possible, including as accurate an inventory of suspected causative agents as can be obtained. This is often a major problem as it involves considerable detective work to determine what agents, in what concentrations, existed in a claimant's workplace 10, 15 or 20 years prior to the claim;

(2)   Researching international medical literature for support. This will include epidemiological data, animal studies and any other scientific material available;

(3)   Reviewing the legal literature to determine if similar claims have been made in other jurisdictions;

(4)   A thorough understanding of the claimant's individual situation, including past medical history, family history of similar conditions and any non-occupational exposure — hobbies, for example; and

(5)   Referrals to knowledgeable specialists. It is often a mistake, however, to rely on doctors who, while they may be expert in *treating* particular diseases, may not be familiar with *causation*. The specialty of "occupational medicine" is only slowly becoming recognized in Ontario.

The percentage ratings for permanent partial disability or permanent impairment resulting from diseases are fraught with the same general perils as other pension ratings involving internal injuries. (See Chapter 14, Permanent Disability Benefits.) One Tribunal decision provided an interesting analysis in arriving at a 100 per cent pension award in a chronic obstructive lung disease case, while in another, the worker's pension was raised from five per cent to 44 per cent for a vibration-induced white finger condition. The Panel noted that there was no specific rating schedule for this condition, so it extrapolated from the AMA guidelines, although anecdotal evidence suggested that this was well beyond the normal pension awarded by the Board for such a condition. In one Tribunal decision, the Panel used the psychotraumatic rating schedule as a guide and awarded a total of 27 per cent for a tinnitus condition, where the normal maximum under Board policy is two per cent.

One interesting case of a disease not covered by the guidelines was addressed by a Tribunal decision. This case awarded benefits to a worker suffering from a neurological disability which, it was claimed, was related to occupational exposure to aluminum dust. This decision relied, in particular, on the evidence of one of the attending specialists despite the fact that the Occupational Disease Panel had reported that "[t]he evidence currently available is inadequate to allow the Panel to conclude that occupational aluminum exposure causes neurological health effects."

This case received prominent media attention and, in November 1997, the Board issued *Operational Policy Manual*, Document No. 04-03-13, stating "dementia, Alzheimer's disease and conditions with neurological effects are not occupational diseases or injuries caused by accidents under the Act when they are alleged to result from occupational aluminum exposure." Despite the findings that the Panel accepted the expert evidence of a neurologist, the Board policy holds that "[t]he available medical and scientific evidence does not establish causal associations between occupational aluminum exposure and dementia, Alzheimer's disease and conditions with neurological effects." For reasons that are not immediately apparent, this policy applies to "all accidents occurring on and after September 23, 1993."

3. EVIDENTIARY ISSUES IN DISEASE CLAIMS

There is a vast array of diseases that may be caused by the workplace and, conversely, a vast array of causes, both occupational and non-occupational, for a particular disease. In establishing a compensable claim, there are two primary areas that must be dealt with: diagnosis and exposure. If a firm diagnosis is established and there is evidence of exposure to a substance which has been shown to result in such a diagnosis, a claim that the disease resulted from workplace exposure will be strengthened.

Several Tribunal decisions have gone into some detail concerning the evidentiary issues in occupational disease claims and are useful references for those facing such a claim. In general, the following guidelines on diagnosis and exposure should be considered.

(a) Diagnosis

While this might appear to be an obvious start, it often happens that a doctor will give a provisional diagnosis or a general one. This may be fine for the treatment of the condition but may be a problem in establishing a claim. For example, a doctor may diagnose a lung cancer and be treating the patient on that basis. However, a diagnosis of lung cancer may not indicate the *primary site* of the disease, that is, the disease may well have started at another location in the body and spread to the lung. It is also the case that, quite understandably, a doctor will focus on what is considered to be the most threatening condition. So, while the cancer may be of occupational origin and spread to the lung, the doctor will not be as concerned with the diagnosis and causation of the primary site.

(b) Exposure

Having established a firm diagnosis, the next step is to establish whether there is an occupational origin. Upon receiving a claim, the WCB will make preliminary inquiries. Often this will entail asking for reports on the workplace from the Ministry of Labour's Occupational Health and Safety Branch. For example, the Board will contact the Ministry and ask about the levels of substance X at workplace Y. If that information is available, it will be forwarded although often the Ministry will conduct an inspection specific to the inquiries by the Board.

In addition, enquiries should be made concerning any other possible origins. Often, establishing a *lack* of such outside causation will strengthen the occupational connection.

CHAPTER 9

Mental and Behavioural Disorders

1. INTRODUCTION

The Board's submissions to the 1967 Royal Commission on Workmen's Compensation (the "McGillivray Commission") stated:

> Patients who have not suffered brain damage may develop severe reactive depressions following prolonged invalidism or progressive conditions. A few of these have little to look forward to and are potential suicidal risks and may be, on the evidence, entitled to compensation.

Since that time the Board's policies on psychological disabilities have gone through a number of revisions and there has been an ongoing attempt to define psychological disability concepts. During that time, in the broader medical community as well as within the workers' compensation system, terminology and treatment have continued to evolve.

The Board has long recognized that an injury can take place to the mind as well as the body. In cases involving accidents which cause brain damage resulting, in turn, in mental disorders, there has been little debate that such disabilities are compensable. The problem areas arise in cases in which there is a claim for a psychological reaction to an accident, a psychological reaction to non-physically injuring *events* at work, or the real or perceived pain resulting from a physical injury. It is obvious that these cases deal with highly subjective areas that are not susceptible to exact, reproducible scientific standards.

In dealing with psychological disabilities, the standard classification system is derived from the American Psychiatric Association (APA) publication, *Diagnostic and Statistical Manual of Mental Disorders* ("DSM-IV").

2. PSYCHOTRAUMATIC DISABILITIES

The Board has developed policies regarding entitlement for what is referred to as "psychotraumatic" disability. It is unclear why the Board used this phrase in referring to mental disorders that result from compensable accidents or the sequelae of accidents. The phrase itself is not defined and it seems to imply the requirement of a traumatic incident as a causative force. As can be seen in the Board policy outlined below, this is clearly not the case. Where a mental disorder results from the sequela of an accident, it will be compensated even though it is quite unlikely that any part of the sequela is "traumatic" in the normal sense of the word. However, it is not unusual to see a claim denied, particularly at the initial levels, on the grounds that the accident was not "traumatic".

In 1986 Dr. M. Tyndel, a Board psychiatrist, testified at the Tribunal's Leading Case on permanent partial disability rating. It would appear from his evidence that the Board used the previous edition of the APA's manual ("DSM-III") categorizations in order to determine the clinical entities that were included in the phrase "psychotraumatic" disability. The most prevalent diagnoses are anxiety disorder, depressive disorder, conversion disorder, psychogenic pain disorder, obsessive compulsive disorder, simple phobia, hypochondriasis, post-traumatic stress disorder, psychological factors affecting physical condition, and factitious disorders.

(a) Entitlement

Of course, establishing that one of the above-mentioned mental disorders is present is not sufficient for entitlement to be granted. The question of causation must first be addressed. Indeed, if any other mental disorder, with the obvious exception of malingering, can be shown to be causally related to an accident or its sequelae, there does not appear to be any reason why entitlement would not be granted.

It would be inappropriate to leave the area of "psychotraumatic" disability without commenting on one of the most frequent sources of incorrect adjudication. This is the failure to distinguish between a predisposition to disability and a pre-existing disability.

If an award for "psychotraumatic" disability is to be denied or reduced on the basis of pre-existing conditions, it must be done on the basis that the pre-existing conditions were themselves disabling. The presence of factors which might have contributed to the predisposition to disability is not sufficient to reduce or deny benefits, although these factors may contribute to an employer's claim for Second Injury and Enhancement Fund Relief. The policy with respect to pre-existing conditions is precisely the same for "psychotraumatic" disability as it is for any other disability. The policy as it is written is quite similar to the common law notion of the "thin-skulled" plaintiff.

It is commonly accepted that some people do not react as well as "normal" people would to various life events. However, when determining whether an accident or its sequelae caused a mental disorder it is important to look at the question of causation in the individual case. Although there is some discussion as to whether the question of causation should be framed as a "but for" test or a "significant cause" test, it is clear, other than in stress cases, that the test must be a subjective one and not an objective one.

The current Board policy has changed very little since a major revision in 1982. The policy now outlines the general entitlement criteria for a psychotraumatic disability if the disability "is attributable to a work-related injury or a condition resulting from a work-related injury ... providing the psychotraumatic disability became manifest within 5 years of the injury, or within 5 years of the last surgical procedure".

The policy specifies the various categories of disability as follows:

Entitlement for psychotraumatic disability may be established when the following circumstances exist or develop.

- Organic brain injury secondary to

    ——— traumatic head injury

    ——— toxic chemicals including gases

    ——— hypoxic conditions, or

    ——— conditions related to decompression sickness.

- As an indirect result of a physical injury

    ——— emotional reaction to the accident or injury

    ——— severe physical disability, or

    ——— reaction to the treatment process.

- The psychotraumatic disability is shown to be related to extended disablement and to non-medical, socio-economic factors, the majority of which can be directly and clearly related to the work related injury.

The first category, organic brain injury, has not generally been contentious, while the second and particularly the third have tended to be far more problematic in that it is usually necessary to determine other non-compensable factors in a worker's life and accurately determine the causal role of the compensable accident and its sequelae.

In general, the decision-maker is to watch for diagnostic labels, such as Conversion Disorder, Personality Disorder, or Post-Traumatic Stress Disorder, Hypochondriasis.

In addition, the policy contains a checklist of things to watch for under the heading "Early Recognition". It is also stressed in the "general rules", that: "psychotraumatic disability is considered to be a temporary condition. Only in exceptional circumstances is this type of disability accepted as a permanent condition."

The term "exceptional circumstances" is not defined, and, despite the above "general rule", the assumption seems to be that such conditions are rarely temporary, and the policy emphasis is on permanent ratings.

Despite the encouragement to detect and treat such conditions at an early stage, there is little in the policy that deals with these claims from a preventive or therapeutic perspective.

(b) Permanent Disability/Impairment

(i) Pre-1990 Claims

In assessing psychotraumatic claims arising from accidents occurring prior to January 2, 1990, the policy considers the presence of one or more of six "clinical entities".

It is very rare, however, to see a specific diagnosis, such as those referred to in the policy, from an attending psychiatrist. It is even rare to see such a diagnosis from a Board doctor. Far more common diagnoses appear to be "post-traumatic stress disorder" and "conversion disorder". Even more common, particularly in older reports, are terms such as a psychological or "functional" overlay or component, or "compensation neurosis". In the past, these terms tended to be interpreted by the Board as code words meaning that the worker was consciously faking his or her symptoms. While some doctors no doubt intended to send that message, others were genuinely mystified as to a more specific diagnosis.

The actual rating of permanent partial disability awards was based on categories dealing with how daily activities of the "total person" are impaired. These categories, which are also applicable to chronic pain disability and fibromyalgia, discussed later in this chapter, are listed in Table 9-1. Reference should be made to the policy for a full description of each category.

(ii) Post-1990 Claims

For impairments arising from accidents occurring on and after January 2, 1990, in addition to Future Economic Loss (FEL) benefits the worker is entitled to a Non-Economic Loss (NEL) award. As with other NEL awards, they are based on a ratings found in the third edition of the American Medical Association (AMA) *Guides to the Evaluation of Permanent Impairment*. Chapter 14 of the AMA *Guides* deals with "mental and behavioural disorders". These guides are used in conjunction with the previous Board rating schedule, discussed above. The result is the scale of five categories — or "classes" — reproduced in Table 9-1, below, page 90. Again, reference should be made to the schedule for detailed descriptions of each class. At the time of writing, there was no specific policy on determining a FEL award arising from any mental or behavioural disorder.

(c) WCAT/WSIAT Decisions

By and large, Tribunal cases have generally tended to follow Board policy with regard to the determination of entitlement and the use of the four-category rating schedule for pre-1990 claims and the five-category schedule for post-1990 claims.

In one Tribunal decision, the Panel upheld a Board ruling that a police officer's head injury, resulting in loss of smell, organic mental impairment and personality change, followed a fainting spell caused by a post-traumatic stress disorder. This, in turn, had resulted from the worker coming into contact with the scene of a previous psychotraumatic event.

In another Panel decision, a fear of driving following a compensable motor vehicle accident was accepted as a secondary psychotraumatic condition.

In one case, the worker's compensable depression resulted from the pressures of Board vocational rehabilitation-sponsored schooling, when he had little English language ability, financial uncertainty and uncertainty regarding future employment.

The Tribunal also upheld an Appeals Officer decision that awarded psychotraumatic benefits as a result of employer surveillance of her activities. The Appeals Officer found that while employer surveillance was sometimes justified and helpful, there are also potentially harmful effects. In this case, the employer surveillance "irrevocably damaged the employer/employee relationship". One of the Appeals Officer's orders was that the worker should not return to work with the accident employer.

3. CHRONIC PAIN

(a) Background

Until the advent of the Workers' Compensation Appeals Tribunal in 1985, the Board took the position that the workers' compensation scheme did not compensate for "pain". If pain resulted from an organic, compensable injury, then the physiological disability, which often implicitly included disabling pain, would be compensated. The Board also recognized that there may be disabling psychological components to an injury. The criteria for accepting a psychological component are discussed above, and include disability "shown to be related to extended disablement and to non-medical, socio-economic factors, the majority of which can be directly and clearly related to the work related injury". Often this extended disablement manifested itself in complaints of pain. Typically, however, a worker would not receive this entitlement without a clear organic basis for the "extended disablement".

Beginning in 1986, however, early Tribunal decisions began to describe cases in which a panel was convinced on the evidence that the worker was suffering pain resulting from a compensable accident. The Panel in one of these early cases considered the problem of specifying the source of pain and concluded:

> We do not have to decide for purposes of this appeal whether the pain is psychogenic in origin or is caused by some undetected organic condition or is a product of some combination of the two. It is enough that we satisfy ourselves on the evidence that it is more likely than not that the pain is and

always was real to the worker, that it is disabling and that it results from the accident. We are so satisfied.

Because of the Tribunal's Leading Case approach to permanent partial disability awards, these early cases only dealt with initial entitlement and temporary benefits.

The next major development arose when it became apparent that the Tribunal's "Leading Case Strategy" for dealing with its review of Board pension cases also required an exhaustive review of the phenomenon of what that Panel called "enigmatic chronic pain". As a result, an important 1987 Tribunal decision dealt at least as much with the medical and policy aspects of the compensability of pain with no apparent source, as with the legal interpretation of the permanent partial disability section of the Act.

The Panel in this case, after considerable review of the Board's practices and the medical literature, noted the category "Psychogenic Pain Disorder" in the DSM-III and considered the constellation of symptoms described. The Panel next considered whether these types of conditions were appropriate considerations in a workers' compensation context, including a consideration of the arguments against compensating for pain. The conclusion was that chronic pain conditions should be compensated where certain basic conditions were met.

Shortly after the release of this decision, the Board published its own policy paper concerning what it then called "chronic pain disorder" (CPD). The date of the publication of that paper, July 3, 1987, was also, initially, the retroactivity date for CPD entitlement; that is, the Board determined that no benefits should be payable for chronic pain conditions prior to July 3, 1987.

As part of the process for this decision, that Panel held further hearings to rule on the retroactivity date of chronic pain benefits. As a result, it was determined by a majority in a related decision in the following year that "chronic pain benefits should be payable from March 27, 1986, the date of publication of the *Pension Assessment Appeals Leading Case Interim Report*".

The Board of Directors reviewed these decisions, and others dealing with chronic pain. As a result, it was agreed that the retroactivity date should be March 27, 1986. The Board of Directors also refined the Board's policy on CPD (now referring to chronic pain *disability*, rather than disorder).

It is the stated intention of the current government in Ontario, and elsewhere, to limit entitlement for CPD. Interestingly, as governments are moving to limit chronic pain entitlement, the courts are declaring such conditions could be "permanent impairment of [important] bodily functions and the impairment is caused by a continuing injury, which is physical in nature", despite the lack of objective testing for such a condition.

(b) Current Board Policy

The current policy holds that CPD will be accepted as compensable when it "results from a work-related injury and there is sufficient credible subjective and objective evidence establishing the disability". The general eligibility criteria include:

- Evidence of a "continuous, consistent and genuine pain" that has existed for six or more months beyond the "usual healing time for the injury";
- That the level of pain is inconsistent with what could be explained by organic findings; and
- That there is evidence that the chronic pain has resulted in a "consistent and marked life disruption". "Marked life disruption" is defined as "the effect of pain on the worker's activities of daily living, vocational activity, physical and psychological functioning, as well as family and social relationships."

Those conditions covered by the CPD policy also include fibromyalgia syndrome, somatoform pain disorder, as diagnosed pursuant to the DSM-III-R, and post-traumatic head pain. With the exception of fibromyalgia, retroactive entitlement for CPD is limited to March 27, 1986.

(c) Permanent Disability/Impairment

For pre-1990 injuries, a worker with a recognized permanent CPD is entitled to a permanent partial disability award. Such an award will be "holistic" and "global" in that all aspects of the worker's disability are supposed to be considered, and benefits will not be "stacked", that is, a worker is not supposed to receive a CPD award *in addition to* a pension for a psychotraumatic disability or an organic disability resulting from the same injury. This is in contrast to a situation in which there is a psychotraumatic injury and an organic one where each disability is rated separately and added together, or "stacked".

While Tribunal decisions have generally taken a similar overall approach, they have noted that if there are two or three distinct disabilities resulting from the same injury, benefits may be "stacked". They have also compared the chronic pain rating to the rating that would result if the complained-of pain had an identifiable organic source.

Under pre-1990 CPD policy the non-stacking aspect became a significant consideration, in that a CPD pension was limited to a maximum of 30 per cent in the severest of cases. If a worker already had a pension for an organic condition, the "no stacking" policy meant that the worker could, in theory, end up with a smaller total pension if the organic pension was removed in favour of a CPD pension. Under the revised policy, however, the Board has determined that a CPD pension will be rated according to the policy on "Psychotraumatic and Behavioural Disorders Rating Schedule". That rating schedule, as noted in Table 9-1, provides four categories of disability ranging from Category 1, "Minor Impairment of the Total Person (10%)" to Category 4, "Severe Impairment of the Total Person (60 - 80%)".

One Tribunal decision noted that, in chronic pain cases, there are two considerations in determining "maximal medical rehabilitation": the stabilizing of the pain symptoms and the worker's capacity for coping with the pain symptoms.

For post-1990 injuries, in addition to any FEL award, the Board's *Operational Policy Manual* provides for a five-class rating schedule for NEL awards. Again, these classes are noted in Table 9-1, below, page 90, and provide for a range between "No Impairment (0%)" to "Extreme Impairment (95%)".

As with other NEL awards, these may be appealed to the Tribunal. Most of these appeals have resulted in the Board's award being upheld.

4. FIBROSITIS/FIBROMYALGIA

(a) WCAT Decision No. 18

Another condition included in the Board's chronic pain policy is that variously referred to as "fibromyalgia", "fibromyalgia syndrome", "fibrositis", and other terms. In one case, the medical controversy surrounding this condition and its nature and symptoms has been considered in some depth, with extensive medical literature and the testimony of two expert medical witnesses presented.

The actual nature and cause of fibromyalgia is unclear, as noted, for example, in one Tribunal decision, which described fibromyalgia as:

> ... a psychophysiological reaction to a number of (often stressful) factors. The extent to which psychological factors or physical factors are important in producing or increasing fibromyalgia symptoms probably varies from case to case. However, even in those cases where the original stressful event is emotional, and there likely are emotional factors affecting ongoing symptoms, there likely is a physiological response (possibly through the interference with stage IV sleep) which appears to be important in producing the fibromyalgia symptoms (including observable physical findings such as tender points).

Generally, in Tribunal decisions dealing with fibromyalgia, the condition has arisen subsequent to a traditional blow or strain type of injury, although there are also examples of fibromyalgia arising as the result of drafts and emotional stress.

(b) Board Policy

The Board has taken the approach that fibromyalgia should be considered as a subcategory of CPD. Board policy notes that, in claims in which the diagnosis is fibromyalgia, workers "will be considered for compensation benefits under the CPD policy", as fibromyalgia is "recognized as a variant of CPD".

(c) Chronic Pain Under Bill 99

Initially, the government was expected to limit chronic pain entitlement. However, as a result of concerns raised during the Committee hearings on Bill 99, the Minister of Labour indicated that changes in the Bill would "ensure that research is immediately targeted towards the pressing issue of chronic pain while compensation for injured workers suffering from chronic pain will continue". The current provisions on chronic pain read:

> **14.** (1) A worker is entitled to benefits under the insurance plan for chronic pain as defined in the regulations but only in such circumstances as may be prescribed.
>
> (2) The benefits to which the worker is entitled for chronic pain are subject to such limits and exclusions as may be prescribed.

The intention to delay any changes to chronic pain entitlement is noted in section 184:

> **184.** (1) This Act, except for section 14 and subsections 40(1) to (7), comes into force on January 1, 1998.
>
> (2) Section 14 comes into force on a day to be named by proclamation of the Lieutenant Governor.

There is no indication at this point when s. 14 will be proclaimed, but the Board has established an "expert advisory panel" to undertake "an independent scientific study" of chronic pain and report back to the Board. The Board sought nominees from the constituency groups representing the university and research community and "health care provider and consumer groups". The panel was scheduled to report to the Board by July 1, 1999.

In April 1998, the Board amended this process by taking a two-stage approach. Stage 1 saw the development of "a scientific consensus on the cause, prognosis and treatment of chronic pain by a panel of experts in the field of chronic pain" chosen by the Board. This Panel was initially scheduled to report its findings by November 1998, but did not do so until June 1999.

At that time a second Panel, comprised of nominees from the stakeholder communities, was "based on the scientific consensus report — [to] develop policy and guideline recommendations on how work-related chronic pain should be prevented, compensated, and managed." The second panel was scheduled to "provide policy recommendations to the WSIB by mid-fall of 1999."

5. MENTAL STRESS

(a) Introduction

Board policy on psychotraumatic disability has long recognized the compensability of *acute* stress reactions to highly emotional workplace events, such as witnessing a co-worker's death or being taken hostage in a robbery. The Board did not, however, recognize manifestations of less dramatic workplace stressors. Therefore, workers who claimed that they were "burnt out" because of the pressures of their jobs, could not expect to get workers' compensation benefits.

In recent years, there has been an increasing recognition of the problems of workplace stress. There is a quarterly academic journal, *Work & Stress*, devoted to the subject, published in London, England. In Japan, in recent years, evidence has emerged of a phenomenon known as "karoshi" — actually working to death. The International Labour Organization has recently published a report detailing what it calls "one of the most serious health issues of the twentieth century".

In Ontario, developments through Tribunal decisions and Board policy proposals placed the question in the public eye at a time when there was considerable pressure to restrict costs. As outlined below, there has been a significant lobby on the part of employers to reverse the trend towards recognizing occupational stress claims under the workers' compensation system. In Manitoba, New Brunswick, and Nova Scotia, legislation was passed that explicitly prevents compensation for "stress, other than an acute reaction to a traumatic event" and "mental stress or a disablement caused by mental stress, other than as an acute reaction to a traumatic event", respectively.

It is of some interest to note a recent decision of the Federal Court of Canada that awarded the plaintiff, a worker for a branch of the federal government, a total of $40,000. On the facts as accepted by the court, it is apparent that, in essence, the plaintiff's claim was for the effects of workplace stress. There is no indication of whether the Court considered and rejected a workers' compensation defence which, presumably, would have barred the suit.

The decision is a useful comparison of how work-related stress claims might be handled as tort claims by the courts, containing commentary on medical evidence and the tests required to be met in establishing an intentional tort (as this case was found to be). This latter discussion is of interest in considering a worker/plaintiff with a predisposition to anxiety:

> It is clear that the plaintiff suffered from feelings of fear and insecurity at the time she was hired at COGLA. What is also clear, however, and in this sense I fully accept the testimony of Ms. Houlding [a social worker], is that the events at COGLA made her condition measurably worse by triggering the severe state of depression from which the plaintiff now suffers.

Another remedy may lie with human rights legislation. In a recent Ontario Human Rights case, the Adjudicator appointed by the Board of Inquiry addressed the question of "mental stress caused by his or her employer's decisions or actions relating to the worker's employment", in the context of damages awarded for a complaint of racial discrimination and harassment. In this case, it was found that the complainant had to work in a poisonous environment and that the respondents had wilfully engaged in creating this environment. It was found that one of the results was that the complainant suffered "work related stress and anxiety for which he is required to take medication".

The decision ordered:

> That the Respondent Ministry [of Correctional Services] compensate the Complainant for the difference between his salary and the actual remuneration received by him while on "sick leave" owing to work-related stress from the time of the first complaint [November 1988] to the date of this award, together with appropriate pre-award interest thereon...

(b) Sexual and Racial Harassment

In recent years there has been an increased awareness of the problems of workplace sexual and racial harassment. The victim of such harassment may indeed suffer disability as a result of this form of workplace stress.

Of note are two Supreme Court of Canada decisions. The first is *Robichaud v. Can. (Treasury Bd.)*, and the second is *Janzen v. Platy Enterprises Ltd.* These decisions discuss the liability of employers for what transpires in the workplace and look at the different definitions of sexual harassment.

In a Tribunal decision, the majority found that the worker had been disabled as the result of workplace stressors. These stressors included derogatory remarks which amounted to racial and gender discrimination. As a result, the worker suffered a major affective depressive disorder with features of anxiety, requiring psychiatric treatment. The majority of the Panel allowed the appeal and granted entitlement.

In a well-publicized case decided at the Hearings Officer level, a black woman claimed that she had been the victim of blatant sexual and racial harassment by her co-workers. (While most Hearings Officer decisions are not available to the public, this decision was widely distributed, with the names of the parties deleted. It is available in the Tribunal library.) The Hearings Officer accepted the worker's evidence, then turning to the question of the lack of a stress policy, noted:

> The Hearings Officer is being invited to adjudicate and allow this case as a "chronic stress" claim. In the circumstances, such consideration is not necessary as it is the opinion of the Hearings Officer that it is not necessary to characterize this claim as "chronic stress" in order to allow it.
>
> Upon review of the evidence, the Hearings Officer is satisfied that the persistent and vexatious harassment endured by this worker and exacerbated particularly by the incident of November 13, 1986, does constitute a significant

event. The instances of insult were over and above that which one might expect in a factory setting; over and above what would be expected for *any* employee to endure.

[Emphasis in original.]

The Hearings Officer found that the worker's case met "the spirit and intent of
the existing psychotraumatic policy". The employer appealed the decision to the
Tribunal, but then withdrew its appeal.

With respect to sexual harassment claims under Bill 99, the then Minister of
Labour stated that they would be compensable under Bill 99, the *Workplace
Safety and Insurance Act, 1997*, notwithstanding an apparent bar for claims
arising from "chronic stress" under s. 12(5). Despite this claim, the Board's
"policy framework" made it clear that:

> A worker [who] is subjected to daily sexual innuendoes, humour in poor
> taste, practical jokes, and other forms of unwanted attention from co-
> workers... is not entitled to benefits for mental stress. The mental stress was
> not due to a sudden and unexpected traumatic event, but arose gradually over
> time due to general workplace conditions.

In addition to these kinds of cases, which tend to be high profile and attract
media attention as "precedent-setting", there are cases of compensation being
paid as the result of sexual assault at the workplace. It could certainly be fore-
seen that one of the results of such an assault might be a psychological disability.

In one Panel decision, a majority found that the worker had not been sexually
attacked as she alleged. On a reconsideration request, it was held that there was
enough new evidence available to call the original decision into question, and a
rehearing on the merits was ordered. The appeal was then allowed.

In another case, the accident employer was denied second injury and enhancement fund relief in a case where a worker, a store clerk, suffered a psychological impairment following a robbery and sexual assault. The Panel noted
that emotional recovery from a rape can take years and "Thus it is difficult to
assess whether this worker's recovery has been 'unduly prolonged'."

(c) Suicide

There have been two Tribunal decisions in which a worker's suicide was accepted as a sequela to a compensable accident. (It should also be noted that there
are two other decisions in which it was ruled that deaths under suspicious circumstances were *not* caused by suicide.) In the first, it was found that the
worker's compensable knee injury and subsequent surgery led to a deteriorating
emotional condition which, in turn, caused him to take his own life. The Panel
put the question as follows:

> The central question in cases of suicide following industrial accident appears
> to be the same in every jurisdiction which has struggled with the topic. The
> threshold problem appears to be this: Suicide which is volitional has been

treated differently from suicide committed in a fit of "insanity". If there was an element of understanding or intention in the victim, the act has been taken to be a new and independent intervening event, breaking the chain of causation between the industrial accident and the death.

That Panel's answer was:

> In the case before us, we have concluded that the factual evidence established the existence of emotional disorder. The factual evidence here paints a complete picture enabling the panel to see the deterioration of this man's experience from joy to despair; from a happy and fulfilling life to intentional violent death. That picture has left no gap in this panel's impression that it was the industrial accident, the intractable pain, the unacceptable lifestyle changes, which contributed to the formation of intent in this worker to take his own life.
>
> We conclude that a volitional element to the suicide does not preclude a finding of compensability. On the facts in this case, we are satisfied that the formation of the intent to commit the act of suicide resulted directly from the accident and its consequences. The formation of that will was a result of, and not a force independent of, the accident and disability.

An Application for judicial review of this decision was denied. The Divisional Court indicated that it was of the view that the decision was correct.

The Board now has a policy which indicates that,

> If the evidence indicates that, as a result of the injury, the worker developed psychosocial problems that led the worker to commit suicide, the suicide may be said to result from the accident. Non-work-related factors are also assessed to determine whether the effect on the worker was so great that the suicide was really the result of factors unconnected to the injury.

(d) Substance Abuse

There are a number of Tribunal decisions in which panels have accepted the compensability of a worker's addiction to drugs prescribed for a compensable accident. In addition, there have been at least two decisions which on the facts of the cases accepted alcohol abuse as a compensable condition, either as an "accident" or as a sequela to an accident.

(e) Stress Claims Arising Under the Pre-1998 Act Under Bill 99

In one Panel decision, the Board had provided the psychotraumatic policy in its *Operational Policy Manual* as the policy applicable in a case in which the worker was claiming a psychiatric disability based on chronic workplace stress. In this interim decision, the hearing panel rejected the argument by the employer's representative that for pre-1997 accidents the Board had a *de facto* policy that refused compensation in claims for chronic stress. It had been argued that the word "policy" contemplated more than just that published in the Board's

Operational Policy Manual, and included Board practice. The Panel rejected this broad an interpretation, noting the importance of published and available policy, although it did not rule out the use of "unpublished changes to Board policies [that] may be effective, where there is evidence that these changes have been authorized by the Board's internal decision-making process".

The Panel also rejected arguments from the worker's representative and the Tribunal Counsel Office that the policy provided was not applicable and that the matter should be returned to the Board for a review pursuant to subs. 126(4). The Panel ruled that the Board's psychotraumatic policy was broad enough to encompass chronic stress claims.

In later cases, however, the Board has been more equivocal, noting that pre-1997 Board practice had been not to compensate for chronic stress claims, although this approach was "not written in any Board minute or official document, but became a standard reference during the adjudication of this type of claim". A further letter from the Board to the Tribunal's General Counsel reiterates that, for chronic stress claims, the Board took the position that there were a number of applicable policies.

This letter also refers to the Bill 99 policies, but notes that they are only applicable to accidents occurring on or after January 1, 1998. In a further letter from the WSIB's General Counsel, however, the reference to the psychotraumatic policy is removed and it is stated that for pre-1998 accidents "the Board's policy" was to compensate only for acute stress claims and "in the absence of such an event, the Board does not compensate".

In response to this letter, the Tribunal Chair received a number of inquiries as to what Board policy was, for s. 126 purposes. The Tribunal Chair wrote to Mr. Holyoke on August 26, 1998, asking for clarification. On December 16, 1998, Mr. Holyoke responded. That response was that "no useful purpose would be served by engaging in a general debate over what constitutes 'policy' within the meaning of s. 126". This letter noted:

> Underlying the more general debate over the meaning of "policy" is my letter of May 28, 1998 in which I stated:
>
> > In addition, the Board's policy on claims for chronic stress prior to 1998 is as follows: the Board only compensates for claims of mental stress/psychological disability resulting from an event that was sudden, shocking or life-threatening in nature. In the absence of such an event, the Board does not compensate.
>
> I would like to reiterate that the above paragraph states the Board's policy for the purposes of s. 126(2). If any of the panels hearing appeals in which this policy has been stated believe that this policy is "inconsistent with, or not authorized by, the Act or does not apply to the case", s. 126(4) provides it with the appropriate route for raising its concerns.

During this period, chronic stress claim have been dealt with in a variety of ways. A final decision was reserved, pending receipt of a response to the Tribunal Chair's letter. Another case allowed a chronic stress claim, based on sexual harassment, without commenting on policy. As of this writing, therefore, the disposition of pre-1998 chronic stress claims at the Tribunal is still not clear.

(i) Post-1998 Claims

With the passage of Bill 99, disability arising from chronic occupational stress has been eliminated as a compensable condition. Section 13(1) of the Schedule to the new Act provides for general entitlement, as follows:

> **13.** (1) A worker who sustains a personal injury by accident arising out of and in the course of his or her employment is entitled to benefits under the insurance plan.

This general entitlement is, however, modified by subss. (4) and (5):

> (4) Except as provided in subsection (5), a worker is not entitled to benefits under the insurance plan for mental stress.
>
> (5) A worker is entitled to benefits for mental stress that is an acute reaction to a sudden and unexpected traumatic event arising out of and in the course of his or her employment. However, the worker is not entitled to benefits for mental stress caused by his or her employer's decisions or actions relating to the worker's employment, including a decision to change the work to be performed or the working conditions, to discipline the worker or to terminate the employment.

"Mental stress" is not defined in the Act, Schedule or policy. Bill 99 *Operational Policy*, 1.1, indicates that, for acute stress claims, "Although a DSM or ISCD diagnosis is not necessary to allow a claim for mental stress, the Board requests such a diagnosis to confirm ongoing entitlement."

Board policy notes that an "acute reaction to a sudden and unexpected traumatic event" need not be an immediate reaction and may be delayed for days, weeks or months, although in the event of a delayed onset claim, the evidence of a relationship to a traumatic workplace event must be "clear and convincing". A "traumatic event" is described as one that would "generally be recognized as [emotionally] traumatic".

Also, "The event must also be uncommon in the normal course of the worker's employment", although, "An event may be considered traumatic even if the worker was exposed to similar events in the past and experienced no ill effects." Events that would, generally, not be recognized as traumatic, but which are traumatic to a worker because of the worker's psychological history, are not considered sudden and unexpected traumatic events.

The policy provides a number of examples of what might be considered compensable and what would not. It also reiterates the legislative protection for employers' activities that might cause stress, that is, termination of employment, demotions, transfers, disciplinary actions, hours of work and productivity expectations.

With statutory elimination of chronic stress as a compensable condition, it is expected that where it is alleged that chronic occupational stress results in impairment, the remedy will be through the courts. In fact, one recent Supreme Court of Canada decision has noted that the kind of "decisions or actions relating to the worker's employment" that are explicitly excluded under the *Workplace Safety and Insurance Act, 1997*, may be recoverable under wrongful dismissal action. The majority decision noted:

> It has long been accepted that a dismissed employee is not entitled to compensation for injuries flowing from the fact of the dismissal itself: see e.g. *Addis, supra*. Thus, although the loss of a job is very often the cause of injured feelings and emotional upset, the law does not recognize these as compensable losses. However, where an employee can establish that an employer engaged in bad faith conduct or unfair dealing in the course of dismissal, injuries such as humiliation, embarrassment and damage to one's sense of self-worth and self-esteem might all be worthy of compensation depending upon the circumstances of the case. In these situations, compensation does not flow from the fact of dismissal itself, but rather from the manner in which the dismissal was effected by the employer.

Table 9-1
Psychotraumatic Ratings

Pre-January 1990 Claims

Category 1 –	Minor Impairment of Total Person (10%)
Category 2 –	Moderate Impairment of Total Person (15%-25%)
Category 3 –	Major Impairment of Total Person (30%-50%)
Category 4 –	Severe Impairment of the Total Person (60%-80%)

Post-January 1990 Claims

Class 1 –	No Impairment (0%) – No impairment noted
Class 2 –	most useful function
Class 3 –	Moderate Impairment (20%-45%) — Impairment levels compatible with some but not all useful function
Class 4 –	Marked Impairment (50%-90%) — Impairment levels significantly impede function
Class 5 –	Extreme Impairment (95%) — Impairment levels preclude useful function

CHAPTER 10

Civil Actions

1. INTRODUCTION

One of the major bargains that resulted in the introduction of workers' compensation in Ontario was that, in return for workers' getting a right to workers' compensation benefits, paid for by their employers, their limited rights to pursue civil actions for work-related injuries against their employers were removed. With a few modifications, the present laws regarding the ability of workers to main- tain civil actions for work-related injuries flow directly from this historical bargain.

Employers included in Sch. 1 are collectively liable for the payment of workers' compensation benefits to the workers of all Sch. 1 employers. Such payments are funded through employer assessments. Along with the collective liability comes collective protection from most civil actions for work-related injuries by the workers of any Sch. 1 employer.

Some employers are individually responsible for the payment of workers' compensation benefits to their workers. These employers are included in Sch. 2 and are only protected against civil actions for work-related injuries brought by their own workers.

Still other employers are not included in either Schs. 1 or 2 of the Act. Most of these employers may opt into Sch. 1. However, if they choose not to, these employers and their workers are not affected by the limitations on a worker's right to sue.

A separate set of restrictions on maintaining civil actions exists for federal government employees within s. 12 of the *Government Employees Compensation Act* (GECA).

While these basic concepts are fairly straightforward, the actual operation of these restrictions on civil actions can be quite complicated. Some of this complexity flows from the different ways that rules apply to workers and employers according to the classification of the relevant employers as Sch. 1 or 2, GECA, or if they are not covered at all. Still more complexity arises from the much criticized, convoluted wording of the relevant provisions of the Act.

Subsection 31(2) gives the Workplace Safety and Insurance Appeals Tribunal exclusive jurisdiction to determine whether a right of action is taken away by the *Workplace Safety And Insurance Act, 1997*. A similar provision exists in subs. 17(1) of the pre-1997 *Workers' Compensation Act*.

It should be noted that, due to delays in litigation, many right to sue cases involve accidents that are years old. Therefore the applicable provisions will be for accidents before January 1, 1998, under the pre-1997 *Workers' Compensation*

Act, rather than the *Workplace Safety And Insurance Act, 1997* for some years to come.

2. PRELIMINARY DETERMINATIONS

Rights of action are taken away under ss. 10(1), (9), and 16 (ss. 26 and 28 of the WSIA). Rights to recover damages are restricted by subss. 10(11) and (12) (subs. 29(3) and (4) of the WSIA). In determining how the right of action and the right to recover damages are affected by these sections in any particular claim, it will often be necessary for determinations to be made regarding the circumstances that surround the civil action.

These preliminary determinations will include whether individuals are workers or employers; whether an employer is in Sch. 1 or 2; whether an accident involving a worker arose out of and in the course of employment; *etc.* In general, the applicable rules in making these determinations are usually found to be the same rules, applied by Board policy in benefit appeals.

In making these preliminary determinations in the context of a hearing under these sections, the Tribunal makes findings that may affect a worker's entitlement to benefits or an employer's classification for assessment purposes. Unlike in appeals, the Tribunal may be making these determinations without the benefit of a WSIB decision and the associated investigations. This means that, unlike in most workers' compensation decisions, the first determination on an issue is effectively also the last.

Where the worker's entitlement to benefits is in issue, the Tribunal would prefer to have a WSIB determination on entitlement first, but will decide a worker's entitlement to benefits so long as the determination is necessary to decide the application and is not an obvious attempt to avoid the "normal channels". In these situations, in contrast with the usual appeal situation, the plaintiff workers are trying to establish that they do not have an entitlement to benefits so that they may proceed with a civil action.

3. ACTIONS BARRED BY STATUTE

(a) Workers Against Their Own Employers

A Sch. 1 or 2 worker's right to bring an action against his or her employer for damages arising from an accident or occupational disease is taken away under s. 16 of the Act (s. 28 of the WSIA). Since amendments in 1985, this protection also applies to executive officers.

These restrictions apply only to the workers of employers in Schs. 1 or 2. Other workers may be affected by s. 12 of the GECA.

Workers who remain eligible to maintain actions for damages arising from accidents or occupational diseases are assisted in doing so by the provisions of Pt. II of the Act (Pt. X of the WSIA) which modify the more restrictive aspects of the common law defences of contributory negligence, assumption of risk, and the fellow servant rule.

(b) Workers Against Other Employers

Providing that the appropriate election is made, there are no restrictions on a worker of a Sch. 1 employer bringing an action against any employer other any other Sch. 1 employer. Again, providing that an appropriate election is made, there are no restrictions on a worker of a Sch. 2 employer bringing an action against any employer other than the worker's own employer. The actions by workers against other employers that are barred by statute are those brought by workers of Sch. 1 employers against other Sch. 1 employers.

Section 10(9) of the Act reads as follows:

> **10.** (9) No employer in Schedule 1 and no worker of an employer in Schedule 1 or dependant of such worker has a right of action for damages against any employer in Schedule 1 or any executive officer or any director or any worker of such employer, for an injury for which benefits are payable under this Act, where the workers of both employers were in the course of their employment at the time of the happening of the injury, but, in any case where the Board is satisfied that the accident giving rise to the injury was caused by the negligence of some other employer or employers in Schedule 1 or their workers, the Board may direct that the benefits awarded in any such case or a proportion of them shall be charged against the class or group to which such other employer or employers belong and to the accident cost record of such individual employer or employers.

Until recently, s. 10(9) has been effective in removing a cause of action where the negligent act was the result of the direct negligence of the employer instead of the vicarious negligence of the employer's worker. In this situation it was necessary to determine if the employer was in the course of his or her "employment" at the time of the accident. An application for judicial review was denied in one case; however, this approach has been rejected in at least two later decisions.

An issue exists as to how to interpret the words "where the workers of both employers were in the course of their employment at the time of the happening of the injury". The question is whether or not these words might require both the injured worker and the negligent worker to be in the course of their employment at the time of the injury. This is referred to as the contemporaneity requirement.

The prevalent trend at the Tribunal is to require only that the injured worker was in the course of employment at the time of the injury. It is sufficient if the negligent worker was in the course of employment when the negligent act or omission took place. However, in one decision, an action arose from the collapse of a wall in 1992. It had been built 12 years earlier. What that Panel found significant was not the time that had passed between the alleged negligence and the accident, but the strong causal connection between the work of the builder and the accident.

At least two other decisions have found s. 10(9) to be ineffective in removing the cause of action as a result of the need for at least some temporal connection between the negligent act or omission and the injury to the worker.

A Supreme Court of Canada decision has recognized the broad jurisdiction of specialized Workers' Compensation tribunals to determine whether a right of action is taken away against other employers.

(c) Workers Against Other Workers

As in the case of actions against employers other than the worker's own employer, if an appropriate election is made, there are no restrictions on a worker of a Sch. 1 employer bringing an action against any other worker, so long as the other worker was not in the course of employment with a Sch. 1 employer.

Tribunal decisions have held that the framing of the cause of action does not affect the barring of the claim, if it can be found that the underlying cause of action was a compensable accident. Thus, decisions have barred claims brought on the grounds of intentional torts, occupiers' liability, breach of contract and claims seeking punitive or exemplary damages.

In one decision, the Panel found that a suit for wrongful dismissal related to an accident could be continued, but a suit against the worker's employer for insurance benefits could not proceed. In the latter case it was argued — an argument that was rejected — that the employer was being sued, not as "the employer", but in its capacity as a provider of private disability insurance.

Accidents involving out-of-province parties have also been addressed. Tribunal decisions and Board policy have relied on a 1985 British Columbia Court of Appeal decision.

The restrictions on workers of Sch. 1 employers bringing actions against other workers of Sch. 1 employers are also found in s. 10(9). This subsection has been found to be applicable in the situation where both workers worked for the same employer even though the subsection states "where the workers of *both* employers were in the course of their employment at the time of the happening of the injury".

In another Tribunal decision, it was found that a sexual assault victim could continue an action against the alleged attacker, a co-worker, although not against their common employer. The Panel noted that:

> In our opinion, the *Worker's Compensation Act* is not intended to shield persons who commit physical or sexual assaults on other workers who are, themselves, in the course of their employment. Where the facts in a case clearly establish that there was an aggressor and a victim, it is, in our view, nonsensical to speak of the action being reasonably incidental to employment.

(d) Actions under the Family Law Act

It is not unusual for the family members of workers injured in accidents to attempt to maintain their own civil actions under the provisions of the *Family Law Act* (FLA). These actions may be affected by the provisions of the *Workers' Compensation Act*. Section 16 of the Act takes away the rights of action of "family members" of the worker against the worker's own employer. Other provisions which affect the worker's own right of action against other employers may also affect the family members' rights as well, where the family members' rights are derivative.

In *Meyer v. Waycon International Trucks Ltd.* the Ontario Court of Appeal decided that the Act does not authorize a determination under s. 10(9) as to whether or not the rights of action of any individuals other than workers or dependants are taken away. The individuals pursuing the action in the *Meyer* case were family members who were not dependants for the purposes of the Act. The question of whether or not other legislation caused those family members to lose their cause of action when the worker's cause of action would have been taken away by the Workers' Compensation Act was left to the courts to decide.

Under s. 10(9), the Appeals Tribunal will now only rule on whether or not the rights of workers and dependants to maintain actions have been taken away. Where the action of a family member who is not a dependant is derivative under the FLA, this determination, while not formally taking away the family member's right of action, will have the practical effect of doing so. The Tribunal has also determined that under the Act, individuals are not considered to be "dependants" for the purpose of s. 10(9) unless the worker is deceased.

The *Meyer* decision does not apply where the cause of action is potentially taken away under s. 16 of the Act. In this situation the Tribunal has jurisdiction to determine the availability of the rights of action of the "family members". This is in contrast to the restrictions under s. 10(9) on "dependants". It should be noted that under s. 16 of the Act, non-dependant family members who cannot sue do not have any right to workers' compensation payments.

Subsection 26(2) of the *Workplace Safety And Insurance Act, 1997* addresses the anomaly of the non-dependent family member being deprived of both compensation benefits *and* a right of action against a worker's employer appears to have been changed. A right of action is barred only for "a worker, a worker's survivor or a worker's spouse, child or dependant", but not a "member of the family". In addition subs. 27(2) of the 1997 Act makes it clear that if a worker's right of action is removed, so is that of family members under the FLA.

4. EXCEPTIONS TO ACTIONS BARRED BY STATUTE

There are three general exceptions to the barring of actions by workers against their employers. These are that:

- The action does not relate to an accident or, it related only to the property damage aspect of an accident;
- The accident was not in Ontario as the Act does not have an extraterritorial effect;
- The Sch. 1 employer being sued by a worker who is not the employer's worker, has supplied a motor vehicle, machinery, or equipment on a purchase or rental basis without also supplying workers to operate the motor vehicle, machinery or equipment. Such actions are allowed by virtue of subs. 10(10) of the act. Similar provisions are fund in subsection 28(4) of the *Workplace Safety and Insurance Act, 1997*.

In circumstances where the actions were framed in terms other than tort, such as breach of contract or wrongful dismissal, the Tribunal has tended to look behind the specific claim to see whether it is being brought "for or by any reason of any accident happening to the worker". One decision reviewed several Tribunal decisions and took away a right of action being brought, in part, for wrongful dismissal.

The Tribunal has considered the meaning to be provided to the phrase "motor vehicle, machinery or equipment" on a number of occasions and has found that the phrase contemplates something that is capable of being operated.

An action against the lessor of a leased vehicle clearly fits within the subs. 10(10) exception. So does an action against a company that sells a vehicle that is involved in an accident.

At least one Tribunal decision has indicated that the manufacturer of equipment may be sued pursuant to subs. 10(10) even though it was not the direct supplier. Foreign manufacturers are, of course, not included in Sch. 1, and may be sued regardless of subs. 10(10).

In cases where subs. 10(10) is an issue, the possibility exists that related companies might supply motor vehicles, machinery and equipment to one another. The Tribunal has refused to "lift the corporate veil" in these circumstances to prevent lawsuits.

5. RESTRICTIONS ON THE RIGHT TO RECOVER DAMAGES

In addition to the provisions of the Act which prevent the bringing of actions, there are also provisions in subss. 10(11) and (12) which restrict the right to recover damages. These sections apply to Sch. 1 and Sch. 2 employers respectively and similar provisions are found at subs. 29(4) of the *Workplace Safety And Insurance Act, 1997*.

The determination of which parties are responsible for what portions of the plaintiff's loss or damages is made by the courts and not by the Tribunal.

The general effect of these damage provisions is that defendants who are not protected by the Act from lawsuits being brought will be protected against liability for the negligence or fault of the defendants, or potential defendants, who are protected.

6. THE ELECTION BETWEEN BENEFITS AND CIVIL ACTIONS

(a) The Requirement to Elect

Sections 10(1), (6) and 9(2) provide that where there is a cause of action for a worker, he or she may "elect" either to claim benefits, or to pursue the action. There is a three-month time limit for such elections. Similar provisions are found in subss. 30(2), (3) and (4) of the *Workplace Safety And Insurance Act, 1997.*

Subsections 10(7) and (8) deal with elections by persons under 18 years of age and workers mentally incapable of making an election.

The Board's legal branch will consider requests to extend the three-month limitation period. The main concern of the Board in dealing with such requests is the possibility of limitation periods being missed that may prejudice the Board.

(b) The Effect of an Election

If an election is made to maintain the civil action, the worker will usually have no entitlement to workers' compensation benefits. However, if the action is not as successful as was originally anticipated, the Act does provide protection for the worker. Sections 10(2) and (3) provide certain protection in that, if the Board approves a settlement, and less is recovered in the law suit than would be payable under the Act, the Board will pay the difference.

Effective January 1, 1994, the amendments introduced by the *Insurance Statute Law Amendment Act, 1993*, came into force. These amendments included an addition to s. 10 — s. 10(2.1) — which provides that this protection is not available for recipients of benefits under s. 268 the *Insurance Act.*

Further subsections — ss. 10(13)-(19) — were added by these amendments to deal with what should occur in these circumstances.

A number of Tribunal decisions have made exceptions to the bar created by s. 10(3) where the settlement by the worker was uninformed.

If an election is made to receive workers' compensation benefits, the Board, or in the case of a worker of a Sch. 2 employer, the employer, is subrogated to the rights of the worker or dependant to maintain the action under s. 10(4) of the Act. Any amount recovered, over and above all amounts expended by the Board or the employer in respect of the workers' compensation claim, including administrative charges and the pursuit of the civil action, are to be paid to the worker. This will have the effect of reducing the worker's future entitlement to workers' compensation benefits once a payout has been made. In practice, the

Board capitalizes the value of benefits that the worker is entitled to in the future, prior to determining if there is a surplus to be paid to the worker. Existing monthly payments are therefore not affected. It has been found that the acceptance of benefits by a worker is sufficient to be considered an election under the Act.

A Tribunal decision found that the Board could change its mind with respect to exercising its subrogated right and that the Tribunal had the jurisdiction to, in effect, re-hear the matter in light of the changed circumstances.

If a worker who has elected to receive benefits subsequently decides that pursuing the civil action would be more advantageous, the Board considers it within its discretion to allow the worker to change the election. In exercising this discretion, the Board will be concerned with protecting its ability to recover benefit expenditures made, the viability of the civil action, the resources of the worker to maintain the action and the adequacy of the worker's representation. The Board will also be concerned with the amount of resources that it has spent on pursuing the action.

The Tribunal has indicated that it will exercise jurisdiction to review decisions by the Board concerning the worker's ability to re-elect. However, the Tribunal also indicated that it would look for exceptional circumstances to warrant such a reversal.

The ability of the Board or of a Sch. 2 employer to maintain the subrogated action is clarified in s. 10(5) of the Act. In one court case, it was determined that this subsection did not make a defendant liable for any amount additional to general and special damages.

The question of whether a defendant can rely on the election of a plaintiff to receive benefits to bar the bringing of an action by the worker is not clear. In the courts it has been found that the election does not eliminate the cause of action but that if the action is brought by the worker it must be for the benefit of the Board. However, should the Board also wish to pursue the claim, the Board is *dominus litis* and can control the action. The defendant would have no complaint against the bringing of the action by the worker in these circumstances unless the defendant is harassed by having to defend two separate actions.

However, other Tribunal decisions have held that while an action is not eliminated when an election to receive benefits is made, the worker is required to have the permission of the Board, or the Sch. 2 employer, prior to proceeding.

An election by a worker to receive workers' compensation benefits will subrogate the worker's rights. However, the worker's election does not affect the rights of the worker's dependants or family members to maintain their own civil actions for their own benefit.

(c) **Considerations in Electing**

Lawyers will often be faced with the task of advising workers whether to elect to receive workers' compensation benefits or to elect to sue.

Where the Board identifies and pursues a cause of action, its stated objective is to recover on the whole claim and not just to recover sufficient funds to cover the expense of the claim to the Board. As noted before, the worker is entitled to recover any surplus funds from the litigation. There may, however, be situations where the worker would desire to control the litigation.

Entering into a final determination of the worker's options will be a consideration of the possibility of maintaining a successful action given the restrictions of the Act, the likelihood of establishing liability, the likelihood of recovery, the size of the potential recovery, the resources available to maintain the action, the ability of the worker to do without income from the Board, and the possibility that the worker might subsequently suffer a recurrence of disability after settlement of the claim. The restrictions contained in the *Insurance Act* on the right to maintain actions in automobile accidents will also have a bearing on this decision in a large number of cases.

Although s. 10(2) does provide some protection in the case of unsuccessful litigation, the plaintiff may be exposed to significant legal expenses.

However, again note the changes resulting from the 1993 amendments to the *Insurance Act*, cited above, under (b) The Effect of an Election.

Where the Board does not intend to pursue a possible action, it may be worthwhile to contact the Board's legal branch to discuss the matter with them. In these circumstances it may also be possible to elect benefits and still proceed with the civil action based on the understanding that so long as its interests are protected the Board will not interfere in the proceedings.

Where the short-term availability of an income for the worker is a consideration, assistance in the form of no fault automobile insurance benefits should not be expected. The Supreme Court of Canada, while dealing with an exclusionary provision in an insurance policy which denied liability for "bodily injury to or death of any person ... who is entitled to receive the benefits of any workmen's compensation law or plan", determined that proof that the insured could successfully claim compensation was sufficient to allow the insurer to rely on the exclusion. It was not necessary for the worker to have actually claimed compensation in order for the exclusion to apply. The manner in which workers' compensation benefits and no fault insurance benefits interact for accidents on or after January 1, 1994, is determined in accordance with s. 10 of the *Workers' Compensation Act*, as am., effective January 1, 1994, and ss. 267.1 and 268 of the *Insurance Act*. The Ontario Court of Appeal has made it clear that workers' compensation benefits take precedence over automobile insurance benefits.

If the claim falls under the *Workplace Safety And Insurance Act, 1997*, in considering whether a party should take legal action, it should be noted that the statutory six-month time limit for filing a claim for benefits with the Board is waived in subs. 31(4), until six months after the Tribunal renders a final decision as to whether a right of action is taken away.

7. PROCEDURAL CONSIDERATIONS

(a) Jurisdiction of the Appeals Tribunal

The exclusive jurisdiction of the Appeals Tribunal to determine whether a plaintiff's right of action or right of recovery are taken away by the Act is found in s. 17(1) of the *Workers' Compensation Act* and s. 31(2) of the *Workplace Safety And Insurance Act, 1997.*

As of January 1, 1994, pursuant to s. 17(2), insurance companies also have the right to apply to the Tribunal for a determination.

There are four decisions of the Supreme Court of Canada dealing with the pre-Tribunal provisions of the Act that conferred exclusive authority on the Board. All four decisions confirmed the exclusive jurisdiction of the Board. The current provisions dealing with the Appeals Tribunal are very similarly worded. The exclusive jurisdiction extends to ousting the jurisdiction of the ordinary courts.

Notwithstanding the exclusive jurisdiction formerly conferred on the Board and now upon the Appeals Tribunal, there is precedent for the courts applying the provisions of the Act to cases before them, without referral to the Board.

However, it would appear to be more appropriate where a defendant seeks to rely on the provisions of the Act before a court, that an application instead be made to the Appeals Tribunal. An early application to the Tribunal may well avoid unnecessary expenditures in preparation for litigation.

The Tribunal has also determined that it has the jurisdiction to determine if a person is entitled to workers' compensation benefits in s. 17 applications brought in the course of litigation over a plaintiff's right to no fault automobile insurance benefits. The finding of entitlement to workers' compensation benefits in these cases would result in findings of no entitlement to no fault benefits.

As discussed above, following the Court of Appeal decision in *Meyer*, the Appeals Tribunal did not determine whether or not causes of action might exist under the FLA.

(b) Procedures on a Section 17 Application

Procedures on s. 17 applications are governed by a Practice Direction of the Appeals Tribunal which was released in July 1986 and last revised on January 2, 1998. Among other things, the Practice Direction deals with the preparation of applicant's and respondent's factums, notice requirements for evidence, scheduling of hearings and summons requests. Where more than one person is injured in an accident the Appeals Tribunal has stressed the importance of a consolidated hearing.

8. THE CANADIAN CHARTER OF RIGHTS AND FREEDOMS

A number of cases have been dealt with by the courts where Charter arguments have been raised in attempts to strike down or restrict the protections against civil actions found in the Ontario Act and in the workers' compensation legislation of other provinces. None of these actions have been successful. The arguments raised have dealt with whether or not the removal of a right to a civil action is an unjustified restriction on the right to security of the person and whether or not the distinctions between who can and cannot sue in particular circumstances are in violation of equality rights.

One Tribunal Panel was asked to remove a right of action being brought as a result of allegations that a plaintiff's Charter rights had been infringed. That Panel found that, even if it was a "court of competent jurisdiction" under s. 24 of the Charter, it had no jurisdiction to effect a remedy and did not bar the constitutional cause of action. See Chapter 25, The Appeals Procedure for further discussion of Charter issues.

CHAPTER 11

Claims and Payments

1. INTRODUCTION

This chapter deals with the claims process, the manner in which payments in a claim are usually made, and how the usual payment processes are modified to deal with matters such as assignments, advances, commutations, overpayments, and orders for family support.

2. NO WAIVER OF RIGHTS

An agreement between a worker and his or her employer to waive or to forego any benefits to which the worker or his or her survivors are or may become entitled to from the WSIB is void.

A negotiated return-to-work agreement or termination settlement might include a provision that the worker not make any claim for benefits arising out of the employer's alleged breach of its return-to-work obligations. Such a provision would not be enforceable against the worker. However, although not binding on the Board or the Appeals Tribunal, a worker may agree that the employer should not be penalized.

3. NO DISCRIMINATION

Neither the *Workplace Safety and Insurance Act, 1997* nor the *Workers' Compensation Act* contain any protection for workers against employer reprisals directed at workers exercising rights under these Acts. However, the Ontario *Human Rights Code* prohibits discrimination in employment based on handicap and the definition of handicap under the Code includes a person who has made a claim pursuant to the *Workplace Safety and Insurance Act, 1997*. Interestingly, the provisions of the *Workers' Compensation Reform Act, 1997* that added a reference to the *Workplace Safety and Insurance Act, 1997* in the *Human Rights Code* deleted the reference to persons with claims under the *Workers' Compensation Act*. The effect of this deletion is not known.

4. WAGES ON THE DAY OF INJURY

The employer must pay a worker entitled to benefits as a result of a work-related injury his or her wages and benefits for the day of the injury as if the accident had not occurred. If the employer does not pay the wages and benefits to the worker, the Board shall. The employer then becomes obligated to pay the same amount back to the Board along with any other penalty or liability.

Enforcement of the employer's obligation to pay wages and benefits for the day of injury is initiated by worker complaint. The Board does not routinely investigate compliance with this obligation.

5. CONTINUATION OF EMPLOYMENT BENEFITS

The employer must, for one year following an injury, make contributions for employment benefits in respect of the worker when the worker is absent from work because of the injury. This obligation exists only to the extent that the employer was making contributions for employment benefits for the worker when the injury occurred and the worker continues to pay his or her contributions, if any, for the employment benefits while absent from work.

The contributions for employment benefits that must be continued by an employer are contributions on behalf of a worker or the worker's spouse, child or dependant for health care, life insurance and pension benefits. Board policy indicates that if accidental death and disability insurance is purchased as part of a life insurance policy that these contributions must continue as well.

No employer is obligated to continue Employment Insurance contributions or Canada Pension Plan contributions on behalf of the injured worker. Both the Employment Insurance system and the Canada Pension Plan system have rules that relieve some of the hardships associated with a lack of contributions caused by a work-related injury.

The actual employer of an "emergency worker" or a member of a municipal volunteer fire brigade or a municipal volunteer ambulance brigade, must make the required contributions for employment benefits but the deemed employer must reimburse the actual employer.

Special rules for the continuation of employment benefits apply to employers who participate in multi-employer benefit plans in respect of the worker.

Failure to comply with the requirement to continue employment benefits may result in a penalty being levied to a maximum of one year's contributions for employment benefits. Failure to comply may also result in the employer becoming liable to the worker for any loss the worker suffers as a result. Enforcement of liability is presumably a civil matter. Seeking enforcement of penalties by the Board often results in voluntary compliance by the employer.

6. THE EMPLOYER'S REPORT OF INJURY

An employer must notify the Board within three days after learning of an accident to a worker, if the accident necessitates health care or results in the worker not being able to earn full wages. The notice must be on a form approved by the Board and the employer must give the Board any other information that the Board may require from time to time in connection with the accident. Failure to report the injury may result in the Board levying an administrative penalty, which may be in addition to any penalty imposed by a court. The accident must be reported by the employer regardless of whether the worker completes an application for benefits.

An injury is considered to have required health care when treatment of the injury required the provision of professional services provided by a health care practitioner, meaning any health professional. The most common health professionals used are, of course, doctors and nurses. It makes no difference if the treatment was provided by an employee of the employer or is otherwise paid for by the employer. An employer must provide a copy of the notice of accident to the worker at the time that the notice is given to the Board.

7. THE WORKER'S CLAIM FOR BENEFITS

For accidents on or after January 1, 1998, the worker must make a claim for benefits on a form approved by the Board. Failure to file the claim will result in no benefits being provided by the Board unless the Board, in its opinion, decides that it is just to do so. The election may be made by the worker on the employer's report of accident to the Board (Form 7). If the employer's report of accident does not contain a completed claim for benefit by the worker benefits may still be paid to a worker for a short period of time prior to the worker's claim being received. This grace period will allow time for the required form to be obtained by, or provided to, the worker and returned to the Board. The obligation to file a claim also applies to persons claiming survivors' benefits.

The claim must be made as soon as possible after the accident and in no case more than six months after the accident or the worker's learning that he or she suffers from an occupational disease. The Board has the authority to permit a late claim if, in its opinion, it is just to do so.

The worker must provide a copy of the claim to the employer. The worker must also consent to the disclosure of his or her employer of information provided by a health professional under the Act concerning the worker's functional abilities. This information is intended to be disclosed solely for the purpose of facilitating the worker's return to work.

Workers or survivors who have the right to bring civil actions or to claim benefits for work-related accidents in another jurisdiction may have to file elections with the Board at the time of making their claims. In these circumstances, the period of time for making a claim may be reduced to three months from six months. In the event that permission to proceed with a lawsuit is denied by the Appeals Tribunal or the claim for benefits may only be made in Ontario and not in another jurisdiction, the worker or survivor may be allowed an extension on the time to claim benefits.

8. FORM AND FREQUENCY OF PAYMENT

For accidents prior to January 1, 1998, the payment of benefits for temporary disability benefits are made every two weeks and the payment of permanent disability benefits, including Future Economic Loss benefits are made monthly. For accidents on or after January 1, 1998, payments are made every two weeks for the first 24 months following injury and then made once a month after that.

Payments from the Board are either by cheque or, with the worker's approval, by direct deposit. With adequate proof, the Board will replace lost or stolen cheques.

A cheque can be cashed without prejudice to the worker's right to dispute any aspect of entitlement, including the payment in question. There is an exception where an election to receive benefits is required, in which case the cashing of the cheque may be taken as an indication of an election to receive benefits.

Benefits for work-related injuries are not considered taxable income. However, the payments may affect entitlement to tax credits and other forms of social assistance. The Board issues information slips for tax purposes. Where there is a delay in receiving entitlement and compensation benefits have previously been assigned to an employer, an insurance company, or a social service provider that paid taxable income to the worker, the worker may benefit from refiling his or her income tax return for the year in question.

9. PAYMENTS TO INCOMPETENT PERSONS, INCARCERATED WORKERS AND DECEASED WORKERS' ESTATES

The Board has the authority to direct payments to someone who will receive the payments on behalf of the injured worker or survivor if the person entitled to benefits is considered by the Board to be incapable of managing his or her own affairs or is a minor.

Where benefits are payable to the estate of a person and there is no person representative of the estate to whom the Board may make the payment, the Board has the authority to make arrangements with other persons as are determined to be appropriate.

An incarcerated worker is not prohibited from receiving benefits from the Board as there are no statutory provisions to allow the Board to treat incarcerated workers any differently from other workers. Incarceration will reduce entitlement to benefits that require the worker's co-operation in medical rehabilitation and return-to-work initiatives. Depending on the sentence, benefits owed to the injured worker may be paid directly to the worker at the penal institution, directly to the worker at the workers' mailing address, or, with written authorization, to a person of the worker's choice.

10. VACATIONING WORKERS AND WORKERS ABSENT FROM ONTARIO

Board policy is to allow up to three weeks of vacation per year to an injured worker who is required to participate in a program of either vocational or medical rehabilitation so long as the vacation does not interfere with the rehabilitation program. Other temporary absences are dealt with by Board policy as well, and focus on the need to keep the Board informed of the worker's medical situation. Leaving Ontario, but remaining in Canada, so long as it does not otherwise interfere with a program of vocational or medical rehabilitation does not have an adverse impact on the receipt of benefits.

Leaving Canada will not affect the entitlement of a worker in receipt of a pension for a permanent partial disability. The Board may even be willing to be flexible with respect to the frequency of payment and the mailing address. The Board may arrange a permanent impairment assessments on a priority basis when it is informed that a worker will be leaving Canada. If the country the worker resides in has a reciprocal agreement with the Board, an permanent impairment assessment may be possible in that country.

Other workers whose benefits are stopped while they are absent from Canada may, subject to cooperation requirements and proof of disability, request payment for the period they were absent upon their return.

11. REDUCTION AND SUSPENSION OF BENEFITS

There are a number of grounds upon which the Board may reduce or suspend benefits to an injured worker based upon a failure to co-operate with the Board or mitigate the consequences of an injury:

- A person receiving benefits under the insurance plan or who may be entitled to do so must give the Board such information as the Board may require from time to time in connection with the person's claim.
- A worker who claims or is receiving benefits shall co-operate in such health care measures as the Board considers appropriate.
- Upon the request of the Board, a worker who claims or is receiving benefits shall submit to a health examination by a health professional selected and paid for by the Board.
- Upon the request of his or her employer, a worker who claims or is receiving benefits shall submit to a health examination selected and paid for by the employer.
- A worker must co-operate in his or her own early and safe return to work and must co-operate in all aspects of a labour market re-entry assessment or plan provided to the worker.

If entitlement to benefits is suspended, no compensation is payable in respect of the period of suspension. However, there are significant differences between the *Workers' Compensation Act* and the *Workplace Safety and Insurance Act, 1997* regarding when suspension of benefits is called for. For injuries on or after January 1, 1998, the Board also appears to be more likely to suspend benefits in situations where it would previously have just withheld benefits pending the receipt of information.

Board policy, as contained in the *Operational Policy Manual* with respect to the reduction and suspension of benefits under the *Workers' Compensation Act* indicates that:

> The *Workers' Compensation Act* provides for the reduction or complete suspension of compensation benefits under certain conditions. In applying the guidelines to specific cases, it is the general practice of the Board, to ensure that every reasonable opportunity is taken to permit the continuation of partial compensation benefits. Complete suspension of benefits will only be employed when all other appropriate measures have failed to resolve the particular situation.

In addition to this formal policy, the Board will in most instances not reduce benefits retroactively. Instead, it will continue benefits until the time of a decision to reduce or terminate takes place plus a further period that is long enough to allow the worker to receive a letter from the Board. The extent to which previous practises and policies will be continued under the *Workplace Safety and Insurance Act, 1997*, with its more numerous provisions regarding the reduction or suspension of benefits, remains to be seen. Given the nature of the decision, it would appear to be particularly important that the Board comply with its requirement to issue decisions promptly and in writing to the parties of record.

12. OBLIGATION TO REPORT MATERIAL CHANGES OF CIRCUMSTANCE — PENALTIES

A person receiving benefits or who may be entitled to do so must notify the Board of a material change in circumstances in connection with the entitlement within 10 days after the material change occurs. A person who wilfully fails to inform the Board of a material change in circumstances within 10 days after the change occurs is guilty of an offence. A person convicted of an offence is liable to a fine not exceeding $25,000 or to imprisonment for up to six months, or to both.

13. EMPLOYER TOP-UPS AND ADVANCES

The Board must have regard to any payment or benefit paid by the worker's employer, or provided wholly at the employer's expense, that relates to the accident. A deduction made from the benefits of a worker receiving an accident related payment or benefit from a Sch. 1 employer, may be paid to the employer by the Board.

While an advance from an employer in anticipation of the worker's receipt of accident related benefits will result in a reduction of the compensation otherwise payable to the worker from the Board, a payment from the employer that is intended to supplement, or top up the compensation will not result in a reduction.

Only some types of benefits payable by the Board will be reduced on account of employer advances. These include temporary disability benefits and Future Economic Loss (FEL) supplementary and pension supplementary benefits.

Pension benefits and FEL benefits will not be reduced on account of advances. At the time of writing the Board did not have any policy on how advances would be dealt with under the *Workplace Safety and Insurance Act, 1997*. Presumably loss of earnings benefits will be reduced by employer advances at least in the early stages of a claim.

Payments from employers in advance of accident-related benefits from the Board should not be recorded as taxable income of the worker from the employer. Tax receipts for compensation payments received are provided by the Board and should include amounts advanced from the employer.

Payments from an employer that represent the worker's holiday or vacation entitlement will not be considered payments in respect of the work-related injury where the worker's injury still prevents a return to work. When payments are made from an employer over a holiday or vacation period, the worker is entitled to both the payments from the employer and the accident benefits from Board.

Benefits paid by the Board cannot be garnisheed but wages payable by an employer may be. The Board will not recognize any amount deducted by an employer on account of a garnishment as an advance on compensation. Amounts deducted by the employer on account of a garnishment order may result in increased payments being made to the worker by the Board.

It is not clear if benefits paid to a worker under an insurance plan where the premiums have been paid for by the employer may be considered an advance so as to reduce benefits payable by the Board.

14. BOARD ADVANCES

If the Board is of the view that the interest or pressing need of the person warrants it, the Board may advance money to the person, or for his or her benefit. An advance will not be considered unless entitlement to the benefits in question has been established. While once used quite extensively, the Board has more recently been reluctant to allow advances.

15. COMMUTATION OF PRE-1989 PERMANENT DISABILITY PENSIONS

(a) Introduction

The amount payable in a lump sum upon the commutation of a permanent disability pension award varies in accordance with the size of the pension being commuted, whether or not the commutation is full or partial, the age and sex of the worker, and the discount rate used in the commutation formula (the higher the discount rate, the lower the amount of the commuted pension).

Prior to indexation of benefits in 1986, the Board used a discount rate of 7 per cent for use in commutations. Commutations of benefits subject to full indexation following January 1, 1986 are discounted at 4 per cent. Following the introduction of Friedland indexing on January 1, 1995, benefits subject to the

Friedland formula were commuted at a 6 per cent discount rate. With the further reduction of inflation protection, it is assumed that these benefits will now be subject to a 7 per cent discount rate. The Board has estimated that the change from a 4 per cent discount to a 6 per cent discount for a 40-year-old male receiving $300 per month would reduce the commuted amount available from $65,400 to $51,102.

(b) Commutations Where Clinical Award is 10 Per Cent or Less

Unless the Board decides that it would not be to the advantage of a worker to do so, upon request, the Board must commute a permanent disability pension of 10 per cent or less. The Board will usually determine that is not in the best interests of the worker where the condition may be subject to deterioration as in the case of pensions for weight bearing joints such as ankles and knees. The Board totals all pensions in all claims to determine whether the 10 per cent figure has been exceeded. The Appeals Tribunal has agreed with this approach. However, in those cases where the Board has declined to grant a commutation of a pension award of less than 10 per cent, the Appeals Tribunal has consistently placed the onus on the Board to demonstrate that the lump sum payment would not be to the advantage of the worker.

(c) Commutations Where Clinical Award is Greater than 10 Per Cent

An initial request for a full or partial commutation can be made orally or in writing. The Board will respond to this with a letter setting out the dollar value of the pension if commuted and also setting out Board policy. For claimants who wish a commutation for a specific purpose, time is often of the essence. In light of the delays in the appeal process an initial denial may be tantamount to a total denial. It is usually very difficult for a worker to obtain a full commutation of a pension award in excess of 10 per cent.

Board policy as contained in the Board's *Operational Policy Manual* is as follows:

> A commutation of a monthly pension may be authorized under section 27(1) [of the Act] when
>
> —— required as a new or continuing rehabilitative measure intended to enable the person to obtain or maintain suitable employment by reducing the effects of a physical and/or psychological disability.
>
> —— medical evidence indicates that the worker's financial situation is producing a disability, which is preventing the worker from obtaining or maintaining employment, and where a commutation will significantly remedy the situation.

"Reducing the effects of a disability" means reducing the precise limitations imposed by that disability. The phrase can be equated with reducing the disability itself. There must be a direct link between the commutation and the reduction of the effects of the disability. There is no direct link between the commutation and employment.

The sequence must be:

commutation → reduced effects → employment.

"Medical evidence" ordinarily means written evidence by a psychiatrist that the worker's financial situation is producing a disability (usually psychological in nature). The evidence must indicate that resolution of the financial problem will allow the worker to obtain employment or maintain an existing job.

The "financial situation producing a disability" does not cover habitual financial problems which predate the work-related accident, but rather, financial problems that have arisen since the worker's accident that result in a disability.

As the primary focus is to reduce the effects of the disability, commutation requests made for purely financial reasons do not conform to the intent of the policy.

A request for commutation must meet the following requirements:

—— it must be intended for a specific rehabilitation purpose
—— alternate resources are not available for the intended purpose
—— it must not jeopardize the applicant's ability to meet ongoing financial obligations
—— counselling must first be explored.

The Appeals Tribunal has tended not to follow the Board's commutation policy too closely, preferring a less rigid approach.

16. INTEREST

For claims registered after January 1, 1990, interest is paid on virtually all delayed payments regardless of the reason for the delay or the decision-making level involved. For claims registered before January 1, 1990, the Board pays interest if there is a Appeals Officer or Appeals Tribunal reversal of a decision regarding entitlement to payments dated January 6, 1989 or later. Except in very limited circumstances involving Board policy reversals, Board policy is that no interest is payable for delays in entitlement payments where the entitlement is determined prior to an appeal level decision. No interest is payable for any period prior to January 6, 1989. Interest accrues from the date of the first standard payment due date or January 6, 1989, whichever is later. The interest entitlement is limited to benefits that should have been received up to the date of the reversal ruling. Benefits payable after the reversal decision are not subject to interest payments.

Interest is paid at a rate equal to the relevant post-judgment interest rate current on the date of the particular ruling, and is calculated on the basis of simple (rather than compound) interest. If the employer advanced to the worker all or part of the payments that should have been paid by the Board, interest is paid only on the portion of benefits that were not covered by the employer. The worker's receipt of E.I. (U.I.) or social assistance benefits does not affect the payment of interest.

17. ASSIGNMENTS, ATTACHMENTS AND FAMILY SUPPORT ORDERS

Benefits may only be assigned with the permission of the Board. The Board will not recognize assignments for legal fees, mortgages or rent accounts, or any other creditors. The Board will recognize assignments for money advanced for income support such as sickness and accident insurance benefits, employment (or unemployment) insurance and social assistance. However, the recognition of the assignment is limited to compensation benefits payable for the same periods of time for which these other forms of income support were payable.

Benefits may only be garnished, charged or attached with the permission of the Board. The Board does not grant permission under any circumstances except as required by statute for family support and maintenance obligations and with respect to Revenue Canada orders to pay. The only other reduction of payments for the repayment of a debt is a reduction to pay for a debt that is owed to the Board itself. There are limits imposed upon the extent to which deductions may be made from benefits payable by the Board.

18. RECONSIDERATIONS

The Board may reconsider any decision made by it and may confirm, amend or revoke it. The Board may do so at any time if it considers it advisable to do so. The authority to reconsider a decision must be exercised by the Board in accordance with the other requirements of the Act governing delegation of authority and the requirement to provide an opportunity for a hearing.

19. FRAUD

Where fraudulent activity is alleged in an allowed claim, a reconsideration of the claim may be made by the Board's Special Investigations Branch (SIB). If the SIB decision-maker proposes that the previous decision be confirmed, amended or reversed, the relevant parties are notified and have three business days to respond to the proposal. Reconsideration decisions by the SIB are considered the final decision of the Board. Any appeal of the SIB decision must be taken directly to the Appeals Tribunal.

20. OVERPAYMENTS

Payments made to workers that are in excess of their actual entitlement have historically, once discovered, been referred to as overpayments. Following legislative changes that took place December 15, 1995, the Board will now often refer to overpayments as "benefit-related debts".

Over the last number of years the laws and policies associated with overpayments have changed numerous times. The Board has presently just completed a further policy review. The most recent review has resulted in overpayment recovery being pursued where there is duplication of employment earnings and benefits; failure to report material change, fraud and/or misrepresentation; or an administrative error that the worker was aware of, or reasonably should have been aware of. On the other hand, overpayment recovery will not be pursued when the decision results from a previous entitlement decision that was overturned on reconsideration or appeal (barring fraud/misrepresentation); the debt is due to an administrative error that the worker reasonably could not have been aware of; the debtor was not notified of the debt within three years of the date the overpayment became due and owing (again barring fraud or misrepresentation); or if recovery would result in severe, long-term financial hardship for the worker.

Decisions creating overpayments may be appealed in the same manner as any other decisions on entitlement matters. However, the Board's decision as to whether and how to proceed with an overpayment recovery has been made subject to restrictions.

For accidents occurring on or after January 1, 1998, the Appeals Tribunal clearly no longer has any authority to deal with appeals respecting overpayments. Although the law is not quite so certain, the Appeals Tribunal may also no longer have any authority to deal with appeals respecting overpayments for claims resulting from accidents prior to January 1, 1998 even if those appeals were initiated prior to January 1, 1998.

For overpayments resulting from payments made on or after January 1, 1997, Board policy is that "debtors" do not have any internal or external appeal rights. The Board's position that its decisions are not reviewable internally or externally would appear to invite a challenge regarding the Board's failure to comply with the basic requirements of procedural fairness. At the present time it is not clear how an injured worker could even insist on the Board following its own policies with respect to overpayment recovery.

Should the Board decide to pursue overpayment recovery, it has a number of recovery methods at its disposal including voluntary repayment plans, offset from future payments (by policy the Board distinguishes between periodic and lump sum payments), recovery through court action and recovery through filing its own certificates with the court for enforcement without initiating a court action.

CHAPTER 12

Earnings Basis

1. INTRODUCTION

Workers' compensation benefits are directly linked to the level of the injured worker's pre-injury earnings. The calculations involved in estimating the pre-injury earnings can therefore have a tremendous impact on the level of benefits paid.

The rules for calculating the pre-injury earnings of workers have undergone a number of significant legislative overhauls over a number of years. Major changes in the method of calculating pre-injury earnings took place on April 1, 1985, and January 1, 1998. In addition, the inflation protection of benefits payable to injured workers has also undergone substantial changes. Very significant changes in the degree to which inflation protection is provided for injured workers' benefits took place on January 1, 1986, January 1, 1995, and January 1, 1998.

Due to space limitations, only the current earnings basis rules will be covered in this chapter.

2. PRE-INJURY GROSS AVERAGE EARNINGS

(a) Introduction

Subsections 53(1) and (3) of the *Workplace Safety and Insurance Act, 1997* provide the Workplace Safety and Insurance Board with a very large discretion to formulate rules to determine the pre-injury wages of injured workers. Most, but not all, of the rules used by the Board to determine wages for injuries occurring after January 1, 1998, are found in Document 4.1 of the WSIB's *Operational Policy* publication.

Earnings or wages include any remuneration capable of being estimated in terms of money but do not include contributions made under s. 25 of the *Workplace Safety and Insurance Act, 1997* for employment benefits.

Average earnings do not include any sum paid to the worker for special expenses incurred because of the nature of the work. This rule is particularly important where remuneration from the employer is intended to cover the costs of materials or equipment supplied by the worker. This practice is quite prevalent in the construction and transportation industries. In these cases, the Board has developed policy documents regarding what portions of the worker's pay is considered to be assessable payroll for assessment purposes, and these documents may be helpful in the determination of earnings basis issues.

For the largest number of claims, Board policy calls for two different calculations of a worker's pre-injury gross average earnings. One calculation is for short-term Loss of Earnings (LOE) benefits and one is for long-term LOE benefits. LOE benefits are recalculated on the basis of the long-term earnings only after 12 consecutive weeks of LOE benefits are paid.

(b) "Short-term" and "Initial" Pre-Injury Gross Average Earnings

The short-term earnings basis is used in most claims until such time as there have been 12 consecutive weeks of LOE benefits. In the 13th consecutive week of LOE benefits, in most claims, the earnings basis is switched from the short-term earnings basis to the long-term earnings basis.

(i) Short-Term Earnings — Regular Rule

Earnings used for the short-term earnings basis include the following earnings from each of the worker's employers at the time of the injury: the base (hourly, daily, or weekly) rate of pay with the accident employer at the time of injury, shift differentials (expressed as a weekly average), vacation pay (only when paid as a percentage of the base rate with each pay cheque), regular overtime, regular production bonuses and commissions, tips, and room and board, if these are a part of the worker's pay.

Board policy contains definitions of what is meant by "regular" overtime and "regular" bonuses and commissions and also contains a more detailed list of what is and what is not included in the short-term earnings.

(ii) Short-Term Earnings — Special Rules

Where the Board does not have complete earnings information to determine an accurate short-term earnings basis, the decision maker may establish a temporary earnings basis, and begin paying LOE benefits based on this amount, until the necessary earnings information is received. Once the actual rate is determined, there is a retroactive adjustment.

If the worker is concurrently employed at the time of injury, the short-term earnings basis is the total of the short-term earnings basis from each of the pre-injury employers. For the purpose of the short-term earnings basis, a worker is considered to be in concurrent employment and thus have more than one employer at the time of the accident if he or she has more than one contract of employment and/or self-employment earnings at the same time, and has received earnings from all the concurrent employers in the four weeks before the accident. If the worker was unable to work in some or all of these four weeks due to illness or vacation, the period may be extended to produce the required four-week period. Earnings from self-employment will only be included if the worker has elected workers' compensation coverage in respect of the self-employment.

If it is not possible to calculate the worker's short-term earnings basis due to the shortness of the worker's time in employment and the fact that he or she is paid in such a way as to make calculation of the average weekly earnings impossible (commission earnings, for example), the Board may look at the short-term earnings of another worker similarly employed by the accident employer or by another employer.

Where the hours of work of the worker are highly variable, in determining the short-term earnings basis, the Board may look at the worker's average earnings in the four weeks prior to this injury.

The Board does not set short-term and long-term earnings basis for individuals who elect personal coverage under s. 12 of the *Workplace Safety and Insurance Act, 1997*. There is one earnings basis used for both short- and long-term benefit payments. Similarly, there is no short-term rate for occupational disease claims or fatal claims.

The earnings basis of apprentices, learners, and students is set by regulation. The division of a worker's earnings basis into short-term and long-term earnings basis does not apply in the same manner to these workers as it does to "ordinary" workers. However, while there is just one method of calculating the pre-injury earnings basis of an apprentice, the earnings basis for learners and students may initially be set at one level and then subsequently adjusted.

Volunteer fire fighters, auxiliary police officers, members of ambulance brigades or first response teams are deemed to be employees of the municipality (or sometimes the police commission or board) they volunteer for. When injured doing their volunteer duties, the short-term earnings basis for the volunteer is set by reference to the earnings with the worker's actual (*i.e.* non-volunteer) employment at the time of the injury in the same manner as any other worker's short-term earnings would be set. Where there are no earnings with an actual employer at the time of the injury, the worker's average earnings are based on the level of coverage selected for the volunteer by the deemed employer.

The short-term earnings of an emergency worker who is summonsed to assist in controlling or extinguishing a fire by an authority empowered to do so, who assists in a search and rescue operation at the request of and under the direction of a member of the Ontario Provincial Police, or who assists in connection with an emergency that has been declared to exist by the Premier of Ontario or the head of a municipal council are calculated based upon the worker's average earnings in actual employment at the time of the accident. If the worker has no actual earnings, the Board will set the earnings based on the average industrial wage.

(c) Long-Term Pre-Injury Gross Average Earnings

The Board uses different methods to calculate the long-term earnings basis of an injured worker depending upon whether the injured worker was employed in "permanent regular" work or "non-permanent irregular" work.

Permanent regular work is considered to be work where the worker is employed 52 weeks a year with no termination date. Permanent, regular employment may involve occasional short-term layoffs of non-earning periods due to shortage of work, plant shutdowns, retoolings, strikes, *etc.* Such temporary layoffs or non-earning periods do not involve a severing of the employment relationship, and workers do not typically obtain work with other employers during such periods.

Non-permanent, irregular work is considered to be work where earnings will typically fluctuate as workers move from job to job and where there will likely be periods of unemployment between jobs. Examples of non-permanent or irregular employment provided by the Board include contract workers, workers hired through a union hall, seasonal and cyclical workers (whether on permanent contract or not) and workers who have received termination notices.

(i) Long-Term Earnings — Regular Rules — Permanent Employment

For workers engaged in permanent employment, the Board will usually set the long-term earnings basis to be equal to the short-term earnings basis unless there is a worker or employer request for a recalculation.

Workers will usually wish to request a recalculation where there was irregular overtime pay, lump sum commissions or bonuses that were not recognized in the short-term earnings basis that was used by the Board. There may also be cases where workers employed in part-time work (less than 32 hours per week) had concurrent employment income during the previous year that was not recognized in the short-term earnings due to the fact that the concurrent employment income was not received in the last four weeks.

Board policy lists a number of items which may not be included in the short-term rate but which may be included in the long-term rate.

Employers will usually wish to request a recalculation where there are periods where the worker did not work due to a lack of work or other similar reason, which are not reflected in the short-term earnings basis. If a recalculation is requested, the long-term earnings basis is set based on the worker's earnings from employment in the 12 months prior to the injury. The 12-month period may be reduced if there has been a break in the employment pattern during that period. The Board considers a permanent change in the employment pattern to include a change in hours from full time to part time or vice versa, a change to permanent work from non-permanent, or a permanent change in job grade or category.

The recalculation is completed by adding together all qualifying employment income during the recalculation period (earnings from the accident employer and earnings from qualifying concurrent employment) and dividing by the number of days in the recalculation period. In determining the number of days in the recalculation period, the Board excludes periods of time where there are no earnings that are not part of the employment pattern. Excluded periods of time include time such as parental leaves, periods of unpaid illness, periods on workers' compensation, long term disability or other insurance benefits, social assistance benefits, and unpaid leaves of absence including leaves for family illnesses, jury duty, funerals, and medical appointments, strikes and periods of full-time study.

(ii) Long-Term Earnings — Regular Rules — Irregular Employment

For workers engaged in irregular, non-permanent work, the Board automatically recalculates the earnings basis from the short-term rate to a long-term rate for benefits paid after the 12th week of consecutive LOE benefits.

The long-term earnings basis of a worker engaged in irregular employment is generally recalculated based upon the worker's earnings with all employers in the 24 months prior to injury. There are, however, circumstances where the 24-month recalculation time period will be varied.

Where there has been a break in the employment pattern in the period prior to the injury, the recalculation period will be restricted to the period of time following the change in the employment pattern. A change in the employment pattern is determined to have occurred where there is a permanent change from permanent, regular employment to non-permanent or irregular employment. The policy does not make clear whether the recalculation period starts with the leaving of the permanent employment or starts with the commencement of the irregular employment. It is expected, however, that the transition from one type of employment to the other will not be clear in most instances until such time as the worker accepts irregular employment.

If necessary, the recalculation period can be shortened or lengthened to the beginning of the calendar year closest to the 24-month mark preceding the injury. This variability of the 24 months is likely intended to deal with the possibility that earnings information from prior employers may only available on a calendar year basis and it may not be possible to obtain earnings information for the precise 24-month period prior to the injury.

As with permanent regular employment, the types of earnings included in the long-term earnings rate are more expansive than for the short-term rate. However, irregularly employed workers may also include earnings from Employment Insurance with the earnings from other employers in the recalculation period prior to the injury.

Periods of unemployment due to lack of work are factored into the calculation of pre-injury earnings of irregularly employed injured workers. However, these workers are still entitled to have periods of unemployment that are not characteristic of their employment pattern excluded from the recalculation in the same manner as regularly employed workers. See the above discussion under Long-Term Earnings — Regular Rules — Permanent Employment.

(iii) Long-Term Earnings — Special Rules

Where the Board does not have complete earnings information to determine an accurate long-term earnings basis, the decision maker may establish a temporary earnings basis and continue to pay LOE benefits based on this temporary rate until the necessary earnings information is received. Once the actual rate is determined there is a retroactive adjustment of benefits.

Long-term earnings calculations may include earnings from concurrent employment held during the recalculation period. However, where workers are injured in permanent employment, for the concurrent earnings to be included (unless the worker was working less than 32 hours per week with the accident employer) the concurrent employment must be held at the time of the accident.

As noted above, concurrent employment exists at the time of the accident if the worker has more than one contract of employment and/or self-employment earnings at the same time and has received earnings from all the concurrent employers in the four weeks before the accident. If the worker was unable to work in some or all of these four weeks due to illness or vacation, the period may be extended to produce the required four-week period.

Because the Board's policies are so complex, no attempt will be made here to summarize the Board's policies on concurrent employment in long-term earnings basis calculations. Reference should be made directly to the Board's policies. However, when reviewing the Board's policies, it should be noted that the recalculation period over which earnings from a particular employment are calculated may be changed by the existence of concurrent employment being taken into consideration. This factor could create unexpected downside risks when requesting recalculations or appeals on earnings basis issues.

Board policy does not specifically mention how long-term earnings calculations will be affected where, due to a short time in employment, it is not possible to compute a worker's earnings from employment. Presumably, the long-term earnings of workers injured in such circumstances will simply reflect the short-term earnings as established under the Board's special rules governing shortness of time in employment when calculating the short-term earnings as discussed above.

Where the special rule regarding irregular work weeks of employment has been used to set the short-term earnings basis, it is to be expected that it is likely in the interests of either the worker or the employer to make an application to the Board for a recalculation of the long-term earnings basis based on the worker's earnings in the one year, or such shorter period as the worker has been employed with the accident employer, prior to the injury.

Workers in non-permanent or irregular employment may not have an employment history that would allow for the establishment of a pre-injury wage using the ordinary rules for irregularly employed workers. This instance will occur where the injury was suffered in the worker's first job or if the worker has been out of the workforce for a prolonged period of time (more than two years). If the job is seasonal or cyclical and the expected season or cycle can be clearly established, the worker's total projected annual earnings from the accident employment are added to the probable employment insurance benefits payable to the worker for the layoff period. If the job is not seasonal or cyclical, and no clear season or cycle may be established, the worker's short-term earnings basis becomes the worker's long-term earnings basis.

Where the injured worker's injury merits a Non Economic Loss (NEL) award in excess of 60 per cent, the long-term earnings basis shall be set at no less than 75 per cent of the short-term earnings basis.

The Board has established very strict policies regarding the establishment of the earnings basis in personal coverage claims. Executive officers with personal coverage are compensated based on the average earnings as reported to Revenue Canada. Independent operators, sole proprietors, and partners pay assessments based upon the earnings reported for assessment purposes. However, compensation is based upon the lower of the earnings reported for assessment purposes or, with limited exceptions, the average earnings from the previous year as reported for income tax purposes. Board policies would not appear to allow any potential for compensation if the injured worker's business showed a net business loss for the year prior to the injury. Individuals in business for less than one year are assumed, irrefutably, it appears, to have average earnings at the time of the injury of one-third of the statutory maximum in effect at the time of the injury.

Any independent operator, sole proprietor, or partner who elects workers' compensation coverage in excess of their year prior's earnings will being paying assessments for more coverage than the Board will ever be willing to grant in the event of an injury. Where the business has been in operation less than one year, the same result will occur for any coverage selected that is in excess of one-third of the statutory maximum.

As indicated above in the discussion of short-term earnings basis, the earnings basis of learners, apprentices and students are set by regulation and reference should be had to the specific provisions of the regulations under the *Workplace Safety and Insurance Act, 1997*.

There is no difference between short-term and long-term rates for occupational disease claims. The worker's average earnings for all benefit payments is the higher of the claimant's current annual earnings or the annual earnings of a fully qualified worker currently engaged in the same trade, occupation, profession or calling to which the claimant's disease is due.

There are no short-term or long-term rates for fatal claims. With the exception of better minimum compensation protection, all survivors' benefits that are based upon wage loss replacement are paid based upon an earnings basis calculated in the same manner as the worker's long-term earnings basis would be if the worker had not died.

The long-term earnings basis for the volunteer is set by reference to the earnings with the worker's actual (*i.e.*, non-volunteer) employment at the time of the injury in the same manner as any other worker's long-term earnings would be set. Where there are no earnings with an actual employer at the time of the injury, the worker's average earnings are based on the level of coverage selected for the volunteer by the deemed employer.

The long-term earnings of an emergency worker injured in the course of duties as an emergency worker are calculated on the worker's average earnings in actual employment at the time of the accident in the same manner as any other worker's long-term earnings would be set. If the worker has no actual earnings, the Board will set the average earnings based on the average industrial wage for Ontario.

(d) Recalculations and Adjustments

For injuries on or after January 1, 1998, a distinction is drawn between recalculations and adjustments of the pre-injury gross earnings. A recalculation is what takes place when the worker moves from the short-term earnings basis to the long-term earnings basis. An adjustment is what takes place when new information comes to light which changes the estimation of the pre-injury earnings. Recalculations are not given retroactive effect, but adjustments are.

What is not clearly specified in Board policy is what happens where an application for a redetermination of a worker's pre-injury earnings is made by a worker or employer where no recalculation was automatically done at 13 weeks due to the fact that the worker was employed in permanent employment. While such an application is referred to in Board policy as a "recalculation" and it might be assumed that the changes would be given no retroactive effect, the statements in Board policy dealing with retroactivity might be read to imply that the changes are fully retroactive. Previous Board policy was that upward adjustments in such circumstances were retroactive but downward adjustments were not. It would not be prudent to assume that the old Board policy under the *Workers' Compensation Act* is being continued under the *Workplace Safety and Insurance Act, 1997*.

(e) Failure to Provide Information

Workers may be required to provide or pursue information required by the Board to determine a worker's pre-injury earnings. Failure to meet such requirements may result in the suspension of benefits. Future compliance will result in reinstatement of full entitlement from the time of compliance but not retroactively.

3. RECURRENCES

In those circumstances where an injured worker returns to work following an injury at a rate of pay higher than the pre-injury earnings, the worker is able to receive compensation benefits for future periods of disability that are the result of the initial injury, on the basis of the higher rate of earnings. For injuries prior to January 1, 1998, the ability to access the higher post-injury earnings is restricted to the payment of temporary benefits. For injuries after January 1, 1998, this ability to access the higher post-injury earnings exists for both short-term and long-term LOE benefits.

Subsection 53(6) of the *Workplace Safety and Insurance Act, 1997*, applicable to injuries on or after January 1, 1998, states the following:

> **53** ... (6) When a worker becomes entitled to payments for a loss of earnings arising out of an accident in respect of which he or she previously received benefits under the insurance plan, the workers' average earnings (for the purpose of calculating the amount payable for the loss of earnings) are the greater of,
>   (*a*) his or her average earnings at the date of the accident; or
>   (*b*) his or her average earnings when he or she was most recently employed.

For the purpose of determining the worker's average earnings at the date of the accident, for post-January 1, 1998, injuries, the Board uses either the short-term earnings basis or the long-term earnings basis, whichever was in use when the worker had returned to work.

In determining whether a subsequent period of disability is the result of a new injury or the result of the original injury, the circumstances surrounding the period of subsequent disability will be examined. The question to be determined is whether the entitlement to benefits is as a result of any matter arising out of the original injury or whether the entitlement is as a result of a new incident.

Workers injured after January 1, 1998, who have recurrences with durations longer than 12 weeks have their earnings basis recalculated in accordance with long-term earnings basis criteria. Not only do these workers have the option of choosing from the higher of the pre-injury earnings and the pre-recurrence earnings for short-term benefits on the recurrence, they also have the same option for determining the long-term basis on the recurrence.

The ability to use pre-recurrence earnings for the calculation of long-term LOE benefits means that for the first time a deterioration of a worker's condition may not only result in a decrease in the estimate of post-injury earnings capacity, the recurrence could also result in an increase in the estimation of the worker's earnings for wage loss calculation purposes.

It is not easy to determine the appropriate method of escalating the pre-injury earnings prior to comparing them to the earnings at the time of the most recent employment.

For injuries subsequent to January 1, 1998, it would appear that full Consumer Price Indexing should be applied to determine benefit entitlement. So long as the worker was considered totally disabled, there would be no subsequent downward Friedland adjustment. (See the discussion in this chapter, below, regarding cost of living adjustments of FEL and LOE benefits). However once the worker was determined to be able to earn some wages in suitable employment or business, the downward Friedland adjustment found in subs. 43(5), para. 3 of the Act would be applied. Unfortunately, at the time of writing, Board policy does not deal with this issue.

The ability to utilize the higher of the pre-injury or the pre-recurrence wages does not allow workers to use the average earnings that were used to calculate the compensation rate for an earlier recurrence. An exception is made where the return to work following the earlier recurrence was for only a brief period of time. For injuries after January 1, 1998, the return to work must be less than four weeks.

4. MINIMUM COMPENSATION RATES

There are two types of minimum compensation rates that have been utilized in the workers' compensation system in Ontario. For lack of a better phrase, these different types of minimums will be referred to soft minimums and hard minimums.

(a) Soft Minimums

A soft minimum does not guarantee that benefits will be based upon a minimum level of pre-injury earnings or guarantee the payment of compensation benefits at or beyond a predetermined level. What a soft minimum does is modify the manner in which the benefit calculation takes place whenever the pre-injury earnings are less than a set minimum level or whenever the compensation payable would be less than a set minimum level.

LOE benefits which are intended to compensate for "full loss of earnings" have a soft minimum of $15,321.51 per year. Benefits for full loss of earnings will only fall below this level to the extent that 100 per cent of the worker's net pre-injury wage are less than this amount. Benefits will be paid at a rate higher than the minimum for full loss of earnings only when 85 per cent of the worker's net pre-injury wage is greater than the stated minimum. This minimum figure was set on January 1, 1998, and is inflation adjusted under the Friedland formula. (See 6. Cost of Living Adjustments, below)

(b) Hard Minimums

The earnings basis used to calculate survivors' benefits is subject to a hard minimum. The minimum was set at $15,321.51 per year as of January 1, 1998. The statutory minimum is subject to annual cost of living adjustment at the Friedland rate.

5. MAXIMUM COMPENSATION RATES

Maximum compensation rates are established by legislative restrictions being placed on the maximum earnings of a worker that are subject to compensation coverage. Starting from January 1, 1992, the maximum is now set using a statutory formula of 175 per cent of the Average Industrial Wage. Maximum annual covered earnings as of January 1, 1999, are $59,200.

Changes to the statutory maximum are applied on a prospective basis so that increases do not have the effect of increasing the maximum earnings basis for injuries taking place prior to the new maximum.

When comparing the earnings at the time of recurrence with earnings at the time of the original injury, the original earnings are restricted by the maximum in effect at the time of injury and then escalated by the appropriate cost-of-living adjustments.

6. COST OF LIVING ADJUSTMENTS

From 1986 to 1994 the Board was required to automatically adjust benefits and dollar amounts set out in the Act on January 1 of each year by using an indexing factor set by reference to the Consumer Price Index (CPI) for Canada on all items for the 12-month period ending October 31 of the previous year as published by Statistics Canada.

From 1995 to 1997, the Board was required to automatically adjust benefits on January 1 of each year by using either the CPI or by what is commonly referred to as the Friedland indexing factor. The Friedland index is actually described in the legislation as the "General indexing factor" and the CPI is referred to as the "Alternate indexing factor" The Friedland factor was set at three-quarters of the CPI factor less one per cent. The Friedland factor had a minimum of zero and a maximum of four. The Friedland factor was also made to apply to the adjustment of dollar amounts set out in the Act.

As of January 1, 1998, the Friedland factor used to index benefits was adjusted to be set at one-half of the CPI factor less one per cent. The minimum of zero and the maximum of four were retained.

The determination of which benefits are to be indexed by the CPI and which benefits are to be indexed by the Friedland factor are set out in subs. 148(1.2) of the *Workers' Compensation Act* and subs. 49(2) of the *Workplace Safety and Insurance Act, 1997*. Generally speaking, the criteria for determining who gets the lower Friedland indexing and who gets the higher CPI indexing, reflect a perception of the relative need of the two groups.

As of January 1, 1998, workers who are in receipt of payments under subs. 147(14) of the *Workers' Compensation Act* had their entitlement to indexing at the CPI rate changed to an entitlement to indexing at the Friedland rate.

In addition to the general indexing provisions referred to above, particular regard must also be had to the indexing rules applied to FEL and LOE redeterminations. See subs. 43(4), (5), and (6.1) of the *Workers' Compensation Act* and subs. 43(5) and (6) of the *Workplace Safety and Insurance Act*. Because FEL and LOE benefits are based on estimated wage loss calculations, whenever a redetermination of the wage loss benefit is required, the pre-injury earnings are escalated by CPI indexing for the purpose of making comparison to the current estimated post-injury earnings. However, paying benefits based on the comparison with CPI indexing being applied to the pre-injury wage would result in the unintended application of full CPI indexing of wage loss benefits for all FEL and LOE recipients whenever a recalculation is performed. As full indexing is not intended for most FEL and LOE recipients the benefit level as determined by applying CPI indexing to the pre-injury wage is then adjusted using a formula that reduces the level of benefits paid to reflect indexing of wage loss benefits at the Friedland rate.

7. NET EARNINGS

Subsection 55(1) of the Act reads as follows:

> **55.** (1) The Board shall determine the amount of a worker's net average earnings by deducting from his or her earnings,
>> (*a*) the probable income tax payable by the worker on his or her earnings;
>> (*b*) the probable Canada Pension Plan or Quebec Pension Plan premiums payable by the worker; and
>> (*c*) the probable employment insurance premiums payable by the worker.

The Board uses one net income tax table, based upon Revenue Canada's tables for source deductions by an employer, to determine net earnings. However, the Board is willing to take into consideration the special circumstances of workers who do not have to pay income tax, employment insurance premiums or CPP premiums. The Board's tables are issued annually. The redetermination takes place following the escalation of the worker's gross average earnings in accordance with the indexing provisions of the Act.

A second variable looked at in determining net average earnings, beyond the gross average earnings, is the worker's net exemption code used to determine the employer's deduction of income tax at source. Information on the worker's net exemption code is forwarded to the Board by the employer on the Form 7 and is usually obtained by the employer when the worker completes the TD1 income tax form at the commencement of employment. The Board has a special rule for determining the net exemption code of workers with optional coverage.

If, subsequent to the injury, the worker's personal situation changes such that the worker's net exemption code status has changed, depending on the type of benefits paid, this change may have an effect on the level of compensation entitlement. LOE benefits will generally only be affected once a redetermination of LOE entitlement takes place.

CHAPTER 13

Temporary Benefits

1. INTRODUCTION

Temporary benefits are administered under one of three legislative schemes, depending upon the date of the injury; and an entirely different compensation scheme exists for workers hurt on or after January 1, 1998. For these workers the concept of temporary benefits has no relevance.

The first scheme (set out in the pre-1985 Act) applies to pre-April 1, 1985 injuries or disabilities (and recurrences). The second scheme (set out in the pre-1989 Act) applies to injuries or disabilities which occurred on or after April 1, 1985 and before January 2, 1990. The third scheme (set out in the pre-1997 Act) applies to injuries or disabilities occurring on or after January 2, 1990 and before January 1, 1998.

The only difference between temporary benefits payable under the pre-1985 Act and those payable under the pre-1989 Act is that under the first scheme payments are calculated based upon 75 per cent of gross pay, while under the second they are based on 90 per cent of "net average earnings".

The pre-1997 Act contains definitions in subs. 1(1) for "disability", "impairment", and "permanent impairment", while these terms were never defined in previous versions of the Act. More importantly, by virtue of the interaction between ss. 37 and 43 there are limits on how long temporary benefits can continue, and how recurrences of temporary total disability will be compensated. These points are discussed below.

In the balance of this chapter, section references will be to the pre-1997 Act provisions unless otherwise indicated.

Temporary benefits may be paid at the total (100 per cent) level either because a worker is totally disabled on a medical basis (subs. 37(1)), or is partially disabled and has not returned to work but is "co-operating" with the Board (subs. 37(2)(*b*)). Workers are often completely unaware of the difference between subs. 37(1) and subs. 37(2)(*b*) since there is no recognizable difference in the form of payment under either provision.

2. TEMPORARY TOTAL DISABILITY

(a) General

Section 36 provides that temporary total (t.t.) disability benefits are payable from the day following the accident. Since April 1, 1985, the accident employer has been responsible for paying full wages for the day of the accident by virtue of subs. 4(2).

Subsection 37(1) provides that where injury to a worker results in t.t. disability, the worker is entitled to wage loss compensation in the form of t.t. benefits so long as t.t. disability continues, or until the worker begins receiving payments under s. 43 (Future Economic Loss (FEL) payments).

Subsection 43(10) provides that where possible the Board shall determine the FEL award payable to a worker in the 12th consecutive month during which the worker is temporarily disabled. In subs. 1(1), "disability" is defined as the loss of earning capacity of the worker that results from an injury. The Appeals Tribunal has held that "disability" is not merely a loss of actual earnings, and that the term "earning capacity" refers to the power to earn, which is a status greater than the facts of a specific employment.

The Board defines t.t. disability as the complete inability to earn full pre-accident wages for a limited period of time as a result of the physical and psychological effects of the injury and the necessity for medical treatment. It is not equated with unemployability. The Board will look at medical information and information regarding the physical requirements of the worker's job and other jobs in deciding whether or not the worker is temporarily totally disabled.

The Appeals Tribunal has held that t.t. disability must be seen in relative, not absolute terms (*i.e.*, was the worker *in general* incapable of performing any work). In one decision the Panel noted that the term "disability" could not refer strictly to a medical assessment of the worker's condition. It has also held that the quantum of a pension award is not an appropriate measure of a worker's level of temporary disability prior to the pension assessment. The reasoning was that temporary benefits and pensions are based on different criteria: pensions are based on generalized data of the average unskilled worker, whereas temporary benefits are based on worker-specific determinations. Appeals Tribunal panels have agreed that competitive unemployability does not equate with total disability, although in one instance a Panel ruled that the Board's conclusion that the worker was unemployable brought the worker within the Board's definition of t.t. disability.

Benefits cannot commence until the worker is disabled from earning wages. This may not coincide with the date of a disabling event (or a recurrence).

Benefits may still be payable even after retirement because there is no requirement that the worker be impaired from an existing job at the time the disability occurs. However a worker over 65 who had been in receipt of a FEL award is probably ineligible for benefits in the event of a recurrence.

(b) Concurrent Employment

A worker may be working concurrently with two employers at the time of an accident and may still be able to work at the non-accident job while disabled from the accident employment. In this case, full compensation with no offset for ongoing non-accident earnings is payable.

(c) Worker in Receipt of Unrelated WSIB Pension

An injured worker who is in receipt of an award for permanent impairment and who is subsequently temporarily disabled through a new work injury (prior to January 1, 1998), which is not a recurrence of the previous injury is entitled to compensation for temporary disability without any deduction for the ongoing award. This is so, even though the two awards together may exceed the maximum set out in s. 38.

(d) Canada Pension Plan/Quebec Pension Plan

The application for or the receipt of a pension under the Canada Pension Plan (C.P.P.) or the Quebec Pension Plan (Q.P.P.) (including the disability provisions) has no bearing on t.t. payments. This follows from subs. 37(3) which limits any C.P.P./Q.P.P. offset to payments under subs. 37(2)(*b*).

(e) Monitoring the Medical Situation

Monitoring is done at the Board through the use of follow-up reports sent out in blank to be completed and returned by the worker and the attending physician. Any ongoing medical documentation (*i.e.*, specialist reports) received will also be reviewed. Consideration will also be given to the expected recovery time of the injury based upon a "Length of Disability Chart" which covers the more common injuries.

(f) Termination of Benefits — General

Depending on the circumstances of an individual case, t.t. benefits may be reduced or terminated if the worker remains disabled because of self-inflicted wounds, unsanitary care of the compensable disability, refusal of treatment or refusal to undergo a Board-ordered medical examination. These topics are dealt with in Chapter 11, Claims and Payments.

Otherwise, t.t. disability benefits will usually cease for one of these reasons:

- There is full recovery (see section (g) Termination of Benefits — Full Recovery, below);
- There is only a temporary partial disability remaining (see 3. Temporary Partial Disability, below);
- The condition of the pre-1985 or pre-1989 Act worker has stabilized and a pension rating has taken place (see Chapter 14 Permanent Disability Benefits);

- A pre-1997 Act worker hurt after January 1, 1990 over 65 years of age has reached Maximum Medical Recovery (MMR) (see section (h) Termination of Benefits — Worker over 65, below);
- A FEL decision (including a zero award) has been rendered (see Chapter 16 Future Economic Loss Benefits); or
- The worker dies (there may be survivor's benefits entitlement if the condition causing the t.t. was the cause of death. See Chapter 19 Health Care Benefits).

(g) Termination of Benefits — Full Recovery

Where there has been full recovery, benefits will be closed regardless of the worker's employment situation. However, where there is a re-employment obligation which has been breached the worker may be eligible for t.t. benefits for up to an additional year under subs. 54(13)(*b*). (See Chapter 21 Labour Market Re-Entry Services).

Occasionally payments may be extended for one week beyond the "full recovery date" to give the worker a chance to adjust to the situation.

The worker or representative who wants to challenge the Board's conclusion that there has been a full recovery or that the condition has stabilized may wish to consider carefully the wisdom of claiming total *medical* disability as opposed to claiming partial disability and a willingness to co-operate.

(h) Termination of Benefits — Worker Over 65 Achieving Maximum Medical Rehabilitation (Recovery)

Board policy is that workers who are 65 years of age or older and injured are entitled to compensation under s. 37 until the date of the maximum medical rehabilitation (MMR) because temporary disability ends on this date. There is no definition of MMR in the Act. The Board defines MMR as a situation where there is unlikely to be any further significant improvement in the worker's medical condition. Board policy provides that MMR may have been achieved even if the worker is still receiving treatment, but the probability of improvement is low.

The date of MMR can be redetermined if new medical documentation indicates further treatment is likely to improve the worker's condition. Although not expressly stated in the policy, it would follow from this that a worker 65 or older could have t.t. benefits reinstated if the compensable condition worsened and further treatment was justified.

3. TEMPORARY PARTIAL DISABILITY

(a) General

Although there is no definition of temporary partial disability in the Act, the concept used by the Board is that the worker is experiencing a reduction in the ability to earn full pre-accident wages for a limited period of time as a result of the labour market's inability to accommodate the worker with the remaining physical effects of the injury. The Appeals Tribunal has held that "disability" means a loss of earning capacity, and that a person could have a disability even if able to return to work at no wage loss. Thus, a determination of entitlement pursuant to subs. 37(2) does not simply require a consideration of fitness to perform the essential duties of the pre-injury job.

Subsections 37(2) and (3) provide:

> **37** (2) Where temporary partial disability results from the injury, the compensation payable shall be,
>
> (*a*) where the worker returns to employment, a weekly payment of 90 per cent of the difference between the net average weekly earnings of the worker before the injury and a net average amount that the worker is able to earn in some suitable employment or business after the injury; or
> (*b*) where the worker does not return to work, a weekly payment in the same amount as would be payable if the worker were temporarily totally disabled, unless the worker
> > (i) fails to co-operate in or is not available for a medical rehabilitation program, an early and safe return to work program or a labour market re-entry plan, as the circumstances require, which would, in the Board's opinion, aid in getting the worker back to work, or
> > (ii) fails to accept or is not available for employment which is available and which in the opinion of the Board is suitable for the worker's capabilities.
>
> (3) In determining the amount to be paid under clause (2)(*b*), the Board shall have regard to any payments the worker receives under the Canada Pension Plan and the Quebec Pension Plan with respect to the injury and, if subclause (2)(*b*)(i) or (ii) applies, the compensation shall be a periodic amount proportionate to the degree of disability resulting from the injury as determined by the Board.

Formerly, instead of "medical rehabilitation program..." the wording in s. 37(2)(b)(i) was "medical or vocational rehabilitation program". The wording was changed because with Bill 99 the concept of vocational rehabilitation disappeared. In the balance of this chapter references are frequently made to "vocational rehabilitation" because complementary changes to Board policy have not been published and older decisions were rendered based upon the previous wording.

Benefits payable under subs. 37(2) may be terminated or reduced for the reasons specified in the provision (as discussed below), or for the reasons discussed above regarding subs. 37(1) benefits. For workers hurt after January 1, 1990 and before January 1, 1998, subs. 43(10) is highly relevant because it drives the Board to implement a FEL award in the 12th consecutive month during which the worker is temporarily disabled.

Subsection 72.1(1)2 provides that if a worker or an employer objects to a decision concerning the worker's co-operation in or availability for a medical or vocational rehabilitation program or availability for employment for the purposes of subs. 37(2)(*b*), the Board shall provide mediation services to deal with that objection. This provision is still in force and may be relevant as an authorizing provision, since the mediation provision in Bill 99 (s. 122) does not specifically apply to pre-1998 injuries.

(b) Events Triggering Entitlement

The Board usually applies subs. 37(2) after it has received a Physician's Progress Report or other information that the disabled worker is now capable of part-time or modified work. At this point the Claims Adjudicator generally should either telephone or write the injured worker advising that the worker is now considered to be partially disabled and must "co-operate" by being "available" for suitable modified work (or be at risk of a reduction of benefits).

(c) Where Worker Returns to Employment

Subsection 37(2)(*a*) authorizes ongoing wage-loss payments as long as there is a temporary partial disability and a wage loss. If the job does not work out, full benefits may be restored if the Board feels that the worker has not otherwise failed to cooperate in terms of subs. 37(2)(*b*).

If the partially disabled worker has returned to work with no wage loss (no benefits payable) there may still be eligibility for a permanent impairment award. The worker should keep in touch with, at least, the treating physician subsequent to the return to work so that there will be "continuity" of complaint and treatment should this become an issue.

(d) Where Worker does Not Return to Employment

(i) Introduction

This situation is covered by subss. 37(2)(*b*) and (3), which are not easy provisions to administer and give rise to a vast number of appeals. In interpreting subs. 37(2)(*b*), the mandatory nature of the provision should be noted. The Board is directed to pay compensation equivalent to t.t. disability benefits as long as the worker does not disqualify him- or herself by either

(i)   failing to co-operate in or not being available for a medical rehabilitation program, an early and safe return to work program or a labour market re-entry plan, as the circumstances require, which would, in the Board's opinion aid in getting the worker back to work, or

(ii)   failing to accept or be available for suitable (as determined by the Board) available employment.

Therefore, there is a presumption of entitlement which can be displaced if it is established that one or more of the disqualification situations has arisen. Appeals Tribunal decisions on subs. 37(2)(*b*) have adopted the "disqualification" approach. Further, the Appeals Tribunal considers that the potential disqualification situations must be viewed as guidelines for the application of the discretion inherent in subs. 37(2)(*b*) and that the circumstances of each case must be considered taking subs. 37(2)(*b*) as a whole into account.

Regarding "refusals of treatment", it is not uncommon for workers to be hesitant to undergo recommended surgery. In some instances, the worker will proceed following a period of consideration. The Board will sometimes cut benefits for the interim period. The Appeals Tribunal has observed that a worker cannot deliberately refuse to undergo treatment to prolong the receipt of benefits, but that a worker will be entitled to a second opinion and to a reasonable period of time to consider the options.

To avoid disqualification, a partially disabled worker must, even in the absence of a specific Board program, take some steps (or at least show a willingness) to get back to work or lessen or remove a handicap, unless the worker has a reasonably held belief in total disability, or an honest conviction (which is objectively substantially based) that there is no chance of finding suitable work.

If it can be established that specific proposed employment is unsuitable, there should be no disqualification under subs. 37(2)(*b*)(ii) if the worker refused the proposed employment but was generally "co-operative". This proposition is not contentious, but there is often contention over whether specific employment which was refused was suitable. What counts is the reality of the proposed employment and the worker's ability to perform it, not the beliefs or hopes of the various parties involved regarding suitability, or of the feasibility of proposed accommodations. The specific employment (*i.e.*, an actual job) has to be offered before the issue of refusal even comes up. However, there need not be total clarification in advance of all the terms and conditions, and the offer need not be in writing. Thus, a refusal of a vague job offer of suitably modified work may disqualify the worker.

If there has been a return to modified work following a period of temporary disability and then, weeks or months later, the worker feels unable to continue with the modified job because of the disability, this could be adjudicated as a refusal of modified employment, or as a fresh disablement, or as a recurrence. Different concerns will have to be addressed depending upon how the situation is characterized.

(ii) Availability of the Worker

The worker must make a "reasonable effort" to be available for suitable employment. This test is subjective and a number of factors may be relevant in reaching a conclusion about a particular worker's availability.

A worker whose job search is restricted to work that he or she knows he or she cannot perform is not "available". Geographic job search restrictions may be reasonable depending on the worker's location. A job search restricted to the accident employer may be reasonable (if it does not exceed six months), where the worker has long-term service (two or more years), or there is a history of the employer being able to supply suitably modified work. During a lawful strike the worker may not be required to look for temporary employment for the duration of the strike.

A worker who moves out of Ontario but stays within Canada may still be considered "available", but this is not so if the worker leaves Canada. If the move is from an area of relatively low unemployment to an area of high unemployment, the Board may take a dim view of the worker's efforts to maintain availability for suitable employment.

Board policy provides that under certain circumstances a worker may take a "vacation" and *not be* disqualified for being unavailable.

A worker who has applied for, or is in receipt of, Canada Pension Disability Benefits is not deemed "unavailable" simply on the basis of this status. The worker would be expected to otherwise demonstrate "availability" through an ongoing job search.

The Appeals Tribunal has articulated that a worker who has an honest conviction — which from an objective perspective may be seen to be substantially based — that there is no chance of finding suitable work (and therefore does not look for any work), may not be considered "unavailable". It has also articulated that a worker who *reasonably* relies on his or her doctor's view that the worker is totally disabled (even if on all of the subsequent evidence this view is wrong) will not be considered unavailable.

A worker's "availability" must be assessed in light of the compensable condition and also any non-compensable conditions. Minor or short-term non-compensable disabilities may narrow the range of suitable employment without detracting from the worker's "availability". More serious non-compensable disabilities may have an adverse effect on entitlement.

Job availability in the area where the worker lives is relevant in assessing the appropriateness and necessary frequency of job search contacts that the worker may be making. A detailed job search list kept by the worker will be very useful in demonstrating a worker's availability.

(iii) Availability of Employment

The Appeals Tribunal has accepted that employment is not available if a doctor's clearance certificate is (or is reasonably thought to be) required by the employer and the worker either cannot or reasonably believes he/she cannot obtain such a certificate.

In cases where benefits were reduced or terminated because of a worker's refusal of a suitable job, and the job becomes *no longer available* while the worker is still temporarily partially disabled, the Board will have to reconsider the worker's benefits entitlement from that point forward. Frequently, the worker will encounter strong resistance from the Board to any reconsideration of benefits entitlement in these situations.

(iv) Suitability of Employment

As with "availability", the concept of "suitability" is subjective. Employment must be suitable to the worker as an individual, given all of his or her characteristics. Factors such as the worker's age, education, training, job skills and employment history will be relevant. Regarding the job itself, lack of potential for improvement (*i.e.*, the dead-end nature of the job) could be a significant factor. Another factor will be the location of the job. A non-compensable condition may limit the options of suitable work for an "available" worker.

In the context of FEL decision-making and re-employment, the Board has created policy defining suitable employment as any job which the worker has the necessary skills to perform, is medically able to perform and which does not pose a health or safety hazard to the worker or any co-worker. The Board will consider the worker's vocational history, educational background and work qualifications. Given the overlap, FEL decisions from the Appeals Tribunal regarding suitability are useful in temporary benefits cases.

(v) Incarcerated Workers

It may be that an incarcerated worker will be automatically disqualified for being "unavailable". On the other hand, within the confines of the institution the worker might well be available for suitable employment. Some institutions do have paid work programs.

4. CALCULATION OF BENEFITS

(a) Temporary Total Disability

For claims arising on or after April 1, 1985, there has been a shift from calculations based upon 75 per cent of gross earnings to those based upon 90 per cent of net average earnings.

(b) Temporary Partial Disability with Return to Employment

Subsection 37(2)(*a*) provides that where temporary partial disability results from the injury and the worker returns to employment, compensation shall be 90 per cent of the difference between the weekly pre-accident (covered) earnings (75 per cent in pre-April 1, 1985 cases), and the current weekly employment earnings. Changes in the wage-loss will be reflected by changes in benefits payable. Therefore, a temporarily partially disabled worker may be working and receiving no temporary compensation payments because there is no ongoing wage-loss. There may still be eligibility for a permanent impairment award.

If the worker receives the same wage loss each week while on modified work the loss will be converted to a percentage of the t.t. rate and paid on a long-term basis without weekly review.

A worker who loses time from work while receiving temporary "wage loss" benefits, may have his or her benefits affected. Board policy is that if the lost time is unrelated to the compensable condition (*e.g.*, lack of work), these lost wages will not increase the "wage loss" benefits payable. If the lost time is related to the compensable condition (*e.g.*, illness due to the compensable condition), these lost wages will be reimbursed to the worker through the "wage loss" benefits payable.

Maximum and minimum compensation rates, apply proportionately. Regarding the very minimum, *i.e.*, where both the pre- and post-accident earnings are below the minimum and there is a post-accident wage loss, the actual difference in wages is paid.

The Board pays "Temporary Partial Helper's Difference" benefits when a partially disabled worker continues working but must hire a helper. The formulae used to calculate temporary partial difference benefits are applied to wages paid to the helper. Where a self-employed individual who has personal coverage hires a helper, the Board bases benefits on the degree of disability.

(c) Temporary Partial Disability with No Return to Employment and Worker has been Disqualified from Receiving Full Compensation

Subsection 37(3) provides that in this situation:

> ... the compensation shall be a periodic amount proportionate to the degree of disability resulting from the injury as determined by the Board ...

The Board has adopted different approaches depending upon the basis of the worker's disqualification.

Where the worker has been found to be unavailable (for a medical program, vocational rehabilitation program or an employment search) benefits will be reduced to 50 per cent.

Where there has been a refusal of a specific job with a wage loss, benefits will be reduced by the amount of the deemed wages. If the refused job entailed no wage loss, temporary compensation benefits are closed.

5. PREDISPOSITION TO DISABILITY

Where there has been a work accident, compensation is payable regardless of whether the worker may have been predisposed to experience disability. In effect, this is simply another facet of the no-fault principle of workers' compensation. The relevant questions is, was the work accident (however defined) sufficient to disable the affected worker, keeping in mind all of the physiological peculiarities of that worker? If the answer is yes, the disability is compensable. The fact that an "ordinary worker" might not have been similarly disabled is irrelevant.

6. PRE-EXISTING CONDITIONS

Prior to a compensable injury a worker may have had a pre-existing condition, such as degenerative disc disease, which was asymptomatic (and possibly unrecognized), or symptomatic.

Board policy regarding temporary disability adjudication is as follows:

> A claim for an occupational injury involving a pre-accident disability is allowed for the acute episode only and entitlement to payment of compensation ceases when the worker's condition has returned to the pre-accident state. In a claim where there is a pre-existing condition but the worker is symptom free at the time of the work-related accident there is no limitation of benefits throughout the period of temporary disability.
>
> Some claims may be allowed for a "once only repair", *e.g.*, strangulated hernia or recurrent shoulder dislocation. Allowance of a claim on this basis recognizes that a work-related accident did occur but that the resulting treatment and period of disability were due, at least in part, to a pre-existing condition.

It is common for the Board, when applying this policy, to allow a claim on an "aggravation basis" with an indication that there will be no compensation *beyond that allowed for the acute episode*. A phrase such as "this concludes the worker's entitlement under the Act for this claim", may be used. In one Appeals Tribunal decision, the Panel deleted such a phrase from a Board decision so the door would remain open for entitlement should future difficulties arise.

The typical issue in the application of policy is determining whether or not the worker was "symptom free" at the time of the accident or whether the worker has reached the "pre-accident stage".

7. NON-OCCUPATIONAL CONDITIONS WHICH AFFECT TREATMENT OF THE COMPENSABLE DISABILITY

Board policy is that where non-occupational unrelated health problems prevent a worker from undergoing treatment for the compensable disability, temporary disability payments may be reduced or suspended until such time as the worker is available for treatment of the compensable condition. Alternatively, a limited period of treatment for the unrelated problem may be considered under s. 24 of the Act, provided that this treatment will reduce the cost of the eventual permanent disability award.

If compensable and non-compensable conditions are all contributing to the ongoing disability, continuing compensation benefits will be paid commensurate with the degree of remaining compensable disability. If the sole cause of the ongoing disability is determined to be a non-compensable condition, benefits will cease.

8. RECURRENCES OF THE COMPENSABLE DISABILITY

Sometimes an injured worker will return to work after a period of disability and then suffer a recurrence of the original disability (as opposed to a new unrelated accident). A home (or non-work) incident may qualify as a compensable recurrence as well.

With amendments to the Act effective April 1, 1985, compensation payable in a recurrence situation can be based on the average earnings at the date of the accident or at *the date of the most recent employment*, whichever is greater.

If the date of the accident is prior to April 1, 1985, but the date of the recurrence is later than that, the most recent earnings will be based on the average of four weeks' earnings rather than the daily or hourly rate prescribed under subs. 40(7).

Where a worker, hurt on or before January 1, 1990, in receipt of an award for permanent impairment suffers a compensable recurrence, there will be a deduction for the pension from the temporary benefits otherwise payable. Any s. 147 payments in the same claim will also be offset from the temporary benefits otherwise payable. Eventually the issue will arise on whether the worker's condition has returned to the permanent impairment level. The Board often determines this issue through a paper review of the file, but, in some instances, a Board medical examination will be arranged.

A major concern for workers hurt after January 1, 1990 and before January 1, 1998, is whether or not, notwithstanding their medical condition, they would be eligible for temporary benefits in a recurrence situation. *If a worker is receiving a FEL payment* the wording of subs. 37(1) precludes the reinstatement of t.t. benefits. One possibility for such a worker is a supplement under subs. 43(9).

9. ENTITLEMENT TO TEMPORARY BENEFITS FOLLOWING LAY-OFF

The Board recognizes that injured workers who return to work and are subsequently laid off may be entitled to benefits if their loss of earning capacity following the lay-off is due to a work-related injury.

It should be noted that a work-related impairment might not be physically disabling but could still entail the loss of earning capacity.

In reality, decision-makers at the Board, when dealing with these situations, often blame the economy and point workers in the direction of Employment Insurance, while denying any loss of earning capacity related to the work-related injury. Achieving entitlement to ongoing benefits will frequently be very difficult.

10. ENTITLEMENT TO TEMPORARY BENEFITS FOR INDIVIDUALS INJURED WHILE ON UNPAID TRAINING PLACEMENTS

Board policy is that these workers are entitled to t.t. disability benefits as long as the injury continues and if it prevents participation in the training program, or, if the program is no longer available, prevents full participation in the labour force. If the worker is capable of suitable work and that work which is available pays less than the pre-injury earnings, temporary partial benefits are paid. The policy also discusses how a placement "will be" modified to accommodate the participant's injury, and how, if it is not modified, the participant "may still continue" with the in-class portion of the training program, if it is still available.

CHAPTER 14

Permanent Disability Benefits

1. INTRODUCTION

It is vital to appreciate that three extremely different schemes of compensation for permanent impairment exist in the Ontario workers' compensation system. This chapter and Chapter 15, Pension Supplements for Pre-January 2, 1990 Claims, deal with the scheme for pre-January 2, 1990 claims.

Sections 144, 145 and 146 of the pre-1997 Act establish that with the exception of the pension supplement provisions (see Chapter 15) the pre-1989 Act continues to apply to injuries or diseases that occurred on or after April 1, 1985 and before January 2, 1990, and the pre-1985 Act continues to apply to injuries or diseases that occurred before April 1, 1985. For the most part there are no relevant significant differences between the pre-1989 Act and the pre-1985 Act. All references in the balance of this chapter are to the pre-1989 Act, unless otherwise indicated.

Under subs. 45(1), where permanent disability results from the injury, the Board will estimate the impairment of earning capacity of the worker from the nature and degree of the injury, and some form of permanent disability payment will follow.

"Permanent disability" is defined in subs. 45(12) as follows:

> any physical or functional abnormality or loss, and any psychological damage arising from such abnormality or loss, after maximal medical rehabilitation has been achieved.

Subsection 45(2) provides that compensation for permanent disability is payable whether or not an award is made for temporary disability.

In December of 1985 the newly-created Appeals Tribunal decided to adopt a "leading case strategy" for pension assessment appeals. The process actually commenced in 1986 and the end product was WCAT *Decision No. 915*, which was released in May of 1987. This decision reviews and essentially endorses the Board's interpretation and application of s. 45, as discussed below.

Pension awards are usually for life, and payable in the form of a monthly pension.

Since January 1, 1995, subs. 147(14) of the pre-1997 Act provides that workers in receipt of pension awards or whose pensions have been paid in lump sum form (commuted) are entitled to an extra $200 per month in pension payments if they are entitled to a subs. 147(4) pension supplement (see Chapter 15) under the pre-1997 Act, or would be but for the fact that they are ineligible under subs. 147(7) (*i.e.*, they are in receipt of old age security payments). In brief, entitlement to a subs. 147(14) payment is contingent upon actual or notional (in the case of workers eligible for old age security) entitlement to a subs. 147(4) supplement, but for calculation purposes, the amount of the subs. 147(14) payment has to be determined before the amount of any subs. 147(4) payment can be determined.

The Board policy document on subs. 147(14) payments closely reflects the legislative provisions and also establishes that these payments cannot be commuted and are assignable. If a worker has more than one pre-1990 claim, there cannot be multiple subs. 147(14) payments. The Board will pay on the oldest claim but, if the payment is less than $200, the balance will be applied in the next oldest claim(s).

2. ESTIMATION OF IMPAIRMENT

(a) General

In practice, the estimate of impairment is made on clinical grounds by a Board doctor who conducts a medical examination of the worker. The doctor assigns a percentage figure which represents:

> the clinical impairment which is a loss of function or loss of part of the body
> and that is expressed as a percentage impairment of the whole person.

Ratings are based on physical impairment, with no discount for artificial improvement in function through prosthetic devices. A worker's occupation is irrelevant in the determination of an appropriate percentage, although the percentage does reflect impairment in all life activities.

The actual impairment of earning capacity of the individual worker is not measured. Socio-economic factors such as age, occupation and skills are not considered. Neither are actual or deemed post-accident earnings. Thus, even if a worker is unemployable, this finding alone would not warrant a full pension.

(b) Permanent Disability Rating Schedule

The statutory authority for the compilation and use of a permanent disability rating schedule is found in subs. 45(3). The Board uses the Ontario Rating Schedule which was prepared by the Board in association with the Canadian Association of Workers' Compensation Boards. It can be found in the Board's policy manual. It is commonly referred to as the "meat chart". The rating schedule was last revised in 1972.

Board policy on the rating schedule can be summarized as follows: The schedule is designed to show in percentage form the approximate impairment of earnings capacity in an average unskilled worker. It provides the Board examiners with standard impairment percentages for "bench-mark" injuries. The injury being examined is related to the most relevant bench-mark injuries in the schedule. If the injury is judged to be two-thirds as serious as the bench-mark injury, it is rated at two-thirds of the bench-mark rating. In off-schedule or "judgment" ratings, awards are to be proportionate to listed items. The schedule is a guide for minimum rating levels for specified disabilities.

In WCAT *Decision 915*, the Appeals Tribunal endorsed the Board's use of a rating schedule, and the Ontario Rating Schedule in particular, even though it acknowledged that the percentages have no scientifically demonstrable relationship to actual impairments of earning capacities.

It is also Board policy that the minimum permanent impairment award is 0.4 per cent. Residual impairment below 0.4 per cent is not regarded as representing an impairment of earning capacity. Even though an impairment might not be serious enough to attract a pension, it could lead to other forms of entitlement (such as health care benefits).

Regarding the maximum permanent impairment award resulting from any accident, Board policy provides that it can amount to, but not exceed, 100 per cent, excluding any lump sum given for facial disfigurement. A 100 per cent pension is relatively rare but will be awarded for total blindness or paraplegia or other catastrophic conditions (such as the sequelae of head injuries).

A worker with two separate and unrelated claims could receive individual awards which, taken together, exceed 100 per cent, given the wording of subs. 45(1) and a Nova Scotia Court of Appeal ruling.

The Board will reassess and physically examine the worker if it appears that additional compensable disability has developed. The award may be increased to reflect a higher level of disability. The effective date for any increase is three months prior to the date of the request for a review, or an earlier date than that if supported by medical evidence. The award may be decreased if it appears that the disability has lessened, or was incorrectly assessed previously.

If it appears that the residual disability may not prove to be permanent (or may worsen) the Board will provide a "provisional" award for a term of not less than one year and not more than five years. The Board will review a provisional award before it expires (or else renew it until a review can be arranged) and extend it provisionally, make it permanent or cancel it.

(c) Timing of Permanent Disability Rating

When residual impairment continues and the maximum medical rehabilitation (MMR) expected has been achieved, the Board will carry out a permanent disability (p.d.) evaluation. MMR is reached if there is unlikely to be any further significant improvement in the worker's medical condition notwithstanding any ongoing treatment, or the fact that a referral to a specialist or further medical investigations may be planned or underway. If it turns out that the MMR finding was premature the worker may be able to have temporary benefits retroactively restored even though a p.d. rating has taken place.

Usually the Adjudicator involved reviews the information on file, possibly in conjunction with the Unit Medical Advisor to determine whether MMR has been achieved. The Board has a Referral Reference Chart which indicates minimum referral times for a variety of disabilities. When the worker has refused corrective surgery, rating may be carried out at the time that would normally have elapsed had the surgery been performed.

Occasionally a claim with an obvious permanent disability is overlooked for a pension assessment. There may be any number of explanations for this. In cases where a long period of time has elapsed since the closure of benefits and a worker's request for a pension assessment, concerns about "continuity" may be raised, *i.e.*, the Board will have to be satisfied that the ongoing disability is medically related to the original injury.

(d) Location of Clinical Assessments

A medical examination is not always carried out. The Board takes the position that some rating can be determined from medical reports in conjunction with the rating schedule. These are typically single digit amputations, visual impairment, or (traumatic) hearing impairment, with no complications or other superimposed conditions.

Permanent disability medical examinations are carried out by Board doctors in Toronto or in the Board's Regional Offices if possible. With workers resident in other provinces, other Canadian Workers' Compensation Boards undertake ratings on request or the Board may pay for the worker to travel to Ontario for the rating.

Workers who reside permanently in Italy, Portugal or Greece are able, by virtue of three international agreements that have been made by the Board, to have their clinical disabilities evaluated or re-evaluated by the compensation authority in the relevant jurisdiction. The authority conducts a medical examination and forwards the report to the Board. A Board doctor reviews this report in conjunction with the rating schedule and chooses a clinical rating.

Board policy also provides that when examination of the worker is not possible (*e.g.*, due to the death of the worker before an examination could be carried out), the Pensions Medical Consultant performs an "indisputable rating" based on available medical documentation in conjunction with the rating schedule.

(e) Assessment Procedure

The worker is examined by a Pensions Medical Advisor. This doctor makes a thorough review of the file prior to the appointment and considers available medical documentation. In most cases the examination is quite brief — 15 minutes or less. Movements while the worker is dressing and undressing or is otherwise distracted are often observed. The examination may not bear any relationship to the worker's normal work activities, and examinations are usually in the morning, rather than at the end of a working day.

The doctor will usually not discuss findings or recommendations with the worker. Afterwards, the doctor provides the patient's file with a written report of the examination findings which includes a recommended p.d. rating and an arrears date. On occasion an Adjudicator may choose to differ with the doctor's recommendations, implementing something different.

(f) Assessment by the Appeals Tribunal

In extraordinary circumstances, an Appeals Tribunal panel may make its own assessment of a worker's disability.

3. SPECIAL RATING SITUATIONS (EXCEPTIONAL CASES)

(a) Cardiac Conditions

An "indisputable rating" may be carried out if the worker is totally permanently disabled and unfit for evaluation at the Board's Head Office. If an examination is possible, the Classification of Cardiovascular Impairment found in the American Medical Association (AMA) *Guides to the Evaluation of Permanent Impairment* (1990), may be used as a guide.

Where death occurs as the result of the compensable cardiac condition, either immediately, shortly after the initial onset, or while the condition is still in the acute phase, Board policy is that the fatal claim may be accepted with resulting entitlement for survivors.

(b) Hearing Loss and Tinnitus

The Board has very specific threshold criteria for granting p.d. awards for traumatic hearing loss and occupational noise-induced hearing loss. It uses the "Hearing Loss Permanent Disability Rating Schedule" to convert the decibel measurement of hearing loss into a percentage. The level of rating is not influenced by any improvement in hearing attained through use of a hearing aid(s). Where applicable there is an apportionment between occupational and non-occupational contributions to the hearing loss.

The Board accepts only claims for occupational noise-induced tinnitus where *inter alia* there is an accepted claim for noise induced hearing loss, and the policy imposes a two per cent cap on p.d. awards for tinnitus which can be exceeded under "unusual circumstances". Both of these points have been successfully challenged at the Appeals Tribunal.

(c) Respiratory Illnesses

The Board has many entitlement policies regarding a variety of respiratory illnesses. The key points from a permanent disability point of view are that:

- The worker is usually examined by the Occupational Chest Disease Review Committee (OCDRC) and its report includes a percentage rating;
- The AMA *Guides* rating schedule for respiratory illness is used; and
- Smoking history may be taken into consideration when establishing the percentage relationship to permanent disability (*i.e.*, there is apportionment).

Various tribunal panels have held that the AMA *Guides* were not appropriate for people with asthma, preferring a more complex rating.

(d) Psychotraumatic Disability and Chronic Pain Disability

These conditions (and fibromyalgia syndrome) are assessed under the Board's "Psychotraumatic and Behavioural Disorders Rating Schedule". (See Chapter 9, Mental and Behavioural Disorders.)

4. IMPOTENCE AND STERILITY

The Board does grant permanent disability awards for impotence and sterility, although it does not compensate for physical scarring and/or partial or total destruction of the genital organs unless it interferes with the ability to carry out normal bodily functions or there is resultant impotence.

Board policy also provides that impotence related to the loss of one or both testes is a psychological problem, and that there may also be entitlement for secondary psychological disability related to impotence or sterility. In these situations p.d. entitlement is determined in keeping with the psychological disability policy.

5. COMPENSATION FOR DISFIGUREMENT

Subsection 45(10) provides that notwithstanding subs. (1) (*i.e.*, even if there is no impairment of earning capacity), where the worker is seriously and permanently disfigured about the face or head, the Board may allow a lump sum in compensation therefore.

Board policy is that, depending upon the degree of disfigurement as determined by the "Disfigurement Committee", the percentage assessed can range from 3 per cent to 25 per cent, spanning four categories of disfigurement: noticeable, substantial, major, and gross.

The lump sum awards paid are based on the maximum compensation rate in effect at the time of the accident, rather than the earnings of the worker.

6. MULTIPLE COMPENSABLE DISABILITIES — ENHANCEMENT FACTORS

The Ontario Rating Schedule provides that multiple compensable disabilities are more disabling than the sum of their individual ratings. It details multiple factors for fingers.

Where there is a bilateral upper limb disability (not restricted to amputations) the disability in each limb is rated separately and then a multiple factor of half the value of the lesser rating is added onto the total rating. A similar multiple factor approach is used with bilateral lower-limb disabilities. In both cases, this multiple factor is applied only when the impairments affect function at comparable levels, or function of the whole limb. A multiple factor is not applied between upper and lower limbs.

The Appeals Tribunal has extended the enhancement factor for multiple disabilities to encompass non-bilateral disabilities.

7. PRE-EXISTING CONDITIONS AND APPORTIONMENT

(a) General Principles

Subsection 45(1) provides that where permanent disability *results from* the injury a pension is payable. It has been held that the Board is therefore required to apportion benefits between compensable and non-compensable disabilities. However, the Board must differentiate between those situations where the worker has an ascertained pre-existing disability and those where the worker only has a propensity to develop a particular disability (*i.e.*, a "thin skull"). In the former case there would be apportionment, while in the latter case the Board is obliged to take the "thin-skulled" victim as found so there would be no discounting or apportionment. Co-existing conditions are conceptually similar to pre-existing conditions.

Another relevant principle is that the compensable injury need only be one of the *significant contributing factors* to the ongoing disability.

The Board defines "pre-accident disability" as a condition that has produced periods of disability in the past requiring treatment and disrupting employment. "Pre-existing condition" is defined as an underlying or asymptomatic condition that only becomes manifest post-accident.

(b) Measurable Condition

Board Policy is that where the prior condition was measurable and the impairment of total body function resulting from the new disability is increased beyond the degree usually associated with such disability because of the prior condition, this will be reflected in the worker's pension award.

The Board considers measurable prior conditions to be conditions such as a prior amputation or loss of movement in which the pre-existing condition has been, or could have been, rated for permanent disability. There are four aspects of evaluation:

(1)   The value of the prior condition by itself;
(2)   The value of the new condition by itself;
(3)   The value of the entire disability; and
(4)   The enhancement factor, which is the value of the entire disability (3) less the sum of the value of the prior and the new condition (1)+(2).

The worker's award is the sum of the value of the new condition by itself (2) and the enhancement factor (4).

The Board makes an exception in cases of total loss of sight or enucleation (removal) of an eye where the pre-existing disability was the loss of sight or enucleation of the other eye. The worker will receive an award which equals the total of:

•   The value of the prior condition by itself;
•   The value of the new condition by itself; plus
•   The enhancement factor.

Where the compensable disability appears to have had no residual effect on the pre-existing condition, there will not be any entitlement to a permanent disability award. This determination, which must be based on medical evidence, may be very difficult to make.

(c) Non-Measurable Condition

Board policy is that where the prior condition was not measurable but enhances the residual disability resulting from the compensable accident, this may be reflected in the worker's pension award. There are three categories used:

(1)   A condition producing minor pre-accident disability — award full assessment;
(2)   A condition producing moderate pre-accident disability — award 75 per cent of total assessment; and
(3)   A condition producing major pre-accident disability — award 50 per cent of total assessment.

The Appeals Tribunal has also followed this approach, although it has chosen in some instances to differ from the Board in its rating of the prior condition.

Where the pre-existing condition was not only non-measurable but non-disabling, there should be no effect whatever on entitlement to the permanent award as assessed, regardless of the severity of the compensable injury.

8. INTERVENING EVENTS AND APPORTIONMENT

It is accepted by both the Board and the Appeals Tribunal that an intervening event (*e.g.*, a non-compensable car accident) may affect entitlement in the permanent disability context. This problem is conceptually similar to the one raised by pre-existing conditions in regard to evaluation and apportionment.

9. CALCULATION OF PERMANENT DISABILITY AWARDS

(a) General

For accidents occurring prior to April 1, 1985, subs. 43(1) (pre-1985 Act) provides that permanent disability awards are based on 75 per cent of the worker's gross earnings. Workers eligible for an additional payment under subs. 147(14) of the pre-1997 Act may receive less than the prescribed amount if that amount plus the pension award plus 75 per cent of any post-injury average earnings plus any old age security payments would exceed 75 per cent of pre-injury average earnings.

For accidents occurring on or after April 1, 1985, subs. 45(1) provides that permanent disability awards are based on 90 per cent of net average earnings. For purposes of the pension award (in contrast with the temporary benefits practice), the Board will not revise the new average earnings figure if the worker's tax exemption code changes. Workers eligible for an additional payment under subs. 147(14) of the pre-1997 Act may receive less than the prescribed amount if that amount plus the pension award plus 90 per cent of any post-injury net average earnings plus any old age security payments would exceed 90 per cent of pre-injury net average earnings.

(b) Lump Sum Payment where Clinical Award is 10 Per Cent or Less

Subsection 45(4) authorizes the payment of a pension as a lump sum where the disability has been rated at ten per cent or less, unless the Board decides that it would not be to the advantage of the worker to do so.

(c) Arrears

The Board defines arrears as retroactive pension benefits, paid as a lump sum, separate from ongoing pension entitlement, dating from the onset of permanent disability. At the time of the initial pension assessment, arrears are paid for all periods where temporary benefits were not paid or were less than the monthly pension payments. At the time of a pension reassessment where the award is increased, the increase (paid as arrears) will date from three months prior to the date of the reassessment request, or an earlier date if supported by medical evidence.

10. OBJECTIONS AND REVIEWS

Subject to the relevant limitation periods, an injured worker and the employer both have the right to object to the percentage of assessed disability, the calculation of the award, the arrears date chosen, etc.

Any objection to the quantum will be referred to the original decision-maker. If an objection is made at the time of the assessment the Board sometimes carries out a second examination within a few weeks. The criteria used are unstated. When a second examination either confirms or denies the award, this decision can be appealed further.

Generally, if a worker's quantum objection is received more than one year after the last assessment, the Board will be inclined to arrange a reassessment, especially if deterioration is obvious from outside medical reports, which may have been received, or the claim has been reopened (*e.g.*, because of a recurrence).

CHAPTER 15

Pension Supplements for Pre-January 2, 1990 Claims

1. INTRODUCTION

Prior to 1975, there were no provisions in the Act authorizing the payment of any supplement to the basic Board pension. The Board had the authority to base a pension on either a clinical rating of the impairment of earning capacity or the actual wage loss of the worker (if the worker had returned to work), but the general rule was to base it on the physical loss or mutilation sustained.

In July 1975, the wage loss pension calculation provision was repealed and a pension supplement provision was substituted. This provision remained in force until April 1, 1985.

As of April 1, 1985, a new supplement provision came into force. It repealed and replaced the original supplement provision, but the repeal was not retroactive. Supplements for periods prior to April 1, 1985, remained payable pursuant to the "old" provision. The new provision — which applied to pre-April 1, 1985, pensioners with supplement claims for periods from, and after, April 1, 1985 — reads as follows:

> **43.** (5) Notwithstanding subsection (1), where the impairment of earning capacity of the worker is significantly greater than is usual for the nature and degree of injury, the Board may supplement the amount awarded for permanent partial disability for such period as the Board may fix unless the worker,
>
> > (*a*) fails to co-operate in or is not available for a medical or vocational rehabilitation program which would, in the Board's opinion, aid in getting the worker back to work; or
> >
> > (*b*) fails to accept or is not available for employment which is available and which in the opinion of the Board is suitable for the worker's capabilities.

For claims arising on, or after, April 1, 1985, a comparable provision is found in subs. 45(5). The wording of the "old" provision was very similar.

From April 1, 1985 until July 26, 1989 "older" injured workers were eligible for the "older worker supplement" pursuant to subs. 45(7) of the pre-1989 Act and subs. 43(5)(*b*) of the pre-1989 Act. These provisions are identical. Although this was a new legislative provision, the payment of this type of benefit was not new. Authorization was given to pay a supplement equivalent to the old age pension to an older worker in a directive from the Corporate Board in January 1976.

There was no definition of "older worker" in the Act. One Appeals Tribunal panel obtained and reviewed the Board's policies on older worker supplements for periods prior to 1985, and found them to be incoherent. The newer Board policy was relatively coherent.

As of July 26, 1989, the supplement provisions then in force were repealed, although the pre-1985 and pre-1989 Acts *otherwise* continued to apply to pre-1985 injuries and pre-1989 injuries (those occurring on, or after, April 1, 1985 and before January 2, 1990) respectively.

The new supplement provisions, applicable from July 26, 1989 onwards, with respect to *all* pre-January 2, 1990 claims, are set out in s. 147 of the pre-1997 Act. Section 147 also establishes the basis for some pre-January 2, 1990 claimants to receive an additional monthly pension payment as of January 1, 1995. To add to the confusion, supplements to Future Economic Loss (FEL) awards (see subs. 43(9)) may be payable for claims arising from January 2, 1990, through December 31, 1997. These are discussed in Chapter 16, Future Economic Loss Benefits.

It should be noted that if an objection to a supplement decision is being pursued, distinct rulings are required for pre- and post-July 26, 1989 periods of entitlement. It is possible to have one decision that deals explicitly with entitlement for both periods. At the time of writing, it is very rare for an injured worker to come forward with a claim for a supplement for a period prior to July 26, 1989. Therefore, these supplements will not be discussed further.

2. PERMANENT PARTIAL DISABILITY SUPPLEMENTS FOR PERIODS AFTER JULY 26, 1989

(a) Introduction

Bill 162 received third reading on July 24, 1989 and received Royal Assent on July 26, 1989. Most of its provisions were to come into force at a later date but the provisions regarding supplements for workers in receipt of pension awards (now set out in s. 147 of the pre-1997 Act) came into force immediately. The Board attempted to determine eligibility in fairly short order for approximately 132,000 injured workers. All pensioners were supposed to have received a letter with a questionnaire attached and eligibility was determined largely on the basis of a worker's answers on the questionnaire. The first step was to determine eligibility for the smaller subs. 147(4) supplement. Emigrant pensioners and pensioners whose pensions had been fully commuted were also eligible for supplements and were also supposed to have been sent questionnaires.

There are a number of points that emerge from the foregoing:

1.   Any number of pensioners probably never received questionnaires, or did not understand them. These pensioners could well be eligible for at least a subs. 147(4) supplement from July 26, 1989.

2. Completed questionnaires may have gone astray at or on their way to the Board and therefore consideration may never have been given to potentially eligible pensioners.
3. Many questionnaires may have been incorrectly filled out and this may have led to improper adjudicative decisions.
4. The Board hired staff ("transitional adjudicators") on a short-term basis. The quality of the decision-making was lower than the usual quality of Board decision-making at the initial levels.

The practical implication of these points is that representatives should always determine why any injured worker with a pre-January 2, 1990 claim and a pension award is not receiving at least a s. 147(4) supplement with full arrears from either July 26, 1989, or the date of the pension determination.

(b) Transition Rules for Workers Who were Receiving Supplements on July 26, 1989

Although entitlement to the supplements payable under the pre-1985 Act or pre-1989 Act ended on July 26, 1989, the Board took the position that any workers in receipt of supplements would continue to receive such payments until the terms of the supplement expired.

In the case of a "co-operation" or "looking for work" supplement, it continued (with any necessary extensions) for as long as the worker was participating in a vocational rehabilitation (VR) program under the auspices of the Board. Then the worker would have been considered for either a subs. 147(2) or (4) supplement.

In the case of a "wage loss" or "work-adjustment" supplement, it expired once its term was up and no extensions were given. Then the worker would have been considered for a subs. 147(4) supplement.

In the case of an older worker supplement, a subs. 147(4) supplement was automatically awarded when the older worker supplement expired (unless, at that point, the worker had become eligible for old age security benefits and therefore ineligible, by virtue of subs. 147(7), for a subs. 147(4) supplement).

(c) General Eligibility for Supplements

Subsection 147(1) has its own definition of "worker": a worker who is permanently disabled as a result of a pre-1985 injury or a pre-1989 injury.

The Board's interpretation of s. 147 is that the worker's wage loss must be at least partially related to the work injury and current Appeals Tribunal decisions favour this approach as well. There is no minimum pension award specified in the Act or Board policy as a threshold for entitlement to a s. 147 supplement.

The normal process (as opposed to the transitional one discussed above) of determining a worker's entitlement under the section is to first determine possible eligibility under subs. 147(2). If there is no entitlement under that provision, then eligibility under subs. 147(4) must be determined.

(d) Eligibility for the Subsection 147(2) Supplement

The wording of subs. 147(2) was as follows:

> **147.** (2) Subject to subsections (9) and (10), the Board shall give a supplement to a worker who, in the opinion of the Board, is likely to benefit from a vocational rehabilitation program which could help to increase the worker's earning capacity to such an extent that the sum of the worker's earning capacity after vocational rehabilitation and the amount awarded for permanent partial disability approximates the worker's average or net average earnings, as the case may be, before the worker's injury.

With the passage of Bill 99, the phrase "vocational rehabilitation program" has been replaced by "labour market re-entry plan" and "vocational rehabilitation" has been replaced by "completion of the plan". Since complementary changes have not yet been made to Board policy, in the balance of this chapter the old phraseology is still used.

As noted in Board policy, the Board is *required* to pay a subs. 147(2) supplement where the Board determines that the worker is *likely to benefit* from a VR program and that program *could help* to increase the worker's earning capacity to the point where earning capacity and pension award approximate the pre-accident earnings.

The "likelihood of benefit" is determined by the Board. A consideration of the worker's age in determining likelihood of benefit may be appropriate and is not contrary to the Ontario *Human Rights Code*. It has been held that historical lack of co-operation with the Board (*i.e.*, in periods prior to July 26, 1989) is not relevant to a determination of likelihood of benefit with respect to s. 147. Another view is that a worker's VR history prior to July 26, 1989, is not determinative but does provide useful and relevant background information.

The Board takes the identified vocational objective (or range of available jobs) for the worker and determines potential wage levels with regard to the objective. Entry level wages will not necessarily be the ones used. The resulting figure (an average) becomes the worker's estimated earning capacity after VR. The vocational objective chosen must be reasonable, realistic and practical in the circumstances of each case. The worker's pension, plus the estimated earning capacity figure, is known as the worker's "total potential earning capacity".

The Board considers the term "approximate" to mean "reasonably close to", or "may approach". There is no mathematical standard applied such as "within ten per cent". In one Appeals Tribunal decision, the Panel concluded that a post-injury earning capacity (including pension) which was between 77 per cent and 88 per cent of pre-injury earnings approximated pre-injury earnings.

The eligible worker must have a "total potential earning capacity" after rehabilitation and return to work that "comes close to or exceeds" the pre-accident earnings within a period of time (*i.e.*, four years). The Board assesses the pre-accident earnings by using the amount stated in the claim to calculate the temporary benefits with no ceiling (*i.e.*, actual earnings are used).

Relatively unskilled high wage earners, such as construction workers, will usually not "approximate" without extensive long-term rehabilitation which the Board is generally not prepared to offer. Low wage earners, on the other hand, will "approximate" if they can find virtually any employment.

(e) Duration of the Subsection 147(2) Supplement

Subsection 147(3) provided that a supplement under subs. (2) is payable for the period during which the worker participates in a Board-approved VR program. With the passage of Bill 99 the wording is now "a Board-approved *labour market re-entry plan*".

Board policy equates "participation" with the date that a worker's VR case was "activated". This date may not accord with the date that the worker's reasonable rehabilitation activities began, or even with the date that the worker first contacted the Board asking for VR assistance. In practice, the Board has been willing to depart from a strict interpretation of its policy on this point.

The Board will be willing to retroactively pay a subs. 147(2) supplement if a decision denying VR is reversed. However, the Board must be satisfied that the worker's self-directed rehabilitation activities could have led to "approximation". If not, a subs. 147(4) supplement could still be considered.

There are no time limits specified in subs. 147(3) regarding duration of the subs. 147(2) supplement. In effect, the Board accepts that the supplement is to continue as long as VR involvement has not been terminated. The Appeals Tribunal has observed that supplements should not be terminated because of their extended duration only.

In reality, the termination of the subs. 147(2) supplement will generally follow soon after the closure of the worker's VR file. The real issue may be an objection to a VR decision, rather than an objection to the termination of the supplement. Representatives should note that a VR decision (or its functional equivalent) must be appealed within 30 days and decisions made prior to January 1, 1998 must have been appealed before January 31, 1998, unless the Board permits otherwise.

Historically, job searching has often been a major component of VR involvement. This may no longer be the case with labour market re-entry programs. Nonetheless, job search activities may be relevant regarding subs. 147(2) entitlement for periods prior to January 1, 1998. In this context, the following should be noted. Subsections 53(12) and (13) arguably limited job search assistance to a maximum of 12 months. However, by virtue of subs. 53(1), these provisions did not apply to pre-January 2, 1990, injured workers. Any limit would be more properly related to Board policy and a consideration of the ongoing rehabilitative purpose of an ongoing job search in the individual circumstances of the case. There are Appeals Tribunal decisions which have granted subs. 147(2) supplements where job searches have extended beyond 12 months.

(f) Entitlement Following a Change in the Worker's Circumstances

There is no limitation period regarding the application for a subs. 147(2) supplement. Workers who may not have been eligible on July 26, 1989 or subsequently can always apply (or re-apply) for the supplement at some time in the future. However, a re-application for the supplement must not be confused with an objection to a previous denial, otherwise there may indeed be a limitation period problem. For example, the Board may have felt that an otherwise eligible worker did not qualify for a subs. 147(2) supplement because of "self-imposed restrictions" that made it unlikely that the worker could have benefitted from VR. If that worker's views have now changed and both the Board and the worker can agree that the worker would benefit from VR, then the worker could now be eligible for a subs. 147(2) supplement. Similarly, an otherwise eligible worker, who had not previously experienced a wage loss, could be laid off. At that point the worker could become eligible for a subs. 147(2) supplement, or alternatively, a subs. 147(4) supplement. In these situations the Board may deny subs. 147(2) entitlement on the basis that a worker's earning capacity has been re-established. In one Appeals Tribunal decision, the Panel noted that this conclusion assumes that a return to work at no wage loss means there is no loss in earning capacity. The Panel held that while this assumption may often be valid, a consideration of a worker's earning capacity must include not only the capacity to earn in suitable employment with the accident employer but also in suitable employment on the open labour market. In another Appeals Tribunal decision, the Panel, in awarding a subs. 147(2) supplement to a worker who had been laid off for economic reasons, observed that there is no requirement in subs. 147(2) that the lay-off be related to the compensable disability.

The receipt of a subs. 147(2) supplement in the past would not preclude its receipt in the future, as long as the worker was able to meet the eligibility requirements set out in the provision.

(g) Calculation of the Subsection 147(2) Supplement

(i) Pre-1985 Injuries

As provided by subs. 147(9), the amount of the supplement plus the permanent disability (p.d.) award plus $200 plus 75 per cent of any average earnings after the injury shall equal 75 per cent of the worker's pre-injury average earnings. For subs. 147(2) recipients, the wording of subs. 147(9) is somewhat misleading because recipients would not be eligible for the $200 payment which (by virtue of subs. 147(14)) is tied to entitlement under subs. 147(4) only. Nothing in the

Act nor in Board policy sets out how to calculate post-accident average earnings for purposes of subs. 147(9).

Subsection 147(11) provides that in calculating the amount of a supplement the Board shall consider the effect of inflation on the worker's pre-injury rate, so *escalated* pre-injury average earnings are used.

Subsection 147(11) also provides that the Board shall consider any payments the worker receives under the C.P.P. or the Q.P.P. with regard to a disability arising from the injury. In practice the Board deducts such payments from the worker's gross pre-injury earnings. The statutory maximum earnings ceiling applies *after* the deduction of the C.P.P./Q.P.P. disability benefit. Decision-makers are supposed to examine any relevant information that may indicate the basis for such payments to determine whether payments received under the C.P.P. or the Q.P.P. are in relation to the work-related injury. The policy does not indicate what the Board will actually do with regard to its findings on this point. In one case the Board had reduced subs. 147(4) payments by the full amount of C.P.P. benefits. An Appeals Tribunal Panel held that only half of the C.P.P. benefits should be taken into account since the C.P.P. benefits were awarded based on both compensable and non-compensable conditions. The Board often adopts this test when integrating C.P.P. benefits and FEL payments.

(ii) Pre-1989 Injuries

As provided by subs. 147(10) the amount of the supplement plus the p.d. award plus $200 plus 90 per cent of any net average earnings after the injury shall equal 90 per cent of the worker's pre-injury net average earnings. The comments above on subs. 147(9) apply here as well.

Subsection 147(11) also applies here, along with the comments above.

(h) Eligibility for the Subsection 147(4) Supplement

Subsection 147(4) provides:

> **147.** (4) Subject to subsections (8), (9) and (10), the Board shall give a supplement to a worker,
>
> > (*a*) who, in the opinion of the Board, is not likely to benefit from a vocational rehabilitation program in the manner described in subsection (2); or
> >
> > (*b*) whose earning capacity after a vocational rehabilitation program is not increased to the extent described in subsection (2) in the opinion of the Board.

As stated earlier, with the passage of Bill 99, the phrase "vocational rehabilitation program" has been replaced by "labour market re-entry plan".

Subsection 147(5) provides:

147. (5) A supplement under subsection (4) for a worker described in clause (4)(*a*) becomes payable as of the later of,

(*a*)　the 26th day of July, 1989; or

(*b*)　the day the Board determines the worker has a permanent disability.

Subsection 147(6) provides:

147. (6) A supplement under subsection (4) for a worker described in clause (4)(*b*) becomes payable as of the latest of,

(*a*)　the 26th day of July, 1989;

(*b*)　the day the Board determines the worker has a permanent disability; or

(*c*)　the day the worker ceases to participate in a vocational rehabilitation program.

Again, as stated earlier, with the passage of Bill 99, the phrase "vocational rehabilitation program" has been replaced by "labour market re-entry plan".

Regarding subs. 147(4)(*a*), Board policy provides that if the Board can determine that the worker is "unlikely to benefit from a vocational rehabilitation program" to the extent required in subs. 147(2), the worker is entitled to a subs. 147(4) supplement whether that worker is willing to co-operate or not. This position is then modified by the following portion of the policy.

However, if the worker's lack of co-operation or unavailability prevents the Board from determining whether that worker can benefit from a VR program, a s. 135(4) [now 147(4)] supplement cannot be determined or paid.

In one Appeals Tribunal decision, the Panel held that the "shall" in subs. 147(4) is mandatory (the Board's position was that it was permissive only) and that in determining entitlement under subs. 147(4)(*a*) there is no requirement to have regard to the reason for a worker's lack of rehabilitation potential. The Board's position was that the lack of rehabilitation potential had to be related to the compensable disability.

Regarding subs. 147(4)(*b*), Board policy provides that as long as the worker has not yet approximated pre-accident earnings, a subs. 147(4) supplement is paid under clause (*b*). It is therefore clear that the Board is equating "earning capacity" with post-injury earnings. In one Appeals Tribunal decision, the Panel held that "earning capacity" is the wage that the worker has the actual or potential ability to secure. The Panel also held that for approximation purposes, it must be determined whether on completion of the VR program the worker's present earning capacity (rather than future potential earnings) together with the worker's pension approximates pre-accident earnings. For the comparison between pre- and post-accident earnings, the Board uses the escalated pre-injury earnings subject to the relevant yearly maximum, and this approach has been endorsed by the Appeals Tribunal.

Even though entitlement to a subs. 147(4) supplement may not be warranted under subs. 147(4)(*a*), a decision-maker should also consider subs. 147(4)(*b*) as an alternative basis for entitlement.

It may be that the Board has awarded a worker a subs. 147(4) supplement, but the worker feels that a subs. 147(2) supplement should have been awarded. It is open to the worker to challenge the Board's decision, although frankly, such a challenge might not be in the worker's best long-term financial interests.

(i) Amount of the Subsection 147(4) Supplement

Subsection 147(8) provides that the amount of a supplement under subs. (4) shall not exceed the amount of a full monthly pension for old age security under s. 3 of the *Old Age Security Act* (Canada). Of course, less than the full amount may be payable subject to subss. 147(9) and (10) as discussed earlier. Subsection 147(13) also applies regarding adjusting a worker's pre-injury earnings for inflation and the offset for C.P.P. or Q.P.P. income received with regard to the work-related disability. In certain cases there may be entitlement to a subs. 147(4) supplement, but no dollar amount payable. The threshold determination of entitlement is relevant, however, for any consideration of entitlement to the pension top up payment provided by subs. 147(14).

(j) Duration of the Subsection 147(4) Supplement and Reviews

Subsection 147(7) provides that a supplement under subs. (4) shall continue until the worker becomes eligible for OAS benefits. Board policy is to presume that a worker who turns 65 is eligible for OAS, but it is open to a worker to establish that the OAS eligibility requirements have not been met.

Subsection 147(13) provides that the Board shall review a subs. 147(4) supplement in the 24th month following the award and in the 60th month following the award and recalculate the amount of the supplement in accordance with subss. 147(9) and (10).

Published Board policy provides that once the subs. 147(4) supplement has been paid, it can be terminated or adjusted only according to the time frames in subs. 147(13), or to coincide with the expiry of a provisional permanent impairment benefit, or on the date the worker dies. It follows that a subs. 147(4) supplement cannot be adjusted "mid-term" to reflect a change in a worker's post-injury earnings, although this position may be out of step with the legislated reporting requirements for material changes in circumstances.

The first subs. 147(13) reviews commenced in 1991. Many supplements were allowed to expire pending review. The Board did (and still does) allow a supplement to expire if the worker fails to return a questionnaire which is supposed to be sent out during the review process. More importantly, the Board was using the subs. 147(13) review to question whether or not the subs. 147(4) supplement was correctly awarded in the first instance, and to question whether or not, on the merits, an extension was warranted. In many cases the Board decided that the supplement should not have been awarded in the first place. The Board defended this practice by arguing that many supplements were initially granted on the basis of inadequate information or the incorrect application of the Act and Board policy by the "transitional adjudicators".

The second reviews commenced in 1994 and the Board's approach was initially similar to that taken in 1991. In some cases the Board maintained that not only was the initial allowance incorrect but also the renewal.

In response to growing concerns about the review process, the Board announced in March 1995, the creation of a special review team to examine approximately 3,000 decisions that had resulted in a discontinuation of the subs. 147(4) supplement. Many reversals followed. Unfortunately, a number of decisions had already worked their way through the appeals system and could not be reviewed by the team.

The Board now accepts that the initial determination through the questionnaire review established entitlement and that subs. 147(13) only mandates a review and recalculation which should properly focus on any changes and new information since the prior decision. These five operating principles apply:

1. A worker's ability to earn is best demonstrated by *actual* earnings. A worker who has been unsuccessful in obtaining employment following a vocational rehabilitation program would be entitled to subs. 147(4) as the worker's injury is likely a significant cause of the worker's inability to secure employment.

2. The review should consider the *current* merits of the worker's situation. A worker's previous failure to co-operate with vocational rehabilitation should not influence the evaluation and decision.

3. The cases where the questionnaire has not been returned will be on the review list. Generally, if the questionnaire has not been returned, it will be assumed that the worker has secured employment with earnings at or greater than pre-accident. Where the file review indicates that there may be a communication problem (address change, infirmity), the adjudicator should consider the probability of ongoing entitlement. If it is apparent entitlement likely exists the adjudicator should take the initiative to make further contact with the client.

4. Only in exceptional situations should the subs. 147(4) entitlement issue be revisited. These could include:

   • no permanent impairment;
   • evidence of misrepresentation;
   • could now benefit from vocational rehabilitation service (high probability of employment being secured) *and* wants to receive vocational rehabilitation assistance.

5. Each decision shall be made upon the real merits and justice of the case.

In 1997 a series of Appeals Tribunal decisions from the same Vice-Chair, but a variety of side members, held that a subs. 147(13) review cannot consider initial entitlement. Only the amount of supplement is open to review. This position has been followed in many subsequent Tribunal decisions.

(k) Objections Regarding Entitlement to a Subsection 147(4) Supplement

Board policy is that in the case of an objection, entitlement to a subs. 147(4) supplement is judged based on the facts at the time of the initial decision. Notwithstanding this provision, Board decision-makers are interested in the worker's circumstances right up to the present, especially with regard to any rehabilitative activities undertaken, and the Appeals Tribunal shares this interest.

(l) Payment of Multiple Benefits

Board policy is that if the worker is receiving a subs. 147(4) supplement and becomes entitled to additional benefits, either in the same claim or in a different claim, the supplement continues. If temporary total (t.t.) disability benefits are payable under the same claim there will be a dollar-for-dollar offset from these benefits. If the t.t. benefits are payable under a different claim, there is no offset. Similarly, there will be no offset from any Future Economic Loss (FEL) benefits payable, and the worker could be eligible for a supplement under subs. 43(9) of the pre-1997 Act.

The Board acknowledges that the Act allows workers to receive more than one s. 147 supplement. The Board's view is that if following the receipt of a subs. 147(4) supplement, a worker is granted a new permanent disability benefit under another claim, *either old or new*, the worker is entitled to be considered for either a subs. 147(2) or (4) supplement under the other claim. The amount of the supplement is calculated based on the provisions of subss. 147(8), (9) or (10). The Appeals Tribunal has ruled that multiple supplements cannot be paid under subs. 147(4)(*a*).

(m) Special Situations

(i) Fully Commuted Pension

If a pension has been fully commuted it in no way affects a worker's eligibility under s. 147. The practical problem is that the Board may have lost or destroyed the worker's file, or may have decided that the pension award was too insignificant to warrant a supplement.

(ii) Emigrant Worker

As noted above, emigrant "workers" as defined in subs. 147(1) are eligible for s. 147 supplements, subject to the provisions in subss. 147(2) and (4). Notification may have posed difficulties however.

Additionally, it would be virtually impossible for an emigrant worker who has left Canada (as opposed to Ontario) to make a case for entitlement to a subs. 147(2) supplement, since the Board does not offer or monitor any vocational rehabilitation to workers residing out of Canada. A subs. 147(4) supplement can be denied where the worker has left Canada and the Board feels that the worker would benefit from a VR program.

(iii) Retired Worker

Board policy is that if a worker "retires" prior to a determination being made regarding s. 147 entitlement and the worker is still interested in pursuing employment, the decision-maker will nevertheless proceed to consider possible entitlement under subs. 147(2). Failing that there could be entitlement under subs. 147(4). A subs. 147(2) supplement will probably be terminated if a worker "retires", but there still could be eligibility for a subs. 147(4) supplement depending upon the reason for the retirement.

If a worker returns to work with no earnings loss and subsequently decides to retire, the worker may not be entitled to a supplement. Board policy provides:

> If the retirement is due to the elimination of a job, a worsening of the permanent disability or a combination of both, in addition to the increasing age of the worker, a supplement may be in order. The decision-maker has to be satisfied that circumstances arising from the permanent impairment have changed in order to consider supplement entitlement.

The policy does not specify which supplement *would* be considered, but earlier in the policy it is noted that even a subs. 147(4) supplement would be denied if a worker has taken early retirement and would benefit from a VR program. The key question is these situations is, was the compensable injury a significant factor in the decision to retire?

A consideration of the basis of an early retirement will be relevant for workers who were never eligible for a subs. 147(4) supplement because of subs. 147(7), but who are seeking entitlement to the pension top up payment available under subs. 147(14). Board policy establishes the following points:

- Wage loss is likely to be at least partially related to the injury if the VR caseworker counselled the worker to retire;
- If the worker retired and the injury was not a significant factor in the retirement, the worker would not have been eligible for the subs.147(4) supplement;

- Wage loss related to the injury cannot be established if the worker's expected retirement date, prior to the injury, was earlier than the date the Board determined that the worker had a permanent disability.

(iv) Incarcerated Worker

Board policy is that if the terms of the sentence do not prevent the worker from benefiting from *and* participating in a VR program, the worker may qualify for a supplement under subs. 147(2). If the terms of the sentence do prevent this, entitlement to a subs. 147(4) supplement will generally also be denied. However, a previously awarded subs. 147(4) supplement cannot be cancelled because of a worker's incarceration.

CHAPTER 16

Future Economic Loss Benefits

1. INTRODUCTION

The Future Economic Loss (FEL) award lies at the heart of the compensation scheme for workers injured after January 1, 1990 and prior to January 1, 1998, and left with a permanent impairment. The basic purpose of the FEL award is to compensate the permanently impaired injured worker for projected wage loss (as determined by the Board) until age 65. A FEL retirement benefit is payable after age 65.

Prior to January 1, 1998, the FEL award was initially paid following the first determination of FEL benefits. This determination is commonly referred to by its acronym "D1". The D1 award was paid for a period of two years and then reviewed. The first review of FEL benefits is referred to as "R1". The R1 award was paid for a period of three years and then reviewed. The second, and likely final, FEL review is referred to as "R2". Barring any further reviews that could occur due to the worker undergoing a significant unanticipated deterioration of the compensable impairment, the R2 award was paid until the worker reached the age of 65.

Following January 1, 1998, the fixed review points of D1, R1, and R2, and the alternative review point (following an unanticipated deterioration) were eliminated. Presently, the review of FEL benefits may be done annually or when the worker experiences a material change of circumstances. Barring fraud or misrepresentation by the worker, the last review of the FEL benefit will take place, at most, 60 months following the initial determination of FEL benefits.

As a matter of practice, the Board still performs regular FEL reviews at 24 months and 60 months past the initial determination of FEL benefits. However, the Board may now also review the FEL benefit whenever the worker experiences a material change of circumstance.

2. ELIGIBILITY FOR THE FUTURE ECONOMIC LOSS AWARD

For a worker to be eligible for a FEL award the following conditions must be met:

- There must be a permanent impairment resulting from the compensable injury; or
- There must have been 12 continuous months of temporary disability resulting from the compensable injury; and
- The worker must be under 65 years of age.

Permanent impairment is defined as impairment that continues to exist after maximum medical recovery (MMR) of the worker has been achieved. A worker reaches MMR when there is unlikely to be any further significant improvement in the worker's medical condition. MMR may have been achieved even if the worker is still receiving treatment, such as physical therapy or drugs, when the probability of improvement is low. By definition, if the worker has received a non-economic loss (NEL) award, there is a permanent impairment.

The Board considers a worker to be temporarily disabled for 12 continuous months if there is no restoration of pre-injury earning capacity for any continuous period of one month or more, for a one-year period. If a worker's post-injury net average earnings equal pre-injury net average earnings the Board will assume that there has been a full restoration of earning capacity. The Board's view on "continuity" is that intermittent resumptions of pre-injury earning capacity of one or two weeks at a time over 12 months are insufficient to break the "continuous months".

A worker over 65 years of age is not entitled to a FEL award, no matter what the state of impairment nor length of time of temporary disability. The Board is required to continue to pay temporary benefits to workers who are 65 years of age or older until MMR is reached. A worker over 65 years of age with a permanent impairment will, however, be eligible for a NEL award.

3. DATE OF DETERMINATION OF THE FUTURE ECONOMIC LOSS AWARD

Subsection 43(10) of the *Workers' Compensation Act* provides:

> **43.** (10) Where possible, the Board shall determine the amount of compensation payable to a worker under this section,
>
> > (a) in the twelfth consecutive month during which the worker is temporarily disabled;
> >
> > (b) within one year after notice of the accident in which the worker was injured is given under section 22, if during that year the Board determines that the worker is permanently impaired; or
> >
> > (c) within eighteen months after notice of the accident in which the worker was injured is given under section 22, if the worker's medical condition precludes a determination within the time stated in clause (a) or (b), whichever applies.

Subsection 43(12) provides that the Board may extend the time limits set out in subs. 43(10) in the case of a worker who is not receiving compensation under the Act and whose entitlement to compensation is in dispute.

Regardless of the requirements of the Act, most initial FEL determinations have not been made within the time frames specified by subs. 43(10)(a) and (b). This has given *de facto* recognition to the opening two words of subs. 43(10), which are "where possible".

Deciding upon what date was, or should have been, the date of determination of the initial FEL benefit had much more significant consequences for benefits payable prior to January 1, 1998, when FEL review dates were fixed and FEL benefits were effectively locked in for years at a time. Changes of circumstance between the date benefits should have been determined and the date when they actually were determined could have a significant effect on the level of benefits paid between reviews. This resulted in many appeals on the date of determination issue.

The timing of the FEL determination in occupational disease claims is different from other claims. Occupational disease claims are rated for a FEL only when there has been 12 consecutive months of temporary disability. A worker with an occupational disease and a permanent impairment but without 12 months of consecutive disability will not be evaluated for a FEL. The classification of a condition as either an occupational disease or a disablement can therefore make a significant difference to the timing of the FEL award. The reason for the differences in procedure between occupational disease claims and other claims is that in a significant number of occupational disease claims, and in particular hearing loss claims, the permanent impairment is unlikely to have an impact on future earnings. The Act, therefore, requires the FEL determination to be made only in this particular group of permanent impairment claims where there is a finding that there has been 12 continuous months of disability. While the FEL rating might be made later in occupational disease claims, wage loss associated with the injury prior to the later than usual FEL determination may be compensated by the payment of temporary benefits.

4. DETERMINATION OF THE FUTURE ECONOMIC LOSS AWARD

(a) General

The FEL award is a projected wage-loss determination based on 90 per cent of the difference between the worker's net average earnings before the injury and the net average earnings that the worker is likely to be able to earn after the injury in suitable and available employment. The determination of pre-injury earnings and the manner in which FEL benefits are adjusted for inflation are dealt with in Chapter 12, Earnings Basis. In determining the amount that a worker is likely to be able to earn in suitable and available employment, the Board is required by subs. 43(7) of the Act to consider:

(*a*) the net average earnings, if any, of the worker at the time the Board determines compensation under this section;

(*b*) any disability payments the worker may receive for the injury under the Canada Pension Plan or the Quebec Pension Plan;

(*c*) the personal and vocational characteristics of the worker;

(*d*) the prospects for successful medical and vocational rehabilitation of the worker;

(*e*) what constitutes suitable and available employment for the worker; and

(*f*) such other factors as may be prescribed in the regulations.

To put these requirements into practice, the Board will first determine whether the worker has actual post-injury earnings. Unless the Board has some reason not to be satisfied with the work being performed by the worker, these earnings will be used as the estimate of the worker's post-injury earning capacity.

If the worker is not working, the Board will look to the projected earnings associated with the labour market re-entry plan (vocational rehabilitation plan) that the worker is involved with, was involved with, or should, in the Board's view, have been involved with, to estimate the worker's post-injury earning capacity.

Where the worker was not offered a labour market re-entry plan because to the accident employer offered suitable work to the worker, which the worker declined or which came to an end for reasons not associated with the work-related injury, the Board will usually estimate the worker's post-injury earning capacity by referring to the wages of the job that was offered.

The Board has developed a number of policies regarding what constitutes suitable work for the purpose of "early and safe return to work with the accident employer" and for the purpose of developing labour market re-entry plans. These policies changed significantly as of January 1, 1998, the same date that most of the changes associated with the *Workplace Safety and Insurance Act, 1997* came into effect. Although there were no significant legislative changes to the requirements for determining the quantum of FEL awards, the determinations of suitability under the newer policies, which will affect the quantum of FEL awards, place much less importance on factors outside of the physical suitability of the job.

In considering Board policies regarding rehabilitation objectives and their role in determining the level of FEL benefit entitlement, it is important to note that while the policy changes effective as of January 1, 1998, appear to remove any considerations of employment availability, employment availability is still a requirement under subs. 43(7) of the *Workers' Compensation Act* before the estimated earnings associated with an employment may be taken into consideration in setting the FEL rate.

Where the Board does not have acceptable actual employment earnings to use in the FEL determination, the Board will determine the worker's likely post-injury earning capacity by categorizing the worker's future employment within specific categories defined by the National Occupational Classification (NOC) system which is administered by Human Resources Development Canada (HRDC). The Board will then seek wage data from HRDC's "wage book" regarding the specific NOC code classifications within which, it is anticipated, the worker will be working. To determine the accuracy of the Board's selection of NOC codes and wages, it is useful to examine the classification descriptions contained in the NOC Code manuals. It is also useful to request wage rate information regarding identified NOC codes, directly from HRDC.

The Appeals Tribunal has disapproved of the use of nominal daily or weekly wage rate information to estimate annual earnings from full time employment in occupations characterized by seasonal employment.

The gross wages associated with the vocational rehabilitation plan should reflect the years of experience that the injured worker has in that occupation or the transferrable occupational experience the worker brings to that occupation. Usually, at the time of the first determination of FEL benefits, injured workers have no experience in the projected occupation and the use of entry level wages is contemplated. It is assumed that the wage rates at the lower range of the wages associated with the chosen NOC code are entry level wage rates.

(b) The Effect of Other Workers' Compensation Benefits

The FEL determination is made independently of a consideration of any other workers' compensation benefits being paid to a worker. The Board will not blend in pensions, temporary disability compensation benefits or other FEL awards when conducting a FEL determination. Similarly, if a worker receiving a FEL award suffers a new work accident, any compensation for temporary disability is calculated without regard to the existing FEL award.

(c) The Effect of Post-Injury Change Unrelated to the Injury

Where a worker experiences a setback in his or her ability to return to work following a work injury that is not related to the work injury, the determination of the post-injury earning capacity is unaffected by any post-injury changes that are not directly related to the work-related injury. On the other hand, the Board is willing, where possible, to modify the vocational rehabilitation assistance offered to a worker who suffers a post-injury change unrelated to the work injury. This is one instance where the earnings associated with the vocational objective will not be used to determine the worker's FEL benefit. The Board will instead use the estimated earnings of the vocational objective that the worker would have pursued but for the post-injury change.

(d) FEL Sustainability Benefits

If the worker is in a Labour Market Re-entry Plan and the vocational objective likely pays net average earnings equalling or exceeding the worker's pre-injury earnings, the worker is entitled to a nominal FEL award (called a FEL sustainability benefit) and a FEL supplement for the duration of the program. The sustainability amount is set at one dollar per year. There is no statutory reference to a sustainability benefit. By granting a "token" FEL award the Board can then pay a FEL supplement to provide income support.

An employed worker with expected post-injury earnings in excess of the pre-injury earnings may be awarded a sustainability FEL benefit. This award will usually occur where there is uncertainty regarding the worker's ability to continue performing the job or where the job the worker has returned to is an accommodated one. This practice was more significant in the period prior to January 1, 1998, where, if the worker was unable to continue in the post-injury job, the complete absence of a FEL would prevent the Board from providing a FEL supplement to support the worker's continuing involvement with some other form of medical or vocational rehabilitation.

To protect the Board's ability to pay a medical rehabilitation supplement where required, a sustainability FEL might be also be awarded to a worker who previously had a wage loss FEL but whose entitlement would otherwise be set at zero on a review. This happens because the Board will not pay temporary benefits to a worker where FEL benefits have previously been paid in the claim.

The Appeals Tribunal's acceptance of the rationale for the sustainability benefit has been mixed. However, a consensus view has emerged that the sustainability award is legal.

(e) The Effect of Canada Pension Plan/Quebec Pension Plan Income

The requirement that the Board take into consideration "any disability payments the worker may receive for the injury under the Canada Pension Plan or the Quebec Pension Plan" has caused a significant controversy within the workers' compensation system.

It is Board policy to add C.P.P./Q.P.P. payments to the worker's post-injury net average earnings capacity as otherwise determined. To determine whether C.P.P./Q.P.P. payments received are in relation to the work-related injury, the FEL decision-maker is required to examine any relevant information that may indicate the basis for such payments (especially medical reports). In practice, it is commonly found that the entire payment is in relation to the work-related injury.

A number of arguments have been raised questioning the authority of the Board to take C.P.P. disability benefits into account at all to reduce FEL entitlement. However, these arguments have been unsuccessful. The narrower issue of whether or not the Board should continue its current practice of stacking C.P.P. disability benefits with deemed earnings to estimate a worker's post-injury earnings capacity is apparently still under review by the Board. The Board's history in this regard is varied. The Appeals Tribunal has itself not been entirely consistent but has previously indicated its acceptance of an earlier Board practice of taking only C.P.P. disability benefits into account to calculate FEL benefits when the Board had accepted that a worker was unemployable.

5. FUTURE ECONOMIC LOSS AWARD SUPPLEMENTS (AND RECURRENCES)

In addition to entitlement to a FEL benefit, an injured worker may also have entitlement to FEL supplementary benefits while co-operating in a Board-authorized medical rehabilitation program, early and safe return to work program or labour market re-entry plan. For decisions on or after January 1, 1998, for a supplement to be payable the medical rehabilitation program, early and safe return to work program or labour market re-entry plan must begin within 24 months of the initial FEL decision or within 12 months of a determination, under subs. 47(9) of the *Workplace Safety and Insurance Act, 1997*, that there has been a significant deterioration of the worker's permanent impairment. Time limits on the payment of FEL supplements are not strictly construed by Board policy, particularly in the case of medical rehabilitation supplements.

The supplement is calculated to ensure that the FEL benefit plus supplement equals 90 per cent of the worker's pre-injury net average earnings. The Board has no discretion to award partial supplements. However, a "full" supplement may be paid for only part of a month.

A worker who wishes to receive a FEL supplement for a period when the Board has not authorized one, for example following the termination of a post-injury job, may obtain FEL supplementary benefits by achieving an opening or re-opening of VR services (LMRP or ESRTW). Once entitlement to these VR services is established, and if other entitlement criteria are satisfied, the entitlement to the FEL supplement follows. Should such services be denied and a subsequent appeal results in a finding that the denial of such services was incorrect, the Board will examine whether or not the worker was involved in a self-directed VR program to determine if supplementary entitlement should be granted retroactively. Good documentation of self-directed VR efforts is usually required.

FEL supplements are used to compensate FEL recipients who are co-operating in Board authorized medical rehabilitation programs as it is not possible for such workers to obtain temporary benefits for recurrences or deteriorations of the compensable condition once FEL benefits have been paid. The Board defines a medical rehabilitation program as any course of medical or paramedical treatment or care for a work injury, or for a recurrence or deterioration of a work injury that is required to bring the worker to maximum medical rehabilitation (MMR) so that the worker may achieve, or return to, suitable work. Board adjudicators quite often will mistakenly indicate that FEL supplements for medical rehabilitation programs are payable only where the worker can demonstrate total disability. Board policy only requires that the medical rehabilitation is necessary for the worker to achieve, or to return to, suitable work.

The payment of a supplement may mask the full impact of the level at which a FEL benefit is set. Problems with the level at which the FEL benefit is set may not be immediately apparent to a worker. This may result in limitation period problems if the worker's decision to appeal a FEL award occurs only after the

FEL supplement is discontinued. However, the elimination of statutorily fixed times for review may lessen this problem as there is now a much greater opportunity for the worker to request a new FEL decision upon the termination of the supplement.

6. THE FUTURE ECONOMIC LOSS REVIEWS

(a) General

As a general rule, the same principles that apply to the initial determination of a FEL benefit also apply at the subsequent FEL reviews. However, some specific considerations apply to the redetermination process.

Since January 1, 1998, FEL reviews at points other than the fixed review points are possible based on changes of circumstance that are considered to be "material". According to Board policy "material" change means a 5 per cent or greater change in the workers post-injury earnings or a change in the level of C.P.P. or Q.P.P. benefits at any amount. The worker and the accident employer should receive a written decision from the Board outlining the basis for the change in the FEL award. This decision will be the starting point for any objection to the FEL award.

A worker who is unemployed at the time of a review for reasons unrelated to the injury has his or her estimated post-injury earnings determined by reference to the greater of the estimated earnings (or actual earnings if employed at suitable work) at the earlier FEL determination, the earnings identified at the completion of the Labour Market Re-entry Plan, or the most recent report of material change.

For an increase in a FEL to take place as a result of a reduction in gross wages it must be established that the decrease is related to the work-related injury. This decrease could be caused by, but is not limited to, a recurrence or deterioration of the worker's condition, or a job change due to the work-related impairment. Board policies do not deal with the effect on FEL benefits of an injured worker being terminated from accommodated employment. However, there may be circumstances where such a termination would result in a recalculation of the wage loss entitlement.

(b) Effect of No Permanent Impairment

Prior to the passage of the *Workplace Safety and Insurance Act, 1997*, the Board would commonly terminate FEL benefits at the first review following a determination that the worker was not entitled to a NEL benefit. This approach to FEL entitlement was commonly referred to as "zero NEL, zero FEL". Despite this prevalent practice, given the provisions of subs. 43(1) of the *Workers' Compensation Act*, it was possible for a worker to argue that the zero NEL did not always indicate an absence of impairment, particularly in cases of chemical sensitization in the workplace or where there were repeated recurrences of disability when a worker was returned to face workplace exposures.

As a result of changes in the *Workplace Safety and Insurance Act, 1997*, for injuries on or after January 1, 1998, there is now statutory authority for a zero NEL, zero loss of earnings (LOE) policy. However, this change in the Act was not made applicable to injuries occurring prior to January 1, 1998. The Board has, through policy, stated that it will be taking the same approach to FEL benefits as it does to LOE benefits whenever a worker receives a zero NEL rating. This means that where there is a zero NEL, there will always be a zero FEL. It would appear likely that the authority of the Board to enforce such a policy will be challenged.

7. COMMUTATION OF THE FUTURE ECONOMIC LOSS AWARD

The Board may commute FEL payments if the FEL payments are less than 10 per cent of the worker's full loss of earnings and the 60-month period following the initial determination of the FEL benefit during which a redetermination may take place has expired. If a worker has multiple FEL awards each at 10 per cent or less, the Board will treat each award separately for the purposes of commutation.

Board policy is that following the Board's review of the FEL award in the 60th month after D1, it informs the worker of payment options. The worker is allowed eight weeks to reach a decision, during which monthly payments are continued. If after that no election has been made, the Board will automatically commute the award. As is Board practice with lump sums payable in other contexts, the Board will not reconstitute a FEL award that has been paid as a lump sum and reinstate monthly payments.

It is not clear if the Board has the authority to commute FEL awards greater than 10 per cent. Although s. 43 does not deal explicitly with this situation, it could be argued that s. 27, which deals with commutations generally, applies. On the other hand, it could be argued that subs. 43(14), which directs monthly or other periodic payments except as provided in subs. (15), precludes commutations of FEL awards greater than 10 per cent. There is no Board policy on this point.

8. THE "OLD AGE SECURITY OPTION" FOR OLDER WORKERS

As an alternative to the usual method of calculating FEL entitlement, subs. 43(8) of the *Workers' Compensation Act* provides that a worker may elect an amount equal to the full monthly pension for Old Age Security (OAS), if the worker

- Is at least 55 years of age when the Board determines or reviews the FEL award;
- Has not returned to work; and

- Is unlikely, in the opinion of the Board, to benefit from a VR program which could help the worker return to work.

This provision is likely to be of assistance only to injured workers who have been unable to benefit from a program of rehabilitation due to a subsequently arising non-compensable condition or to injured workers whose pre-injury net average earnings are very low.

The Board has developed policies to precisely define who is eligible to request the OAS option and to deal with such matters as the timing of the election to receive OAS benefits and the possibility of re-election of regular FEL benefits.

9. THE IMPACT OF PRE-EXISTING CONDITIONS ON THE FUTURE ECONOMIC LOSS AWARD

Second Injury and Enhancement Fund (SIEF) relief is available to employers for costs associated with FEL benefits.

Generally, the Board accepts injured workers as they are at the time of an injury. Whatever the pre-existing disability might have been, the worker's pre-injury earnings are what they are prior to the injury and demonstrate an earnings capacity that existed regardless of the disability. The estimated post-injury earnings must also take into account limitations imposed by the worker's pre-existing disability. However, as mentioned earlier, projected post-injury wages are estimated without reference to non-compensable post-injury changes in the worker's medical condition.

As discussed in Chapter 18, Non-Economic Loss Awards, there may be situations where a worker with a permanent impairment from a work-related injury ends up being awarded a zero per cent NEL award because of the manner in which the Board integrates a pre-existing pre-1990 permanent disability award with the NEL awards for the subsequent injury. If not appealed, the worker could end up with a zero FEL, despite the fact that the worker has suffered a permanent economic loss as a result of the second injury. This is a further illustration of the difficulties that may be presented by the Board's zero NEL, zero FEL policy.

On the other hand, if the reality of the situation is that the worker's condition has resolved to the level of impairment arising from the first compensable injury, there should be no FEL benefit payable as a result of the subsequent injury which did not cause an ongoing impairment.

10. THE RETIREMENT PENSION

For each worker in receipt of a FEL benefit the Board sets aside an additional amount equivalent to 10 per cent of all FEL payments made to the worker for the purpose of providing the worker with a retirement pension. Where FEL payments are made retroactively, so are the contributions to the FEL retirement benefit.

The retirement pension is payable to the worker at the age of 65. The value of the pension is the value of the contributions made on behalf of the injured worker plus the accumulated growth generated by the investments made with the contributions. The Board sends periodic notices to injured workers to update them on the value of their retirement pensions.

Upon approaching the age of 65 an injured worker is presented with a list of options regarding the manner in which the retirement pension shall be paid. The options the Board makes available are dictated by regulation. The worker, and the worker's spouse in some instances, choose amongst various options including survivorship of the pension, minimum guarantee periods, and alternative levels of inflation protection. However, if the annual value of the pension is less than a minimum amount, the benefit is paid as a lump sum. The minimum amount was $1,000 per year in 1990. This amount is partially indexed by inflation.

If the worker dies before beginning to receive the retirement pension, the spouse and dependants of the worker may receive benefits as set out by regulation under the Act unless survivor benefits are payable.

11. OBJECTIONS

Objections to FEL decisions and to the underlying vocational rehabilitation and return to work decisions are now, following January 1, 1998, the subject of time limits.

The Board's policy document regarding objections is titled "Objections to FEL Determination" and the entire policy is as follows:

> Any worker or employer whose interests are affected by compensation for future loss of earnings arising from a work-related injury has a right to object to that decision based on the circumstances as they were, at the time of original determination.
>
> The issues on objection may be that
>
> — the Board did not properly consider all the evidence available at the time of the determination or review, or that
> — the Board did not properly interpret the available evidence in calculating the worker's future loss of earnings.
>
> These guidelines apply to all decisions made on or after January 1, 1991.

There may be issues on objection other than those outlined in the policy. For example, the date of determination of the FEL award could be challenged on the basis that it was inappropriate. An objection could also be based on an argument that the Board did not have sufficient evidence to make a fair and realistic determination of projected post-injury net average earnings.

To determine what evidence should be taken into consideration in a FEL objection, it may be helpful to distinguish between economic circumstances for projection purposes and a worker's medical impairment. While the Board might be justifiably reluctant to consider evidence of changed economic circumstances since the FEL determination involves a projection, a reluctance to accept new medical evidence clarifying a worker's impairment would be less well-founded. All Appeals Tribunal decisions that have considered this issue appear to agree that the FEL decision must be a projection. Exactly what this means for the consideration of new evidence is, however, still somewhat unclear.

Now that FEL review dates are more flexible than they were prior to January 1, 1998, it may be the case that a request for a new FEL decision to deal with changed circumstances may provide a more satisfactory way of dealing with an inappropriate FEL award than an objection to a FEL decision which may have been fine when it was first made but which has since failed to address the changed circumstance.

An objection to a FEL award may have its roots in a VR decision (*e.g.*, that the worker has not been co-operative) rather than a FEL decision *per se*. It may be appropriate to pursue an objection to the VR decision, and if that is successful, request the FEL decision-maker to reconsider the FEL decision in light of the fresh VR ruling. If a delay in pursuing a FEL objection is anticipated, care must be taken to avoid limitation period problems.

CHAPTER 17

Loss of Earnings Benefits

1. INTRODUCTION

With the passage of Bill 99, *Workplace Safety and Insurance Act, 1997*, a new benefits scheme was introduced for workers hurt on or after January 1, 1998 who experience a loss of earnings called the Loss of Earnings (LOE) benefit. Sections 43, 44, and 45 are the relevant statutory provisions. Unlike the benefits schemes for workers hurt prior to January 1, 1998 (temporary benefits/permanent pension, temporary benefits/future economic loss (FEL)) the new scheme covers both initial and permanent loss of earnings situations.

The LOE benefit is 85 per cent of the difference between the worker's pre-injury net average earnings and the worker's post-injury net average earnings from suitable employment or business, either actual or deemed.

2. DURATION OF BENEFIT

The employer is required under s. 24 to pay the worker's full wages and employment benefits for the day of injury. It is Board policy to presume that this has occurred unless informed otherwise. LOE benefits start the day following the injury, or whenever the loss of earnings begins. Benefits continue until the earliest of:

- The day on which the worker's loss of earnings ceases;
- The day on which the worker reaches ages 65 (if the worker was less than 63 years old on the date of injury);
- Two years after the date of injury if the worker was 63 or older on the date of injury;
- The day on which the worker is no longer impaired as a result of the injury.

It is also Board policy to terminate LOE benefits where it is determined that the worker has no impairment following a NEL (see Chapter 18, Non-Economic Loss Awards) assessment. Specifically, Board policy in cases of recovery is to terminate the LOE benefit the day after a health care practitioner advises the worker to return to full employment. If the Board makes the determination that there is no longer an impairment, presumably payments would stop as of that day. In the 0 per cent NEL situation, the LOE benefit may continue until the worker is "fully notified", but only to a maximum of two weeks. The benefit will be paid for the full month when the worker turns 65.

LOE benefits can be reduced or suspended pursuant to subs. 43(7) if the worker fails to co-operate in:

* Health care measures;
* His or her early and safe return to work (see Chapter 21, Labour Market Re-Entry Services);
* All aspects of a labour market re-entry (LMR) assessment or plan (see Chapter 21, Labour Market Re-Entry Services).

The Board interprets health care measures to be those recommended by the attending health care practitioner and approved by the Board. Co-operation in early and safe return to work (ESRTW) includes contacting and keeping in touch with the accident employer, fulfilling Board reporting obligations, participating in health care measures, and working towards identifying an appropriate job. A return to work may be possible while a worker is still undergoing treatment, in the Board's view.

3. CALCULATION AND FREQUENCY OF PAYMENTS

LOE benefits are subject to the minimum and maximum amounts set out in the Act. Note that the minimum amount of a full LOE benefit is the lesser of the statutory minimum or the worker's net average earnings before the injury. (See subss. 43(2) and 54(1) and Chapter 12, Earnings Basis.)

Board policy is that for the first 12 weeks of LOE benefits, the benefit is based on the worker's average earnings from each of the worker's employers at the time of the injury. This is called the short-term earnings basis. If the worker receives 12 consecutive weeks of LOE benefits, the benefit is re-calculated using the worker's long-term earnings basis. This re-calculation could result in a change in the LOE payment. (See Chapter 12, Earnings Basis.)

By virtue of subs. 43(5) pre-injury net average earnings are adjusted annually by the alternate indexing factor. Accordingly, the LOE benefit can change annually. Any disability payments paid to the worker under the C.P.P. or the Q.P.P. in regard to the injury will be considered part of post-injury net average earnings, as required by subs. 43(5). This inclusion will lead to a reduction in the LOE benefit payable. Retroactive awards will trigger retroactive adjustments in the LOE benefit. LOE benefits are annually indexed to partially reflect changes in the cost of living.

LOE benefits are paid bi-weekly in the first 24 months after the injury. From then on the payments are monthly.

4. FULL LOE BENEFITS

Full LOE benefits are payable if the nature or seriousness of the injury completely prevents the worker from returning to any type of work, or if the worker has not returned to work (and is still impaired) and is participating in ESRTW or LMR activities. No time limit exists as such regarding duration of full LOE payments. In particular, while subs. 43(4) directs the Board to deem post injury net average earnings, there is no fixed determination date or deadline. The deeming date is tied to the date a worker completes a LMR plan (subs. 43(4)(*a*)), or to the date that the Board determines that the worker does not require a LMR plan (subs. 43(4)(b)). There are review provisions, however, and these are discussed below.

5. PARTIAL LOE BENEFITS

Partial LOE benefits are payable where there has been a return to work at a wage loss or where the Board has deemed post-accident net average earnings. Note that there can be a return to work prior to the completion of an LMR plan, in which case the LOE benefit will be adjusted to reflect any earnings. If the employment ceases and co-operation in the plan continues, there is no reason why the LOE benefit could not be readjusted upwards.

Board policy is to calculate post-accident net average earnings using either deemed earnings or actual earnings, whichever is greater. Workers and their representatives would be well advised to consider this point while a Board decision-maker is determining suitable employment or business (SEB) or the LMR plan employment objective. There may be a gap of many years between this determination and the implementation of partial LOE benefits, so the effect of the determination on future LOE payments may not be appreciated initially by workers and their representatives.

Partial LOE benefits may also be payable during any periods of worker non-co-operation. Subsection 43(7) is silent on the level of benefits payable under these circumstances, and so to a great extent is Board policy. However, the Board's position is that non-co-operation in ESRTW will result in a reduction in LOE benefits, as if the worker had returned to appropriate employment (and its wage) if such employment has been identified or arranged by the accident employer. If no such employment exists, Board policy is silent on how any LOE benefit reduction will be determined. If there is non-co-operation in an LMR plan the Board reduces the LOE benefits to what they would have been had the worker completed the plan.

6. REVIEWS OF PAYMENTS

(a) Yearly Reviews

Subsection 44(1) authorizes the Board to review LOE payments to a worker every year, and the Board can confirm, vary, or discontinue the payments. It does not seem that the Board intends to do this (see (c) Variable Reviews below).

Subsection 44(2) restricts the Board's review powers. It provides that the Board shall not review LOE payments more than 72 months after the date of the worker's injury, unless, if before the 72-month period expires, the worker has failed to notify the Board of a material change in circumstances or has engaged in claim-related fraud or misrepresentation.

(b) Material Change In Circumstances Reviews

Subsection 44(1) also authorizes the Board to review LOE payments to a worker if a material change in circumstances occurs. The subs. 44(2) review restriction also applies. If a material change in circumstances occurs after the 72-month period, the Board could probably reconsider an LOE decision pursuant to s. 121 which reads: "The Board may reconsider any decision made by it and may confirm, amend or revoke it. The Board may do so at any time if it considers it advisable to do so."

The Board has commented that the LOE benefit review system is largely driven by material change reporting. Subsection 23(3) provides that a person receiving benefits, or who may be entitled to do so, shall notify the Board of a material change in circumstances in connection with the entitlement within ten days after the material change occurs.

The following types of changes that must be reported include, but are not limited to:

Changes in a person's medical status

- Improvement or deterioration in the work injury;
- Need for further or different type of treatment, or surgery;
- Termination of treatment;
- Need for, or a change to assistive or prosthetic device.

Changes in a person's earnings/income

- Wages from employment increase or decrease;
- Begins to receive C.P.P./Q.P.P. disability benefits arising in whole, or in part, from the work-related injury.

Changes in a person's work status

- Job duties or hours have been altered due to work-related injury;
- Employment has been terminated due to work-related injury;
- Has retired or otherwise voluntarily moved him- or herself from the workforce.

Changes in a person's availability or co-operation in health care, ESRTW activities, or LMR programs

- Has changed address or left the province;
- Has been sentenced to prison or is imprisoned;
- Has a non-work-related medical condition that impedes ability to work;
- Work visa has expired or worker is about to be deported.

Changes in optional insurance coverage

- Has optional insurance coverage, and the earnings used to elect the amount of coverage change.

Once a material change is reported, a Board decision-maker has to decide if it is sufficient to affect a worker's entitlement to LOE benefits. The Board uses a 5 per cent threshold test regarding earnings changes. A decision-maker compares recently reported gross earnings with the escalated gross earnings being used to pay the LOE benefit. A 5 per cent or greater change in the gross earnings is considered a material change. LOE benefits will be changed accordingly as long as it is also determined that the reduction in post accident earnings is due to the work-related injury, or that any additional income can be considered part of a worker's post-accident earnings. The 5 per cent threshold test does not apply to the receipt of C.P.P./Q.P.P. disability benefits arising in whole or in part from the injury. It also does not apply if there has been a recovery of full earnings where the LOE benefit was less than 5 per cent.

(c) Variable Reviews

It is Board policy to review LOE benefits if, at any time during the first 6 years of a claim, a period of 24 months of continuous payment passes in which no benefit review has taken place. The worker will be asked to provide earnings and employment status information. If this information still has not been provided after two follow-ups, the LOE benefit will be suspended.

(d) Final Reviews

It is Board policy to conduct a "final review" of the LOE benefit shortly before six years post-injury. At 63 months a decision-maker will initiate the review by requesting earnings and employment status information from the worker. If there is no response after 2 follow-ups, benefits will be withheld at 67 months. The LOE benefit will not be restored until a "full review" can take place. If this review does not occur by the 72-month point, the LOE benefit is "locked in" at $0, subject to change only if the worker later reports a material change that occurred before the end of the 72nd month.

(e) Older Workers and the No Review Option

Subsection 44(3) provides that older workers may direct the Board not to review their LOE payments if:

- They are 55 or older when the Board determines that they are entitled to LOE payments;
- They have reached maximum medical recovery (MMR) (as defined and determined by the Board);
- Their labour market re-entry plan has been fully implemented.

Subsection 44(4) provides that this direction must be given within 30 days after the later of:

- The date on which MMR is reached;
- The date on which the LMR plan is fully implemented.

Because MMR is determined by the Board, a worker may be unaware of the MMR date. Further, the Board frequently determines the MMR date retroactively. It would have been preferable if the provision read "the date on which *the worker is advised* that MMR has been reached". On this point Board policy simply provides that:

- Decision-makers are responsible for ensuring that workers are notified of their "no review" eligibility by letter as soon as possible once they reach MMR or complete the LMR plan;
- Workers have 30 calendar days from the MMR date or LMR plan completion date to respond.

By virtue of subs. 44(5), once the direction is given, the worker is entitled to the same LOE payments until age 65. The direction is irrevocable. However, subs. 44(6) provides that the Board shall review the LOE payment (only) if before the direction was given the worker failed to notify the Board of a material change in circumstances or engaged in fraud or misrepresentation with regard to the claim.

What follows from subss. 43(1) and 44(5) is also stated in Board policy: workers between the ages of 63 and 65 years old who choose the "no review" option are entitled to receive LOE benefits only until age 65, and workers 65 years of age or older are not eligible for the option. It is hard to understand why a worker 63 or older at the time of injury would want to choose the "no review" option, thereby limiting the potential LOE benefit entitlement.

7. COMMUTATIONS

The circumstances under which LOE benefits can be commuted are set out in s. 62 of the Act. The relevant provisions read:

(2) Subject to subsection (3), the Board may commute payments to a worker under section 43 (loss of earnings) and pay him or her a lump sum instead,

> (*a*) if the amount of the payments is 10 per cent or less of the worker's full loss of earnings; and
> (*b*) if the 72-month period for reviewing payments to the worker has expired or if the Board is not permitted to review the payments.

(3) The worker referred to in subsection (2) may elect to receive periodic payments instead of the lump sum, and if he or she does so, the Board shall make the periodic payments. The election is irrevocable.

The Board has policy on this topic. Essentially, the Board intends to send letters to eligible workers explaining the option and providing the value of the commuted benefit. These workers will receive two monthly payments after the letter is mailed, and then, if no preference is expressed, the Board will commute the benefit. For older workers who have chosen the "no review" option and whose payments may still be biweekly, four further biweekly payments will be made and, if no preference is expressed, the Board will commute the benefit.

If a worker is eligible for LOE benefits in more than one claim, the Board treats them as discrete entities, so that when determining eligibility for a commutation, each LOE benefit in each claim is considered individually. This is in marked contrast to the Board's position regarding pre-Bill 162 pensions (see Chapter 11, Claims and Payments and Chapter 14, Permanent Disability Benefits).

8. RECURRENCES

This topic is dealt with in Chapter 6, Entitlement: Personal Injury by Accident. The concern in this chapter is with the LOE payments implications of a compensable recurrence.

If there is a recurrence within six years of the accident (or disablement) date, the Board could review the LOE payments and make appropriate adjustments, unless the worker has chosen the "no review" option. After that, a recurrence will not affect LOE payments because of the limitation in subs. 44(2). Board policy seems to be that even if there are no LOE payments at the time of a recurrence, a recurrence six years or more following the accident date cannot trigger LOE payments at that point in time. This decision may not follow from subs. 44(2), depending upon how the wording "the Board shall not review the payments" is interpreted. If there are no LOE payments in a claim, is a consideration of entitlement following a recurrence a review of "the payments" in that claim?

It is noted in Board policy that even if it is too late for LOE payments, there may still be entitlement to further treatment, or a re-determination of the worker's NEL benefit following a compensable recurrence.

9. THE RETIREMENT PENSION

Fairly detailed retirement pension provisions are set out in s. 45. Note that these provisions apply only to post-January 1, 1998 claims.

Workers under 64 years of age at the date of injury who have received LOE payments for 12 continuous months are entitled to have the Board set aside an amount equal to 5 per cent of every subsequent LOE payment. They are also entitled to contribute another 5 per cent of their own money to the amount being set aside. If this election is made, subs. 45(4) directs the Board to deduct the worker's contribution from each LOE payment.

10. OBJECTIONS

Objections to LOE decisions and any related decisions are the subject of time limits set out in s. 120.

Many issues and decision points overlap for workers hurt before and after January 1, 1998. Workers and their representatives would be well advised to keep this in mind when considering or preparing an objection. Some of the more obvious overlaps are:

- Determinations regarding co-operation;
- Determinations regarding the earnings basis;
- Determinations of the date of injury/disablement;
- Determinations of the seriousness of the injury and/or stages of recovery (including the MMR date);
- Determinations regarding material change in circumstances;
- Determinations regarding recurrences versus new injuries.

In the early days of policy development and interpretation with regard to LOE and related issues, a certain amount of confusion and revision exists at the Board. As a preliminary step in an objection, it may make sense to double-check that the relevant policy has been applied and that the decision-maker is aware of all relevant factors, policies and legislative provisions.

CHAPTER 18

Non-Economic Loss Awards

1. INTRODUCTION

The Non-Economic Loss award (NEL) is intended to compensate injured workers for the effects of their permanent impairments other than those associated with wage loss, health care costs, or rehabilitation. Although not precisely correct, the award is sometimes referred to as an award for pain and suffering. The award is payable regardless of whether the worker suffers any wage loss as a result of the injury.

The NEL award was introduced into the compensation system on January 1, 1990. The essence of the NEL award remained virtually unchanged with the introduction of the *Workplace Safety and Insurance Act, 1997* for injuries on or after January 1, 1998. Although previously the NEL co-existed and complemented the Future Economic Loss (FEL) wage loss benefit, it now co-exists in the compensation system with the Loss of Earnings (LOE) benefit. However, the procedures associated with the NEL determination process, for injuries before and after January 1, 1998, were substantially changed and simplified with the more recent Act.

The NEL award is payable only to workers who suffer permanent impairments. Permanent impairment is often referred to as simply "P.I." and is defined under subs. 45 (1) of the *Workplace Safety and Insurance Act, 1997*, as follows:

> "permanent impairment" means impairment that continues to exist after the worker reaches maximum medical recovery.

Impairment is defined as a physical or functional abnormality or loss (including disfigurement) which results from an injury and any psychological damage arising from the abnormality or loss.

2. DETERMINING WHEN MAXIMUM MEDICAL RECOVERY OCCURS

The Board monitors a claim in order to determine when a worker has achieved Maximum Medical Recovery (MMR). It is the achievement of MMR that triggers the NEL determination process for workers with residual impairments. However, a determination that MMR has been achieved with no residual PI means that the Board is of the view that no NEL award is payable. The date of MMR is also when a NEL payment is regarded as due by the Board. Interest is payable on the NEL award between the date of MMR and the date of payment.

Workers are considered to have reached MMR when it is not likely that there will be any further significant improvement in their medical condition. However, once the MMR date has been identified, the Board may change its determination of the MMR date based upon new medical information indicating that further treatment is likely to improve the worker's condition. Generally speaking, a worker with multiple impairments from one claim will only be assigned one MMR date. However, in some cases of delayed recognition of an additional impairment, a second MMR date may be set for the purpose of starting the NEL determination process regarding the additional impairment. A NEL award may be set aside if it is determined that the NEL assessment took place prior to MMR being reached.

3. DETERMINING THE PERCENTAGE IMPAIRMENT

(a) The Steps Required to Assign a NEL Percentage Rating

The first thing to be done in calculating the amount of the NEL award is to express the effects of the work related permanent impairment as a percentage of total impairment of the person. This process consists of three steps:

- the medical assessment of the injured worker is conducted to provide a NEL medical assessment report;
- a percentage impairment is assigned to the permanent impairment by application of the prescribed rating schedule to the worker's permanent impairment as described in the NEL medical assessment report, with regard to the other health information about the worker on file with the Board;
- adjustments to the NEL percentage are made to account for pre-existing impairments.

(b) Medical Assessment of the Worker

The Board may, and usually does, require a worker to undergo a NEL medical assessment after the worker reaches MMR. The requirement may be waived in exceptional cases such as when workers move from Ontario or are too ill to attend a NEL medical, or die before the NEL medical can take place.

The worker selects a physician from a roster maintained by the Board to perform such assessments. The Board does not provide the worker with the names of all doctors on the roster but instead provides the worker with a list naming at least three roster physicians who practice in an appropriate area of clinical expertise and within the worker's region. If there are not enough suitable physicians in a worker's region, the Board may include on the list the name(s) of physicians from another region which is convenient for the worker. If the worker does not make the selection within 30 days after the Board gives the worker a copy of the roster, the Board shall select the physician.

The Board requires that the physicians on the list provided to the worker must not:

- Be employed by the Board;
- Have examined the worker for the same condition;
- Have treated the worker or a member of the worker's family;
- Have acted as a consultant in the treatment of the worker or as a consultant to the employer; or
- Be, or have been, a partner of a physician who has done any of the above.

These conditions may be waived for workers who live in small or remote communities, or by consent of the worker and employer.

The worker may be eligible for reimbursement of travel costs to attend the NEL medical in accordance with the Board's policies on travel expenses. The worker is also eligible for compensation for wage loss because of a required absence from work.

The physician who is selected to perform the assessment shall examine the worker and assess the extent of the worker's permanent impairment. When performing the assessment, the physician shall consider any reports by the worker's treating health professional. The physician is required to promptly give the Board a report on the assessment. The Board may request further clarification or elaboration regarding the report. The information may be obtained by phone. The collection of additional information should be noted in the Board file.

Only the Board may request a second NEL medical exam. The Board will request a second assessment if there is a significant difference between the findings of the NEL medical and the other medical information on file or if it is not possible to obtain a complete and accurate assessment. Where a second assessment is requested, the Board attempts to obtain a joint selection of a physician by the worker and the employer. However, if this is not possible within 30 days, the Board selects a physician. Once the second assessment is obtained, the first assessment report is disregarded by the Board.

The Board is required to give a copy of the assessment report to the worker and to the employer. Where there is a second assessment, it, too, is sent to the worker and the employer. Personal information irrelevant to the NEL determination is to be removed from the report before it is provided.

(c) Assigning a Percentage Impairment

The Board uses a rating schedule to assign a percentage impairment based upon the assessment report and other medical information in the file. The rating schedule used is the third edition of the American Medical Association's *Guides to the Evaluation of Permanent Impairment* (AMA *Guides*). Because there are some gaps in the types of impairments covered by the AMA *Guides* the Board has adopted its own rating scales to be used by decision-makers in conjunction with the AMA *Guides* when assessing mental and behavioural impairments (specifically, psychotraumatic disability, chronic pain disability and fibromyalgia syndrome) or when rating Hand Arm Vibration Syndrome (HAVS) or asthma.

While the AMA *Guides* appear very precise and comprehensive, difficulties often occur in using the *Guides* because of their complexity, the fact that they do not cover all types of injuries, and the fact that some injuries have both objective and subjective components which are not easily evaluated by the *Guides*. A significant amount of academic writing has been done on the strengths and shortcomings of the AMA *Guides*.

In addition to any other concerns expressed about the accuracy and fairness of the AMA *Guides*, it must be noted that their application to any given claim can be very complex. The efforts of the Board's adjudicators to transform the information provided by the Board's assessors into a percentage using the AMA *Guides* are documented in individual claims on the NEL Assessment Worksheets in the Board's claim file. It is perhaps as a result of the complexity of the *Guides* that it is often worthwhile for advocates to carefully review the NEL Assessment Worksheet in light of the NEL Medical Assessment and a copy of the *Guides*. Mistakes are not uncommon and may be appealed. Time limits apply.

(d) Adjustments for Pre-Existing Conditions

The NEL percentage rating assigned to an injury may be affected by a worker's pre-existing medical condition.

Conditions that did not result in pre-existing impairments that create predispositions to injury should not affect the NEL determination. These types of conditions could, however, give rise to the employer's ability to claim cost relief under the Second Injury and Enhancement Fund (SIEF). In these circumstances, an employer's entitlement to SIEF relief is dependent upon whether or not the pre-existing condition was minor, moderate, or major, with varying levels of SIEF relief according to the severity of the accident. The SIEF reduction to the employer might be 25, 50, 75, or 90 to 100 per cent.

Where the pre-existing medical condition did result in an impairment to the same area of the worker's body that was injured in the workplace accident, the NEL rating will be affected. Where it is possible for the Board to rate the earlier impairment, the rating of the worker's post-accident impairment is reduced by the rating of the pre-existing impairment. If the pre-existing impairment is not rateable, the worker's total impairment is rated and then an adjustment is made to the total impairment according to whether or not the pre-existing impairment is considered to have been minor, moderate, or major. The associated reductions are 0, 25, or 50 per cent.

Although a pre-disposition to injury or a pre-existing condition without preexisting impairment should not affect a NEL rating, perhaps due to the similarity of the concepts and structures of the NEL and SIEF percentage reductions, instances may exist where, instead of making the appropriate adjustment to the employer's SIEF relief, the Board adjudicator mistakenly makes a downward adjustment in the NEL payment to the worker. Such occurrences may be successfully appealed.

A further difficulty with the manner in which the Board accounts for pre-existing impairments in the NEL process may occur where the pre-existing impairment is rated under the pre-January 2, 1990 Act under the WCB's own Ontario Rating Schedule and not in accordance with the AMA *Guides*. Where the prior rating schedule is less generous than the AMA *Guides*, the NEL rating will be set too high. Where the prior rating schedule is more generous than the AMA *Guides*, the NEL rating will be set too low, and may, in fact, be zero despite the most recent injury having increased the worker's permanent impairment and having also resulted in increased disability. The zero NEL rating could result in the worker experiencing great difficulty in obtaining FEL or LOE entitlement.

4. CALCULATING THE DOLLAR VALUE

Subsection 46(2) of the *Workplace Safety and Insurance Act, 1997* indicates that:

> The amount of compensation is calculated by multiplying the percentage of the worker's permanent impairment from the injury (as determined by the Board) and,
>
> (a) $51,535.37 plus $1,145.63 for each year by which the worker's age at the time of the injury was less than 45; or
> (b) $51,535.37 less $1,145.63 for each year by which the worker's age at the time of the injury was greater than 45.
>
> However, the maximum amount to be multiplied by the percentage of the worker's impairment is $74,439.52 and the minimum amount is $28,631.22.

The dollar figures contained in subs. 46(2) are for injuries occurring in 1998. The dollar figures are partially indexed for inflation.

For injuries prior to January 1, 1998, the equivalent NEL dollar amounts are slightly lower and are set by reference to dollar amounts that are contained in subs. 42(2) of the *Workers' Compensation Act*. The base rate for 1990 injuries was $45,000 with the increase or decrease based on the worker's age at the time of the accident being $1,000 per year. These dollar figures were indexed for inflation (partially indexed after January 1, 1995).

The amount of indexing adjustment applied when calculating an injured worker's entitlement is determined according to the date upon which MMR is achieved.

5. FORM OF PAYMENT

Where the amount of the NEL award is less than the minimum threshold specified by the Act, the NEL award must be paid as a lump sum. In 1998, the amount specified by the *Workplace Safety and Insurance Act, 1997* was $11,456.30. Amounts specified by the Act are partially indexed for inflation.

If the NEL benefit is over the threshold amount, the NEL is paid as a monthly payment for the life of the worker unless the worker elects to receive the payment as a lump sum. For NEL awards first paid after January 1, 1998, the worker's election to receive benefits as a lump sum must be made within 30 days of being notified by the Board of the amount of the NEL award. The election is irrevocable.

6. REDETERMINATIONS

A reconsideration of a NEL award may be requested in the following circumstances:

> 47(9) If the degree of the worker's permanent impairment is greater than zero and if the worker suffers a significant deterioration in his or her condition, the worker may request that the Board redetermine the degree of the permanent impairment.
>
> 47(10) The worker is not entitled to request a redetermination until 12 months have elapsed since the most recent determination by the Board concerning the degree of his or her impairment.

To obtain a redetermination from the Board, the worker bears the burden of demonstrating that a deterioration has taken place by obtaining the appropriate medical documentation from the treating physician. The Board may pay for such reports where they contain relevant information that assists in the adjudication of the claim. The Board is of the view that, in exceptional cases, the NEL may be reviewed without applying the 12-month restriction or following the usual NEL assessment process.

If the Board accepts that a deterioration has taken place, the Board establishes a permanent worsening date (PWD) that basically acts as a new MMR date. It is the PWD date that is used to determine the appropriate level of indexing to the NEL base amounts.

The worker is entitled to an increased NEL payment based upon the increase in the percentage of the NEL assessment under the AMA *Guides*. Where the NEL is already being received as a monthly award, the increased NEL entitlement will also be paid monthly. Where the NEL had previously been paid as a lump sum, the additional award will also be paid as a lump sum except in those cases where the amount of the increase is in excess of the minimum threshold amount for monthly payments, in which case the payment would be monthly unless the worker elects to receive the payment as a lump sum.

CHAPTER 19

Health Care Benefits

1. INTRODUCTION AND GENERAL PRINCIPLES

For workers injured prior to January 1, 1998, health care benefits are authorized by subs. 50(1)(a) of the pre-1997 Act, which entitles the worker to "such health care as may be necessary as a result of the injury". In subs. 50(2) "health care" is defined as:

> medical, surgical, optometrical and dental aid, the aid of drugless practitioners under the *Drugless Practitioners Act*, the aid of chiropodists under the *Chiropody Act*, hospital and skilled nursing services, such artificial members and such appliances or apparatus as may be necessary as a result of the injury and the replacement or repair thereof when deemed necessary by the Board.

For workers injured on or after January 1, 1998, subs. 33(1) of the current Act provides:

> A worker who sustains an injury is entitled to such health care as may be necessary, appropriate and sufficient as a result of the injury and is entitled to make the initial choice of health professional for the purposes of this section.

Section 32 defines "health care" as:

> (a) professional services provided by a health care practitioner;
> (b) services provided by or at hospitals and health facilities;
> (c) drugs;
> (d) the services of an attendant;
> (e) modifications to a person's home and vehicle and other measures to facilitate independent living as in the Board's opinion are appropriate;
> (f) assistive devices and prostheses;
> (g) extraordinary transportation costs to obtain health care;
> (h) such measures to improve the quality of life of severely impaired workers as, in the Board's opinion, are appropriate.

A number of Appeals Tribunal decisions have been fairly critical of Board health care policies and have adopted a more liberal approach.

2. INDEPENDENT LIVING AND QUALITY OF LIFE MEASURES

Two provisions in the current Act broaden the Board's specific legislative authority to assist injured workers either directly or indirectly with health care needs. Section 32(e) defines "health care" as "modifications to a person's home and vehicle and other measures to facilitate independent living as in the Board's opinion are appropriate". Section 32(*h*) defines "health care" as "such measures to improve the quality of life of severely impaired workers as, in the Board's opinion, are appropriate". There is no definition of "severe impairment" in the current Act. For workers covered by the pre-1997 Act, the broad wording of ss. 50 and 52 is used by the Board to support a variety of special needs policies.

In 1998 the Board introduced an Independent Living Allowance. It is currently $2,800 yearly, retroactive to January 1, 1998, payable annually to workers with a 100 per cent pension (pre-January 2, 1990 claims) or a 60 per cent non-economic loss (NEL) award. No proof of expenditures is required. Payment could be affected by a material change in circumstances, two of which would be the worker's move to a long-term care facility, or death. This allowance is paid over and above the Attendant's Allowance (see Topic 4 below).

Additionally, the Board will pay for "independent living devices" that cost more than $250. These are defined as devices that help to restore a worker's ability to communicate, be mobile, perform personal hygiene, or prevent further injury or health complications from work injury/disease.

Both versions of the Act provide entitlement for the replacement or repair of an artificial member or apparatus of a worker that is damaged as a result of an accident in the course of employment.

3. CLOTHING ALLOWANCE

Upon application, a "Clothing Allowance" is payable on an annual basis, pursuant to subs. 50(3)(*b*) of the pre-1997 Act and subs. 39(3) of the current Act. Payments are indexed to changes in the cost-of-living. In cases of permanent disability where clothing damage is caused by the use of a Harris-type back brace, leg prosthesis, permanent leg brace, manual wheelchair, or a custom-made knee brace, a full clothing allowance may be payable. For clothing damage caused by the permanent use of an arm prosthesis, arm brace, back support or corset, cervical brace, wrist gauntlet(s), off-the-shelf knee brace, power wheelchair, forearm-supported or under-arm crutches, up to half of the value of a full clothing allowance may be payable. The dollar amounts of the allowance are obtainable from the Board.

In many instances the Board will not advise a worker that the clothing allowance exists. There is no limitation period regarding an application for a clothing allowance, and payments should be retroactive to the date the worker first purchased the device or reached maximum medical rehabilitation (MMR) (whichever is later), bearing in mind that clothing allowances have been payable only since July 1, 1975.

It is Board policy that these criteria must be met: the worker must be in receipt of a permanent impairment benefit (or a provisional award); the Board must have authorized and/or supplied the device; the worker must have worn the device one full year after reaching MMR; the worker must submit a written application annually, verifying the frequency with which the device is used and the resulting damage to clothing. A worker who uses the device less than 25 hours per week may find that the Board will award only a partial allowance according to a scale set out in the policy. Regardless of the number of devices approved by the Board, the worker is allowed no more than one clothing allowance for an upper body device and one for a lower body device per year.

The Appeals Tribunal has authorized a clothing allowance under s. 52 of the pre-1997 Act as a general rehabilitation measure.

4. ATTENDANT'S ALLOWANCE

Under subs. 50(1)(*c*) of the pre-1997 Act, a permanently totally impaired worker who has been "rendered helpless" through the impairment is eligible for such other treatment, services or attendance that may be necessary as a result of the injury. The Board pays an "Attendant's Allowance" under the authority of this provision. Under the current Act, authority for an attendant's allowance would follow from s. 32(*d*) in conjunction with subss. 33(1) and (2).

Since 1989, workers eligible for an attendant's allowance have had the amount and level of attendant care determined by the Board using an "Activities of Daily Living Scale" which is an eight-page form. The allowance will vary depending on individual worker needs for three levels of attendant care: skilled, personal, and basic/supervisory. The dollar amount is based on the total hours monthly of each level of care required with an hourly rate for each level as set by the Board. The allowance will be paid monthly, generally directly to the worker. Entitlement and quality of care are reassessed annually. The Appeals Tribunal has awarded an attendant's allowance under s. 52 of the pre-1997 Act as discretionary rehabilitation assistance, but the Panel left it to the Board to determine its duration and level.

5. TRAVEL AND RELATED EXPENSES

It has been Board policy to pay all reasonable expenses incurred when, on the direction or approval of the Board, a worker or another person designated by the Board must travel in relation to a claim. This includes transportation and related expenses incurred while attending Board-sponsored training-on-the-job programs. For claims falling under the current Act, the Board could end up with a more restrictive approach, since s. 32(*g*) specifies "extraordinary transportation costs to obtain health care".

Where the Board determines that an escort is necessary it will pay for a professional or non-professional escort (or both at once) and payment includes a *per diem* rate along with necessary travel and related expenses.

Under subs. 50(11) of the pre-1997 Act, and subs. 38(1) of the current Act, employers are obliged to furnish at their expense, to any injured worker in their employment, immediate transportation to a hospital or physician located within the area or within a reasonable distance of the place of injury or to the worker's home, where such is necessary.

6. DENTAL SERVICES

For all injured workers there is entitlement to such dental aid that may be necessary as a result of the injury. All dental services, except emergency services, must be authorized by the Board. The Board will authorize a treatment plan and if the worker does not follow it up promptly and the dental condition deteriorates as a result of the delay, entitlement may be limited to the treatment originally approved.

Board policy also deals with entitlement regarding restoration of teeth, broken dentures and the removal of diseased teeth impeding recovery from compensable dental injuries. Although there is no Board policy on dental implants, this topic has received consideration at the Appeals Tribunal.

7. REIMBURSEMENT TO WORKER

(a) Wage Loss

The Board takes the position that wage loss incurred because of absence from work for medical reasons is compensable. The Board defines "absence from work" as time off from the worker's normally scheduled working hours. The Board defines "medical reasons" as consultation with, examination by or treatment from a medical practitioner, relating to a work-related injury or disease. Time loss from work for the purpose of repairing, refitting or replacing an artificial appliance supplied by the Board is also covered. Amounts payable vary with the date of injury, and the Board is often remiss in advising workers of the availability of this compensation.

(b) Worker's Personal Health Care Insurance

Absent an assignment of benefits, the Board will reimburse a worker whose insurance policy pays for health care benefits and medical accounts, as if the account was paid for by the worker.

(c) Payment of Interest on Health Care Benefits

The Board does not pay interest on health care benefits. However, in one instance the Appeals Tribunal ruled that the worker was entitled to be reimbursed for the cost of a surgical procedure and held that interest was also payable.

8. DRUG PAYMENTS

The Board will pay for an injured worker's drugs that are necessary as a result of the injury. Entitlement for a specific drug may be accepted, rejected, or accepted for a limited period, and the worker will be so notified. Ordinarily, the Board makes payments directly to the dispensing pharmacy for drugs on the basis of cost plus a dispensing fee. If the worker has paid for accepted drugs from his or her own funds, the Board will reimburse the worker directly. Payment of these accounts is often slow. It is not unusual for the Board to perform an unannounced audit of a claimant's medications and to decide without advance notice to the claimant or the dispensing pharmacy that certain medications will no longer be paid for.

9. CHIROPRACTIC TREATMENT

Chiropractic treatment may be part of the worker's entitlement in an allowed claim, or the chiropractor may be considered the "treating physician" by the Board. The Board encourages reporting from chiropractors similar to that sought from treating physicians. Treatment will be closely monitored by the Board after 12 weeks.

Board policy on chiropractic treatment has been criticized as lacking objective criteria to assist adjudicators in determining appropriate circumstances for continued treatment. Generally, the Board will not authorize ongoing treatment if it is characterized as "palliative" or in the nature of maintenance. In some instances the Appeals Tribunal has been more generous in authorizing treatment.

10. PHYSIOTHERAPY

Physiotherapy is frequently an essential part of an injured worker's medical rehabilitation and the Board will pay for it. The initial period of physiotherapy is limited to 12 weeks. Authorization to extend physiotherapy beyond this time must be obtained from the Board by the attending physician and/or physiotherapist/physiotherapy centre and extensions will be reviewed every four weeks.

In cases of extended disability or permanent disability, ongoing physiotherapy will not be authorized unless it is felt by the Board that it will significantly improve the worker's condition.

11. HOSPITAL TREATMENT

Hospitalization services for in-patient care in public and private hospitals are paid at a rate established by the Board. Unless there are exceptional circumstances, only standard ward accommodation will be paid for.

12. SKIN DONORS

The Board has been prepared to pay to a skin donor who suffers loss of earnings: all hospital expenses plus ten dollars a day for each day in hospital.

13. HEALTH CARE FOR OUT OF PROVINCE/COUNTRY WORKERS

The Board has a detailed policy regarding necessary health care outside of Ontario which sets out entitlement guidelines and fees for both Ontario and non-Ontario residents. The Board has Memoranda of Understanding with Italy, Portugal and Greece which are applicable for workers who have transferred their residences to these countries.

14. TREATING NON-WORK-RELATED CONDITIONS TO LESSEN IMPACT OF WORK-RELATED INJURIES

The Board has interpreted s. 24 of the pre-1997 Act as authorizing it to pay for treatment of a worker's non-work-related medical condition, if, in the Board's opinion, this is the only way of avoiding heavy payment for compensation. The Board has very specific guidelines for both pre- and post-January 2, 1990 accidents.

CHAPTER 20

Survivors' Benefits

1. INTRODUCTION

There are three different legislative schemes in place to compensate the survivors of workers whose deaths are compensable.

- The survivors of workers who died before April 1, 1985 are dealt with under s. 36 of the pre-1985 Act;
- The survivors of workers injured at any time prior to January 1, 1998, and whose deaths occur on or after April 1, 1985, are dealt with under s. 35 of the most recent *Workers' Compensation Act* (injuries between January 2, 1990 and December 31, 1997) or under the substantially similar terms of s. 36 of the pre-1989 *Workers' Compensation Act* (injuries prior to January 2, 1990);
- The survivors of workers who died on or after January 1, 1998, who were also injured on or after January 1, 1998, are dealt with under s. 48 of the *Workplace Safety and Insurance Act*, 1997.

This introduction contains some discussion of relevance to all three legislative schemes. The balance of this chapter is devoted to the current scheme. Readers who are interested in the most recent earlier legislative scheme may find the discussion of the current scheme useful as there are many similarities between the most recent scheme and the current one. However, care must be exercised as there are also a significant number of differences regarding matters such as the percentage income replacement awarded, the treatment of separated spouses and the apportionment of benefits between eligible recipients.

Where there is a passage of time between the work injury and the worker's death, survivors' benefits are payable if the injury was a significant contributing factor in the worker's death.

There is an exception to the requirement that survivors' benefits are payable only where the death results from the work injury for workers injured prior to January 2, 1990 who are eligible, or who would have become eligible, to receive 100 per cent pension benefits in one claim at the time of their death.

Prior to April 1, 1985, survivors' benefits to widows and widowers under the pre-1985 legislative scheme ended upon remarriage. As of January 1, 1998, any person whose benefits were terminated for this reason may apply to the Board for reinstatement of benefits, and the Board shall reinstate the benefits, as of April 1, 1985.

The survivors of a worker injured after January 2, 1990, who are not eligible for survivors' benefits in regard to the worker's injury may qualify to receive the worker's Future Economic Loss (FEL) retirement benefits or Loss of Earnings (LOE) retirement benefits.

Representatives of a worker's estate have the right to pursue any interest that the worker had at the time of death to benefit payments the worker could have claimed, or did claim, eligibility for prior to the worker's death.

2. SURVIVORS' BENEFITS FOR DEATHS RESULTING FROM INJURIES AFTER JANUARY 1, 1998

The types of survivors' benefits paid include:

- Lump sum payments;
- Periodic payments;
- Vocational rehabilitation assistance to spouses;
- Bereavement counselling; and
- Burial expenses.

Precisely who is entitled to the lump sum and periodic payments varies with the worker's domestic circumstances at the time of death. In straightforward domestic situations, it is relatively easy to determine who is entitled to what. Examples of straightforward situations are: the worker has never had a spouse or children, or the worker has had just one spouse and all of the worker's children have been with, and reside with, that spouse.

Where the worker's domestic affairs are more complicated, determining who is entitled to what is also more complicated. In these cases, determining all of the persons who may have entitlement and defining the precise status of the various persons under the Act becomes very important.

(a) Classes of Potentially Entitled Survivors

The following are some of the people who may have entitlement to survivors' benefits under the Act:

- Spouses cohabiting with the worker at the time of death;
- Spouses not cohabiting with the worker at the time of death;
- Separated spouses;
- Persons acting in the role of a parent who are not spouses;
- Dependant children; and
- Other dependants.

The term "spouse" is no longer defined by legislation but is, instead, defined by Board policy as follows:

A spouse is either of two persons who are cohabiting in a conjugal relationship, and

> (*a*) are married to each other, or
> (*b*) are not married to each other and,
>> (*i*)   have cohabited at least for one year
>> (*ii*) are together the parents of a child and have cohabited in a relationship of some permanence, or:
>> (*iii*) have together entered into a cohabitation agreement under s. 53 of the *Family Law Act*.

Although not stated in the relevant Board policy, this definition of spouse would appear to contemplate survivors' benefits for same sex spouses.

A person who has been a spouse, referred to by Board policy as a separated spouse, may be entitled to benefits under the Act as a spouse. Entitlement exists if, immediately prior to the worker's death, the worker was required to make support or maintenance payments under a separation agreement or judicial order to a person who had been his or her spouse. In the absence of such an agreement or order, it is sufficient if the person was dependent on the worker at the time of the worker's death.

The term "child" is defined in s. 2 of the Act as having the same meaning as the definition of "child" in subs. 1(1) of the *Family Law Act*. Board policy indicates that this definition of child:

> means a person whom a parent has demonstrated a settled intention to treat as a child of his or her family, except under an arrangement where the child is placed for valuable consideration in a foster home by a person having lawful custody.

Board policy defines a "dependent child" as:

> a child of the worker who was wholly or partly dependent on the worker's earnings at the time of the worker's death. This includes a child to whom the worker has demonstrated a settled intention to treat as a child of the family.

Given this definition, Appeals Tribunal decisions dealing with the definition of dependency under the earlier versions of the Act will likely continue to be relevant here. Dependency is evaluated as of the time of death of the worker.

A child of the worker who is not yet born at the time of the worker's death is considered to be a dependent child at the time of birth.

The term "dependants" is now defined in s. 2 of the Act in such a way as to exclude dependent children of the deceased worker. The exclusion of dependent children from the definition is presumably done to achieve greater clarity in describing the differences of entitlement between dependent children and other dependants.

Only certain persons may qualify as "dependants" for the purpose of establishing entitlement under the Act. These are: parents, stepparents, persons who stood in the role of a parent to the worker, siblings or half-siblings, grandparents, and grandchildren.

(b) Periodic Payments

Periodic payments are based upon a percentage of the deceased worker's pre-injury net average earnings. Pre-injury net average earnings are reduced in accordance with C.P.P./Q.P.P. periodic benefits that are payable upon the death of the worker. Pre-injury net average earnings are also indexed by the consumer price index. The minimum pre-injury net average earnings used for the calculation of survivors' benefits is $15,312.51 per year based on a January 1, 1998, base rate subject to indexing at less than the Consumer Price Index.

The entitlement that a person or group of persons would usually be entitled to (that are described in the following paragraphs) may be reduced by the need to apportion survivors' benefits between two or more persons who are simultaneously entitled to survivors' benefits in regard to the same deceased worker. See further discussion of apportionment is contained below.

A surviving spouse without children is entitled to periodic payments of between 20 and 60 per cent of the deceased worker's pre-injury net average earnings. The minimum percentage would be payable to a surviving spouse aged 20 or less at the time of the worker's death. The maximum percentage would be payable to a spouse aged 60 or more at the time of the worker's death. The percentage entitlement for surviving spouses between the ages of 20 and 60 at the time of the worker's death matches the surviving spouse's age at the time of the worker's death. These benefits are payable for the lifetime of the surviving spouse.

A surviving spouse with children is entitled to periodic payments of 85 per cent of the deceased worker's pre-injury net average earnings until the youngest child reaches 19 years of age. When the youngest child reaches 19 years of age, the spouse's entitlement will be recalculated in accordance with his or her entitlement as a surviving spouse without children. For the purpose of the recalculation, the usual method of determining the percentage entitlement to periodic payments is varied by making the calculation referred to in the preceding paragraph as if the worker had died immediately after the day on which the youngest child reached 19 years of age.

When there is no surviving spouse, or if the surviving spouse dies, a sole surviving child is entitled to receive periodic payments of 30 per cent of the deceased worker's pre-injury net average earnings. Entitlement at this level usually lasts until the child reaches 19 years of age. The percentage entitlement is increased by 10 per cent for each additional child. The entitlement of the children is as a group. The entitlement of surviving children may also be affected by the existence of a person acting in the role of a parent to the children. See the discussion below.

A surviving child over the age of 19 who is attending school may be entitled to compensation benefits at the rate of 10 per cent of the deceased workers' pre-injury net average earnings for as long as the Board considers it advisable for the child to continue in education.

For a child who is physically or mentally incapable of earning wages, periodic benefits are payable until the child is able to earn wages or until his or her death. Because no benefits are payable to the child if there are benefits being paid to the spouse, a child who is physically or mentally incapable of earning wages may become entitled to benefits as a surviving dependent child only upon the death of the deceased worker's spouse. The child may be considerably beyond the age of 19 at that time. However, the incapacity of the child must pre-exist either:

- The death of the worker; or
- The child reaching 19 years of age; or
- If the child is past 19 years of age, the child leaving Board approved education.

If a surviving child (or children) is being maintained by a parent who is not the spouse of the deceased worker or by another person who is acting in the role of parent to the child (or children), the parent or person acting in the role of a parent is entitled to periodic payments of 85 per cent of the worker's pre-injury net average earnings. These periodic payments are in lieu of the periodic payments that the child (or children) would otherwise be entitled to.

Other "dependants" as defined by the Act may be entitled to periodic benefits as follows:

> If the deceased worker has no spouse or children but is survived by other dependants, the dependants are entitled to reasonable compensation proportionate to the loss occasioned to each of them. The following rules apply with respect to that compensation:
>
> 1. The Board shall determine the amount of compensation.
> 2. The total periodic payments to the dependants must not exceed 50 per cent of the deceased worker's net average earnings.
> 3. The periodic payments to a dependant are payable only as long as the worker could have been reasonably expected to continue to support the dependant if the deceased worker had not suffered injury.

(c) Apportioning Periodic Payments

There is no limit to the number of permutations and combinations that may exist with regard to the circumstances of the survivors of the deceased worker at the time of the worker's death and beyond. The Act recognizes that there may be circumstances where the Board will be required to make periodic payments to more than one person in regard to the same deceased worker.

Apportionment of periodic payments between spouses and children who do not reside with a spouse takes place pursuant to subs. 48(5) of the Act. Apportionment in these circumstances may also take place pursuant to subs. 48(19). Apportionment between existing spouses and separated spouses is dealt with under subs. 48(8). Apportionment between persons acting in the role of parents to a child takes place pursuant to subs. 48(2), para. 3.

The *Workplace Safety and Insurance Act, 1997*, provides greater flexibility to the Board in apportioning benefits than was previously possible under the *Workers' Compensation Act*. When dealing with any question regarding apportionment of survivors' benefits, it is extremely important to reference the applicable Board policy.

(d) Lump Sum Payments

A surviving spouse who was cohabiting with the deceased worker at the time of the worker's death is entitled to a lump sum payment varying between $27,777.76 for a spouse age 60 or more and $83,330.30, for a spouse age 20 or less. The value of the lump sum decreases by $1,388.88 for every year of the spouse's age between the ages of 20 and 60. All figures use a January 1, 1998 base rate and are subject to inflation indexing at less than the rate of the Consumer Price Index.

Separated spouses are entitled to benefits under subs. 48(7) "as spouses". Rules governing the apportionment of benefits between spouses in subs. 48(8) and in Board policy discuss the manner in which lump sum benefits may be apportioned. There is no question that spouses and separated spouses under the prior *Workers' Compensation Act* could apportion lump sum awards. However, subs. 48(2) of the *Workplace Safety and Insurance Act, 1997*, that authorizes lump sum awards for spouses, now specifically authorizes payments only in regard to a surviving spouse "who was cohabiting with the worker at the time of the worker's death".

If there is no spouse when the worker dies and if the deceased worker is survived by one or more dependent children, the dependent children, as a class, are entitled to a lump sum of $55,555.55. This figure is a January 1, 1998, base rate with indexing at less than the Consumer Price Index. The Act appears to leave open the absurd result of dependent children being denied a lump sum should the deceased worker leave a spouse who was not co-habitating with the deceased at the time of death. The spouse would not receive the lump sum either.

(e) Other Survivors' Benefits

If a request from a spouse is received within one year after the death of a worker, the Board may provide vocational rehabilitation assessments and services.

Upon request, the Board may pay for bereavement counselling for the spouse of the children of the worker. The request must be received within one year after the worker's death.

The necessary expenses of burial or cremation of the deceased worker will be paid for by the Board. The minimum award established by the Act is $2,083.32. This is a January 1, 1998, base rate with indexing at less than the Consumer Price Index. The maximum award is set by Board policy. For the year 1998, Board policy allowed up to $8,650.

The Act and Board policy both indicate that additional necessary expenses, as determined by the Board, will be paid if, owing to circumstances, the body of the worker must be transported a considerable distance for burial or cremation.

CHAPTER 21

Labour Market Re-Entry Services

1. INTRODUCTION

With the passage of Bill 99, substantial legislative changes have been introduced that affect how the Board works towards re-integrating injured workers into the workforce. This process used to be called "vocational rehabilitation" (VR). For workers covered by the pre-1997 Act, there is no longer any statutory reference to VR. Instead, the terminology is "an early and safe return to work program" (ESRTW) or a "labour market re-entry plan" (LMRP). This terminology is also applicable to workers hurt on or after January 1, 1998. In light of these changes, the Board has changed its focus in its delivery of what were formerly known as Vocational Rehabilitation Services (VRS) and what are now known as Labour Market Re-entry Services.

Entitlement to specific labour market re-entry services is related to a worker's benefits scheme (the scheme varies with the date of injury). Section 52 of the pre-1997 Act, which is a very broadly worded provision, applies to all workers hurt prior to January 1, 1998. It provides:

> To aid in getting injured workers back to work and to assist in lessening or removing any handicap resulting from their injuries, the Board may take such measures and make such expenditures as it may deem necessary or expedient, and the expense thereof shall be borne, in Schedule 1 cases, out of the accident fund and, in Schedule 2 cases, by the employer individually, and may be collected in the same manner as compensation or expenses of administration.

Section 53 of the pre-1997 Act has been substantially altered by Bill 99, but applies only to workers hurt after January 1, 1990 and before January 1, 1998. It reads as follows:

> **53.** (1) This section applies in respect of a worker who is receiving or has received benefits under section 37 and in respect of the employer.
>
> (2) *Early assessment* — Within forty-five days after notice of an accident under section 22 is filed, the Board shall contact a worker who has not returned to work, for the purpose of deciding if assistance is required to facilitate the worker's early and safe return to work or whether a labour market re-entry assessment is to be provided to the worker and section 42 of the *Workplace Safety and Insurance Act, 1997*, applies.
>
> (2.1) *Same* — Promptly after contacting the worker, the Board shall contact the employer for the purpose of deciding if assistance is required to facilitate the worker's early and safe return to work or whether a labour market re-entry assessment is to be provided to the worker and section 42 of the *Workplace Safety and Insurance Act, 1997*, applies.

(3) *Assistance re: return to work* — The Board shall assist the worker and the employer with the worker's early and safe return to work if the Board considers it appropriate to do so.

The balance of s. 53 has been repealed, but subss. 42(3) to (7) of the current Act apply instead with regard to the preparation of a LMRP for the worker. Subsections 108(5) and (6) of the current Act provide:

(5) *Idem* — If, before January 1, 1998, the Board has provided the worker with a vocational rehabilitation assessment but not a vocational rehabilitation program under subsection 53(9) of the pre-1997 Act, the Board shall determine whether a labour market re-entry plan is to be prepared for the worker. Subsections 42(3) to (8) of the *Workplace Safety and Insurance Act, 1997*, apply in the circumstances.

(6) *Idem* — If a worker was provided with a vocational rehabilitation program under the pre-1997 Act, it shall be deemed either as an early and safe return to work program or a labour market re-entry plan, as the circumstances require.

For workers hurt on or after January 1, 1998, the key provisions are ss. 40 and 42 of the current Act. Section 40 sets out duties of employers and workers regarding a worker's early and safe return to work and the Board's role in this process. Section 42 reads as follows:

42. (1) The Board shall provide a worker with a labour market re-entry assessment if any of the following circumstances exist:

1. If it is unlikely that the worker will be re-employed by his or her employer because of the nature of the injury.
2. If the worker's employer has been unable to arrange work for the worker that is consistent with the worker's functional abilities and that restores the worker's pre-injury earnings.
3. If the worker's employer is not co-operating in the early and safe return to work of the worker.

(2) *Labour market re-entry plan* — Based on the results of the assessment, the Board shall decide if a worker requires a labour market re-entry plan in order to enable the worker to re-enter the labour market and reduce or eliminate the loss of earnings that may result from the injury.

(3) *Suitable employment or business* — In deciding whether a plan is required for a worker, the Board shall determine the employment or business that is suitable for the worker.

(4) *Preparation of plan* — The Board shall arrange for a plan to be prepared for a worker if the Board determines that the worker requires a labour market re-entry plan.

(5) *Consultation required* — The labour market re-entry plan shall be prepared in consultation with,

(*a*) the worker and, unless the Board considers it inappropriate to do so, the worker's employer; and
(*b*) the worker's health practitioners if the Board considers it necessary to do so.

(6) *Contents of plan* — The plan shall contain the steps necessary to enable the worker to re-enter the labour market in the employment or business that is suitable for the worker.

(7) *Duty to co-operate* — The worker shall co-operate in all aspects of the labour market re-entry assessment or plan provided to the worker.

(8) *Expenses* — The Board shall pay such expenses related to the plan as the Board considers appropriate to enable the worker to re-enter the labour market.

2. THE SELF-RELIANCE MODEL

Regardless of the date of injury, the Board sees its strategic role as promoting and supporting workplace party self-reliance in managing return to work. It is felt that "fostering employer and worker self-reliance in the workplace will allow Ontario businesses to be better positioned to identify best practices and improve their return to work outcomes". An implicit aspect of the new model is the privatization (or outsourcing) of labour market re-entry services. The Board seems intent on eliminating its capacity to provide anything other than information resources and a monitoring/mediation function. The biggest change will probably be felt with early and safe return to work. Under the self-reliance model the Board is reluctant to get involved, whereas in the past Board employees would often facilitate a return to work with the accident employer.

3. SOME OBSERVATIONS FROM AND ABOUT THE APPEALS TRIBUNAL

If an Appeals Tribunal panel can be made to appreciate what an injured worker actually experienced, it may be prepared to be quite critical of the Board's labour market re-entry activities in any particular case. The Appeals Tribunal has demonstrated an interest in giving a very broad interpretation to s. 52.

An early Tribunal decision laid down some guidelines on the Appeals Tribunal's approach to the Board's VR decisions. These were:

- Decisions must be reviewed on the basis of the actual wording of Board policy;
- The Tribunal must first determine whether there is any eligibility for VR services before considering specific programs;
- The Board's discretion regarding VR must be exercised in a non-arbitrary and non-discriminatory manner;
- VR personnel are making judgments when applying Board policy and the question upon review for the Tribunal is, was the judgment right?

In decisions considering the appropriateness of a worker's activity with or without involvement from the Board's staff, the worker will be held by the Appeals Tribunal to a standard of good faith and reasonableness of activity, although this will be evaluated very much on the individual circumstances of each case.

The Appeals Tribunal has also observed that the language of s. 52 implies that the Board has a right to participate in the rehabilitation process and should have a fair degree of control over it. Therefore "unauthorized" actions on the part of a worker may deprive the worker of discretionary entitlements (*e.g.*, specific programs) flowing from s. 52.

4. PARTICIPATION OF A WORKER'S REPRESENTATIVE

Board policy is that:

> If a worker requests the presence of a representative during consultation, the provision of information, and the planning and design of a VR plan, the caseworker invites the representative to be present, whenever reasonably possible (i.e., if it does not cause a delay of more than one week).

External service providers are generally willing to allow the participation of a worker's representative.

The more controversial aspect of a representative's involvement revolves around a representative's presence with the injured worker on job sites (either with the accident employer or a new employer) where a work trial or actual job is being considered. Many employers refuse to allow a representative onto the job site, especially if it is a non-unionized workplace.

5. POLICIES AND PROCEDURES EXISTING PRIOR TO JANUARY 1, 1998 (PARTICULARLY RELEVANT FOR PRE-1997 ACT WORKERS)

(a) General

Although the Board has created new policies regarding workplace re-entry, which are deemed to apply to all claimants regardless of date of injury, old policies (which have not been deleted yet) are also relevant for pre-January 1998 claimants. This is because the Board has decided that pre-Bill 99 commitments regarding services and benefits are to be honoured, and old policies apply for periods prior to January 1, 1998. These old policies may also be relevant for current Act claimants since there are gaps in the new policies.

While written in the present tense, this material must be considered in the context of current developments at the Board, specifically the restructuring of service delivery with elimination of most VR staff. In the main, references are to "VR", *etc.* rather than "LMR", *etc.*, since this reflects how the policies are written.

(b) Vocational Rehabilitation: Setting Goals, Identifying an Objective and Writing a Plan

In the Board's view, the VR goal is to re-establish the worker's pre-injury earnings profile, the VR objective is a job that will do this, and the VR plan specifies how it is to be done. The lower the pre-injury earnings profile, the less likely it is that substantive VR will be offered by the Board. The Board has a five-tiered hierarchy that it uses to achieve the VR goal:

—— return to the pre-injury job with the accident employer;
—— return to work with the accident employer in a job that is comparable to the pre-injury job;
—— return to work with another employer in a job that is comparable to the pre-injury job;
—— return to appropriate alternative work with the accident employer;
—— return to appropriate alternative work with any employer.

A key concept in this hierarchy is "alternative comparable work". The Board assesses this by comparing:

—— the duties actually performed;
—— the working conditions, including the working environment, geographic location, hours of work and right to work overtime;
—— the degree of skill, effort and responsibility;
—— the rights, privileges and perquisites;
—— the opportunities for the worker continuing in, advancing in, and being promoted in the employment;
—— the required vocational qualifications; and
—— whether the jobs are covered by the same collective agreement.

The Board normally uses the worker's pre-accident gross earnings (including the monetary value of employer-provided benefits) to represent the worker's pre-injury earnings profile with *no cap* for the statutory maximum. The gross earnings figure will be escalated by identifiable scheduled salary or wage increases since the injury, by inflation factors, and by any increases that are part of any established wage grid that would have applied had the worker not been injured.

In setting the VR objective the Board projects the job's gross earnings *over time* rather than using entry level wage. According to Board policy, the VR objective is supposed to be realistic and practical, based on a consideration of the worker's personal and vocational characteristics, and suitability and availability of the objective. Personal and vocational characteristics include:

—— age
—— gender
—— language facility
—— place of residence
—— physical capabilities
—— family status
—— likelihood of permanent impairment

—— employment history
—— vocational interests
—— vocational aptitude
—— union membership
—— vocational qualifications
—— education
—— technical skills that the worker can exercise given the worker's physical capabilities.

According to Board policy a job (or VR objective) is suitable if the worker:

—— has the necessary skills to perform the job
—— is physically able to perform the job, and if
—— the job does not pose a health and safety hazard to the worker or co-workers.

The caseworker is supposed to determine availability of the VR objective by considering:

—— the existence and location of potential employment opportunities in the worker's local labour market, and
—— the likelihood of the worker securing the objective.

The policy defines the local labour market as within 60 kilometres of the worker's home and the regional labour market within 120 kilometres. The regional labour market will replace the local labour market if time passes and the worker has not found employment.

Unfortunately, because of new wording in Bill 99 and related wording in some new policies, many Board personnel feel that availability is no longer a relevant concept. It is, however, because of the wording of various provisions in the pre-1997 Act which was unchanged by Bill 99.

The VR plan itself is usually written. The plan sets out the VR objectives, activities, programs and the time frames necessary to achieve the objectives. By having signed the plan, the injured worker is considered to have accepted all of its terms. As of January 1, 1998 VR plans that were still operating were converted to either ESRTW plans or LMRPs, depending upon the nature of the plan.

Board policy provides that a VR plan may be changed if the caseworker determines (after consultation with the worker and employer) that the occupation required to achieve the VR goal has disappeared or that the VR objective is no longer "suitable, realistic or attainable because of changed circumstances".

(c) Special Evaluations

Special evaluations are professional assessments arranged when there is insufficient information to enable the Board to decide what to do next. Generally, two types of special evaluations are undertaken: functional abilities evaluations (FAEs), and vocational evaluations. FAEs are assessments to determine a worker's physical abilities and limitations, either generally or regarding a specific job. The Board defines vocational evaluations as a "series of tests, evaluations and work samples designed to identify an individual's cognitive functioning, academic standing, interests, aptitudes and personality traits".

(d) Situational (Agency) Assessments

These assessments are on a fee-for-service basis in a rehabilitation workshop where various job situations are simulated. The assessment usually lasts for a few weeks and there may be some flexibility in the daily hours of attendance, especially at the start of the assessment. The typical injured worker referred for a situational assessment has been out of the work environment for some time and the likely vocational objective is semi-skilled modified work at low wages.

(e) Work Trials

The Board defines a work trial as a trial placement of a worker with an employer, usually for a maximum of two months, to ascertain worker-job compatibility. If the trial is successful, the employer will (it is hoped) employ the worker. Generally the employer will be the pre-accident employer.

(f) Transitional Work Programs

Although not defined as such by the Board, a transitional work program is essentially a longer-term work trial (*i.e.*, in the range of four months) which involves more of a learning component along with a gradual increase in hours and work demands. The prospective employer must pay the worker at least 50 per cent of the starting weekly salary for that job over the duration of the program, irrespective of the number of hours actually worked. The Board will top up the worker's wages to the 100 per cent level.

(g) Training-on-the-Job

The aim of a training-on-the-job (TOJ) program is to teach new skills in a hands-on manner. The TOJ employer must pay the worker at least 50 per cent of the starting weekly salary for that job over the duration of the program, irrespective of the number of hours actually worked. The Board will top up the worker's wages to the 100 per cent level.

(h) Special Work Placements

A special work placement is a job in a real work setting, usually of a one-year duration. The aim of the placement is to provide a worker who has restricted employment opportunities because of the compensable permanent impairment with a "meaningful work experience" so the worker may acquire specific job skills that will improve the worker's prospects for successful return to work.

(i) Formal Training

Formal training does not appear in the Board's hierarchy of VR goals.

Board policy is that it will consider upgrading, post-secondary education and business/trades training for injured workers when:

—— Placement of the workers in appropriate alternative work is not possible without training;

—— Training will enable the workers to achieve specific, long-term vocational objectives;

—— Vocational testing indicates that the workers have the interest, aptitude and ability to complete the programs; and

—— Employment opportunities exist or may be reasonably expected to exist for the workers in the chosen field.

The policy also provides:

The Board sets no limits on the length of a formal academic or training program other than what is appropriate and feasible in bringing workers as close as possible to the vocational goal.

One major limitation on formal training is the worker's pre-injury earnings level, because the Board is usually unwilling to train a worker for an occupation that would pay wages higher than the pre-injury wages. Another limitation is a worker's age. Formal training generally will not be considered for workers in their mid-40s or older, unless the program is of relatively short duration.

What if an injured worker wishes to pursue formal training or a specific program but the Board disagrees? Should the worker pursue the goal without Board sponsorship with the financial consequences that VR file closure entails (and then object to the denial of sponsorship), or should the worker go along with whatever the Board *is* offering?

At the Appeals Tribunal level, decisions regarding formal training have gone both ways with fairly similar fact situations. It is unwise to assume that formal training will be supported at the Appeals Tribunal level, even if the program has been successfully completed.

A worker being sponsored by the Board in a formal training program may run into difficulties with the program for any number of reasons. The amount of latitude given to a worker can vary tremendously, but it is not uncommon for a worker to be given a second chance to pass a portion of the program, or a short time extension (or both). Lack of success may be viewed by the Board as lack of co-operation, although it could be that the program is not suitable for the worker.

(j) Job Search Assistance

In a job search assistance "program" the injured worker is directed to look for work and report back to the caseworker every few weeks with documentation of the job search. If the number of documented job contacts is too low (below 3 to 5 contacts per day or 25 per week) the worker will be considered "unco-operative". The caseworker may be more lenient if the injured worker has completed a special work placement or a formal training program and is conducting a more specialized job search.

The Board sometimes provides what it calls "job-search training" and "job-search planning" through either a very short program called "Creative Job-Search Techniques" (CJST) or programs with outside agencies, or through "one-on-one sessions" with Board staff.

Subsection 53(12) (now repealed) authorized a period of job-search assistance of up to six months for workers hurt after January 1, 1990. Subsection 53(13) (now repealed) authorized an extension for up to a further six months. Although it could be argued that job-search assistance entitlement with no time limit could be extended pursuant to s. 52, regardless of a worker's date of injury, Board policy does specify a 12-month limit on job-search assistance with no differentiation for date of injury.

Decision-makers at the Board and the Appeals Tribunal have made decisions that have had the effect of overriding any 12-month time limit on job-search assistance. Nevertheless, in its March 1998 clarification memo, the Board still sets a 12-month cap on job search assistance. The provision of less than six months of job search assistance in the first instance had become more common at the Board in 1996-97.

(k) Co-Operation Policies

A finding of non-co-operation will result in the closure of the VR file and, in most cases, a reduction or cessation of payments. The Board policy on "Co-operating With Vocational Rehabilitation" lists five grounds for a finding of non-co-operation:

> —— refusing to participate in the creation of a VR plan
> —— failing to fulfil the commitments of the plan
> —— declining employment which is in accordance with plan objectives
> —— having unrealistic employment expectations, or
> —— displaying abusive/threatening behaviour.

(l) File Closure Policies

The Board has a separate policy on file closure which incorporates the co-operation policy discussed immediately above, but also lists other grounds for file closure as follows:

—— successful completion of the VR plan by a return to work of one
  sort or another
—— a worker's inability or unavailability to complete the VR plan because of
—— intervening events (such as illnesses) which preclude any vocational
  activities contemplated
—— death
—— retirement or voluntary withdrawal from the workforce
—— emigration from Canada
—— incarceration
—— a worker's unco-operative behaviour
—— a worker has "had extensive VR service in the past without benefit
  and further involvement by the caseworker would not likely lead to
  successful placement or resolution of ongoing obstacles to employment".

A compensable recurrence (which could be characterized as an intervening event
of sorts) may not lead to file closure, but rather to revisions of the VR plan.

(m) Re-Activating the VR File

The general threshold for re-activation is that it must appear that the worker
would benefit from further VR. The onus will generally be on the worker to request renewed VR services, as the Board cannot be expected to monitor closed
cases in the abstract. Board policy is that a caseworker will re-activate cases if:

—— previous VR did not meet the vocational objectives and earnings
  profile, as evidenced by the worker's post-injury work experience
—— the worker is laid off from temporary, modified work and is still
  temporarily partially disabled
—— the employer has failed to fulfil one or more "critical commitments"
  made in a previous VR plan, or
—— if there is such an increase in the worker's impairment that the
  worker is unlikely to return to the most recent employment.

A caseworker *does not usually* re-activate a claim for new VR services

—— if the worker previously received VR services without benefit and it
  is *unlikely* that a new period of VR services or a VR plan would
  bring the worker any closer to the VR goal or to re-establishing the
  pre-injury earnings profile, or
—— if the worker did not co-operate in previous attempts at vocational
  rehabilitation or failed to fulfil one or more of the commitments in a
  previously established plan, *unless the worker shows a new willingness to co-operate or fulfil commitments.*

[Emphasis added.]

Although the policy on re-activating closely parallels the policy on VR file closure, it clearly contemplates giving the worker a second (or third) chance.

Situations where a worker's earnings basis has increased may require the Board to re-visit the VR goal and perhaps re-activate VR. Similarly, an increased pension, or a revised Future Economic Loss (FEL)/Loss of Earnings (LOE) award may lead to a change in a worker's VR goal and warrant re-activation of the VR file.

A new policy, entitled "Labour Market Re-Entry Re-Assessments", outlines the circumstances under which a LMR Re-Assessment may be conducted and a LMR Plan may be implemented for workers injured prior to January 1, 1998. It is much more restrictive than the policy outlined above. Essentially, this is available only to workers who have experienced a deterioration in the work-related impairment rendering the former suitable employment or business inappropriate.

(n) Entitlement to Vocational Rehabilitation Following Termination

Historically, the Board's position has been that injured workers who return to work and are subsequently laid off are entitled to vocational rehabilitation if their work-related injuries are an obstacle to re-employment. The new policy, "Labour Market Re-Entry Re-Assessments" outlines the circumstances under which a LMR Re-Assessment may be conducted and a LMR Plan may be implemented for workers injured prior to January 1, 1998. It specifies that a worker is not re-assessed for reasons unrelated to the work-related injury, such as unemployment because of plant layoff, closure, strikes, or other employment or labour market-related situations. There is no mention of the concept of an obstacle to re-employment.

A request for VR following a termination related to economic conditions has been considered in a number of Appeals Tribunal decisions with varying results.

6. EARLY AND SAFE RETURN TO WORK (ESRTW)

(Particularly relevant for workers hurt on or after January 1, 1998)

(a) General

As set out in s. 40 of the Act employers and workers have an obligation to co-operate in the worker's ESRTW with the employer. The concept of ESRTW is also relevant in pre-January 1, 1998 claims if workplace re-entry services are being considered for periods from January 1, 1998. The Board's new policies regarding ESRTW apply to all claims regardless of accident date effective January 1, 1998. Thus, for all injured workers with lost time injuries, the initial focus will be on a return to work with the accident employer. (This was the previous practice.) The Board sees the desired outcome of ESRTW programs as an early return to safe and suitable employment that is within the worker's functional abilities, and, if possible, restores the worker's pre-injury earnings.

The Board defines suitable work as work that:

- The worker has the necessary skills to perform or is able to acquire the necessary skills to perform; and
- Does not pose a health or safety risk to the worker or co-workers.

Available work is defined as:

- The first opportunity of appropriate work that exists with the employer.

With such open-ended definitions, employers may be inclined to create "make-work" jobs to keep time loss (and compensation costs) to a minimum, if it looks as if the disability will be of relatively short duration.

(b) The Board's Role

The Board does not see itself involved in the ESRTW process, except to:

- Suggest a list of return to work resources that are available and that can be purchased by the workplace parties to assist in ESRTW programs;
- Monitor activities, progress and co-operation of the workplace parties;
- Provide dispute resolution; and
- Determine compliance with the obligations to co-operate and re-employ.

As discussed in Topic 5 above, prior to January 1998, different types of evaluations were utilized by the Board to determine a worker's "fit" for workplace re-entry, and the costs of these evaluations were covered by the Board. In the ESRTW context, the employer must now purchase these services from an appropriate provider.

Board policy regarding cost responsibility for work/workplace accommodations and/or assistive devices is less clear. The policy found under the heading Early and Safe Return to Work states that the Board pays for this, while the policy found under the heading Re-Employment Provisions states that the employer must pay, unless the employer demonstrates that the resulting expenses will cause undue hardship.

(c) The Role of the Workplace Parties

In its policy on this topic, the Board has basically restated the Act (mostly s. 40). Note that while s. 40 obligations apply only in claims occurring from and after January 1, 1998, the Board policy applies to all claims regardless of accident date, effective January 1, 1998. The employer is required to co-operate in the ESRTW of the worker by:

- Contacting the worker as soon as possible after the injury occurs and maintaining communication throughout the period of the worker's recovery or disability;
- Attempting to identify and arrange suitable employment;

- Giving the Board any information the Board requests concerning the worker's return to work; and
- Notifying the Board of any material change in circumstances within 10 days of the change occurring.

The worker is required to co-operate in the ESRTW by:

- Contacting the accident employer as soon as possible after the injury occurs and maintaining communication throughout the period of recovery or disability;
- Assisting the employer as required or requested, to identify suitable employment;
- Giving the Board any information the Board requests concerning the worker's return to work; and
- Notifying the Board of any material change in circumstances with 10 days of the change occurring.

With the "self-reliance" model, and noting the Board's conception of its own role, in the first instance the workplace parties will be left to their own devices to sort out an ESRTW. It is fair to say that many employers, and most injured workers, will have no idea of how this should work. From a worker's point of view, ignorance coupled with unequal bargaining power may produce a less than optimal result.

(d) Resolving Disputes

No doubt, there will be disputes between the workplace parties regarding the suitability of offered work. Because the Board may not be involved in the ESRTW process, one or both of the parties may want the Board to become involved. Board policy is that if either party notifies the Board of a dispute or disagreement, the Board will offer to try to resolve the dispute. If dispute resolution is unsuccessful or refused, one or both of the parties may be found by the Board to be non-co-operative. This finding, for a worker, means that benefits may be reduced or suspended. For an employer, it means that the Board will provide the worker with a Labour Market Re-Entry (LMR) assessment and, perhaps, LMR assistance, with costs consequences for the employer. In certain cases the Board could also determine that there has been a breach of the employer's obligation to re-employ.

7. LABOUR MARKET RE-ENTRY (LMR)

(a) General

If an ESRTW has failed through no fault of the worker's, or if it is unlikely that re-employment with the accident employer will be possible because of the nature of the injury, the Board is obliged under subs. 42(1) to provide the worker with a labour market re-entry (LMR) assessment. Following from that, a LMR plan may then be necessary. This terminology and related policies will also be relevant for workers hurt prior to January 1, 1998 who were still receiving VR services after January 1, 1998, or who are seeking a re-instatement of services. As discussed under Topic 5, however, the Board's old policies may be relevant for these workers as well.

The Board sees the goal of the LMR assessment as ensuring that a worker has the skills, knowledge and abilities to re-enter the labour market into a job that is consistent with the worker's functional abilities and that reduces or eliminates loss of earnings from the injury. Assessment tools can include psycho-vocational evaluations, vocational/transferrable skills assessments, functional abilities evaluations, controlled environment assessments and work assessments. A Board decision-maker must then identify a potential suitable employment or business for a worker to determine whether or not an LMR plan is required. The LMR plan is tailored to enhance transferable job skills, or, if necessary, provide new skills for re-entry into the labour market.

External service providers are used by the Board to conduct the assessment and formulate the plan. Unfortunately, the Board contemplates a turn-around time of 30 days from initial contact to completion of plan preparation. Also, any plan must be approved by a Board decision-maker before being implemented.

(b) Determining Suitable Employment or Business (SEB)

The Board's view is that the suitable employment or business (SEB) represents the category or categories of jobs suited to the worker's transferable skills, that is/are safe, within the worker's functional abilities, and reduce(s) or eliminate(s) the loss of earnings (LOE) resulting from the injury. The Board is using the National Occupation Classification (NOC) to help to identify a worker's SEB. Board policy is that "the decision-maker" determines the SEB for the worker. The decision-maker also determines (deemed) post-injury earnings using wage information related to the job(s) chosen, taking the wage range based on the decision-maker's assessment of the worker's skill level (actual or acquirable). Generally, these determinations are made by the external service providers and adopted by the Board.

(c) Labour Market Re-Entry (LMR) Plans

The Board's interpretation of subs. 42(2) is that an LMR plan will be provided if it is the most appropriate and cost-effective approach to enable a worker to re-enter the labour market. More particularly, the policy provides:

> In addition to the information obtained through the LMR assessment for each suitable employment or business (SEB) option identified, the decision-maker considers if:

- The worker has transferable job skills or skills that can be improved to enable labour market re-entry
- An LMR plan is required to attain job skills
- The identified SEB will result in reducing of eliminating any loss of earnings resulting from the injury
- A continuing loss of earnings is expected if the worker is not provided with an LMR plan
- The worker has the aptitude and ability to complete the activities set out in the LMR plan, and
- The worker is likely to be successful in completing the LMR plan.

The decision-maker evaluates the cost-effectiveness by comparing:

- The total estimated cost(s) of the proposed plan and the benefits to be paid for future LOE;
- The estimated costs of alternative plans; and
- The estimated cost of future LOE benefits if an LMR plan is not provided.

The use of the terminology "future loss of earnings benefits" is unfortunate because this policy applies to all claims regardless of accident date. Essentially, the decision-maker has to consider the appropriate benefit system based upon the date of injury (pre-Bill 162, FEL, LOE) when making this cost-effectiveness assessment. In practice, the cost-effectiveness assessment is prepared by the external service provider.

Board policy repeats the statutory provisions regarding LMR plans; it also establishes that there is no fixed duration for a plan. Rather the "program and/or plan" is to continue as long as necessary, but the duration is to be agreed to by the decision-maker and the worker during the preparation of the plan. The policy provides that the plan must describe the

- Name of each training agency or institution;
- Details and outline of programs;
- Start and end dates for each program;
- All [sic] costs for each program or activity, and any associated costs.

(d) Labour Market Re-Entry (LMR) Services

Board policy lists the following five "programs" or services that can be provided in a plan:

- English as a second language;
- Academic upgrading;
- Skills training;
- Formal training;
- Creative job search techniques.

Notably absent as a program is job search assistance. This absence has already caused some confusion at the Board and consternation among injured workers and their representatives. In January 1998, the Board took the position that job search assistance would not be provided to any claimant regardless of the date of injury, unless it had been included in a written VR Plan (and not necessarily in that event). This position was modified in March 1998 to allow for job search assistance for up to 12 months for claimants injured prior to January 1, 1998, regardless of whether or not this had been written up in a VR Plan.

Workplace modifications and assistive devices or other accommodations may be provided (and specified in the LMR plan) if the Board decision-maker determines that they are necessary for the worker to perform the SEB.

(e) Monitoring Participation Progress and Co-Operation

The worker is obliged, by virtue of subs. 42(7), to co-operate in all aspects of the LMR process. In the first instance the monitoring is done by the external service provider, who, in turn, reports to the Board. A failure to co-operate will result in the termination of the LMR plan and will affect payments (specifics depending upon the applicable payment scheme for the worker). New Board policy does not elaborate upon examples of non-co-operative behaviour, and so the old policies may be relevant.

The LMR plan may be changed if the worker's condition improves or worsens, but the Board will be reluctant to reconsider the SEB. The LMR plan will be discontinued if the worker receives an offer of "appropriate employment". There may also be a LMR Re-Assessment, perhaps leading to a new SEB or new LMR plan, in certain circumstances. Overall, the policy on these topics is sketchy.

(f) Payment of Expenses

Historically, the Board was prepared to pay incidental expenses including tuition fees, relocation costs, and other expenses associated with VR programs and certain policies were developed. New Board policy allows for similar payments with LMR programs, but only if the expenses are documented in detail in advance. There are also transitional rules for programs started before January 1, 1998.

(g) Home Modifications for Homebound Employment

In the past, the Board was willing to consider paying for home modifications to facilitate homebound employment, but the eligible worker had to be totally and permanently impaired while medically capable of homebound employment, with no other employment alternatives available. The Board is still willing to do this. The new policy is more liberal in that these payments are available to workers with "limited functional abilities".

8. VOCATIONAL REHABILITATION/LABOUR MARKET RE-ENTRY (LMR) FOR SURVIVING SPOUSES

Regardless of the date of injury, surviving spouses of deceased workers can apply to the Board within one year after the worker's death for a LMR assessment (and a related plan). These "rights" are provided under both the current Act and the pre-1997 Act.

9. OBJECTIONS

If at all possible, negotiation with the decision-maker is preferred over an objection because if services are cut, payments will be affected. However, subs. 120(1)(*a*) specifies that once a negative decision has been made concerning return to work or a LMR plan (or program), any objection must be made within 30 days after the decision is made. Subsection 120(2) requires the notice of objection to be written and to indicate why the decision is incorrect or why it should be changed. Vocational rehabilitation decisions rendered prior to January 1, 1998 had an appeal deadline of January 31, 1998 (see subs. 112(3)). The legislation provides that the Board can extend these time limits but criteria are not specified.

It is open to the Board to mediate these objections, but if mediation is unsuccessful subs. 122(2) provides that the Board should try to decide the matter within 60 days after receiving the notice of objection.

CHAPTER 22

Re-Employment

1. INTRODUCTION

A long-standing grievance of injured workers has been that when a worker was injured at work, there was no statutory protection of the worker's job. It is true that the Ontario Human Rights Commission included injured workers among those protected from discrimination because of handicap, and that s. 9(*b*) of the Ontario *Human Rights Code* was amended, in 1985, by the terms of Bill 101, to include the words "an injury for which benefits were claimed or received under the *Workers' Compensation Act*", under the definition "because of handicap". These forms of protection, however, were often unknown to injured workers. And many Workers' Compensation Board (WCB) personnel either did not know of the existence of these provisions, or they did not see it as their responsibility to inform injured workers of this recourse.

In 1987, a critical report commissioned by the government called for major changes to the WCB system of Vocational Rehabilitation (VR). As a result, one of the major focuses of Bill 162 amendments was on VR. In this chapter we consider the provisions that are generally intended to ensure that an accident employer provides, to the best of its ability, work for workers who have suffered disabilities while in its service.

To accomplish this protection, s. 41 of the *Workplace Safety and Insurance Act, 1997* (the Act) (s. 54 of the *Workers' Compensation Act*) sets out an elaborate code for employers' obligations to re-employ injured workers. This code contains provisions for penalty sanctions against employers and the payment of compensation benefits to workers, even in cases where there is no longer any disability. These provisions may be, at times, at odds with provisions in collective agreements and with other statutes. It should be stressed that the provisions set out that there is an employer's *obligation* to re-employ, not a worker's *right* to be re-employed. Although this may appear to be a subtle difference, the difference will become apparent when considering the remedies.

With the introduction of the re-employment provisions, it was anticipated that there would be a significant number of disputes between employers and workers. In anticipation, the Board set out a new appeal area: the Re-employment Hearings Branch. However, for reasons that are not clear, the anticipated rush of litigation did not materialize. As Table 22-1 shows, the Tribunal has not been overwhelmed with re-employment cases.

Table 22-1
Re-Employment Appeals Heard at the Tribunal, 1990-1998

Year	Re-employment Appeals	Year	Re-employment Appeals
1990	1	1995	26
1991	19	1996	28
1992	26	1997	12
1993*	28	1998**	6
1994	17		

* The highest level of re-employment appeals, as a percentage of all appeals (1,069), was in 1993 — 2.6%

** The percentage of all appeals (1,772) in the last full year before publication — 0.34%

2. THE APPLICATION

Before it is determined that the re-employment provisions apply to the employer, there are certain threshold issues that must be met. These provisions apply only to claims for compensable injuries occurring on or after January 2, 1990. For those workers, subs. 41(1) provides that re-employment rights are triggered where an injured worker had been "employed continuously for at least one year".

The re-employment provisions, however, do not apply to employers "who regularly employ fewer than 20 workers or such classes of employers as may be prescribed" (subs. 41(2)). To determine the number of workers the Board first looks at the number of workers employed at the time of the injury. If the worker or the employer feels that this number does not fairly represent the number of workers "regularly employed", a variety of formulas, depending on the circumstances, are used to arrive at the "average number of workers".

In this context questions may arise as to whether the employer of record is, in fact, *the* employer, or whether nominally separate corporations with joint ownership may be combined to produce the required 20 workers. One such attempt at "piercing the corporate veil" was accepted by the Reinstatement Officer, but rejected on the specific facts of the case by the Tribunal.

Certain parts of the re-employment provisions do not apply to "employers engaged primarily in construction" whose workers "perform construction work" (subs. 41(8)). These workers are covered by Ontario Regulation 259/92 under the *Workers' Compensation Act*, as continued by subs. 41(9) of the *Workplace Safety And Insurance Act, 1997*.

(a) The Date of the Injury

The "the date of an injury" is interpreted in Board policy to mean the date that a disablement or occupational disease results in an "impairment". For traumatic injuries, the actual date is used unless there are circumstances in which the onset of impairment is delayed, in which case, the latter date is used. If the impairment results from a *recurrence*, the date of the original injury is used. See Bill 99 *Operational Policies*, 9.10.

(b) Employed Continuously for at Least One Year

In determining whether a worker has been "continuously" employed, Board policy (Bill 99 *Operational Policies*, 9.1) states:

> Workers who are hired for one year or more before their injury are considered to be continuously employed unless the year was interrupted by a work cessation intended by the worker or the employer to sever the employment relationship.

The policy goes on to provide further detail concerning exceptions such as strikes/lockouts, various leaves of absence and lay-offs. The general rule of thumb is that a lay-off of three months or less is not considered a break in employment. The policy also considers seasonal workers and training participants.

(c) Duration of Obligation

If the employer meets the general obligations, subs. 41(7) stipulates that it remains obligated for a period of two years after the injury, one year after the date that the Board notifies the employer that a worker is able to perform the essential duties of his or her pre-injury job, or until the worker reaches 65 years of age, whichever comes first.

In one Tribunal decision, the worker continued working after the compensable accident. The worker was laid off 18 months after the accident date. By the time that a claim was filed and allowed by the Board, the two-year period had expired. The Panel found that the employer's obligation continued at the time that the worker was laid off. The fact that the claim was not recognized until after the two-year period did not relieve the employer of its obligation. What was important, in that Panel's opinion, was that at the time of the lay-off effective notice had been given and the employer continued to be obligated even if the claim had yet to be accepted by the Board.

In another variation on this scenario, however, a Tribunal ruled that there was no obligation for the employer to re-employ when a worker was terminated *before* he had filed a claim. In that case, the worker was terminated in December 1990, for poor work performance and only subsequently claimed WCB benefits for a back condition. The Panel found that at the time of termination the employer was not aware of the claim for compensation and, therefore, the reasons for termination could not be related to the compensable condition.

(d) Jurisdiction

A number of cases have arisen in which employers under the federal *Government Employees Compensation Act* (GECA) argued that the s. 54 provisions did not fall within the jurisdiction of GECA.

The jurisdictional issue was considered by the Ontario Divisional Court and the Ontario Court of Appeal, and they rejected an application for judicial review challenging the applicability of s. 54 to GECA employers.

3. THE SUBSTANTIVE REQUIREMENTS

To adjudicate these claims the Board had created a new area — the Re-employment Hearings Branch. In 1994, 68 per cent of re-employment complaints were settled through the mediation process. When a complaint was first lodged, the Branch appointed a mediator who discussed the facts of the case with the worker and the employer to encourage a mutually acceptable accommodation. Such settlements included complaints withdrawn, the satisfactory reinstatement of the worker or a mutually acceptable severance deal.

If a mediated settlement could not be arrived at, the matter was referred to the appeal process, where a hearing was convened by a Reinstatement Officer. Reinstatement Officer decisions, as opposed to other WCB appeal decisions, have been published by the Re-employment Hearings Branch. Unfortunately, they have not been indexed or summarized.

There was, however, a major change in re-employment provisions wrought by Bill 99 and a transfer of "the Board's central role for returning the worker to work to the employer and the worker". With this transfer of responsibility, the Board no longer automatically provides the mediation services that it did in the pre-Bill 99 days. Mediation services may arise in re-employment circumstances, secondary to the return to work provisions. Also, the Board's internal appeal system will no longer provide a separate appeal structure for these cases. The Board's final decision will be rendered by an "Appeals Resolution Officer".

In the first few years of decision-making, it was apparent that there were a number of complex issues in the section which lent themselves to different interpretations. These differences appear within Reinstatement Officer decisions, and between those decisions and Tribunal decisions.

(a) The Nature of the Employer's Obligation

The Workplace, Safety and Insurance Board (WSIB) no longer has a supervisory role in determining fitness and is no longer required to notify the employer of the worker's fitness; that will, presumably, become part of the move to "encourage the workplace parties to be more self-reliant". However, the Board still *"may* determine the following matters on its own initiative or *shall* determine them *if the worker and the employer disagree* about the fitness of the worker to return to work" [emphasis added] (subs. 41(3)). The "following matters" are essentially the same as the determinations under subs. 54(2)(*a*) and (*b*) of the pre-1997 Act; that is, whether the worker is medically able to perform the essential duties of the pre-injury employment or to perform suitable work.

(i) The Strategic Determination

If it is accepted that the worker is fit to return to work, then the employer has re-employment obligations. However, such an action may be seen as a *de facto* acceptance of a determination of fitness. And, if suitable work is not forthcoming, neither are benefits, at least until a re-employment obligation determination is made.

If the worker disagrees with a determination of fitness, then his or her challenge will be through the normal entitlement channels and, obviously, he or she will not be interested in arguing that the employer did not fulfil its re-employment obligations. By the time that a possibly negative decision has been upheld through to the Tribunal, the worker's re-employment claim will be, at best, tenuous.

Finally, a decision on fitness has ramifications on the worker's loss of earnings (LOE) award. If the worker is unsuccessful in challenging the determination of fitness — assuming the determination was that the worker was fit for the pre-injury job with no loss in pay — he or she may be in the position of having a zero LOE award *and* no job.

Another complication can arise when a re-employment question is combined with questions of initial entitlement. In one Tribunal decision, for example, an employer wanted to challenge the Board finding that a 1991 event was a new accident, and therefore subject to the re-employment provisions. The employer sought a ruling that it was a recurrence of a 1985 accident and therefore re-employment would not apply. At the Board, as re-employment questions are "fast tracked", the Reinstatement Officer refused to adjudicate the question of entitlement. The Tribunal Panel ruled that the determination of whether there was a new accident was integral to determining the re-employment issue and that it would, therefore, rule on both issues.

It should also be noted that it is, typically, an employer appealing a re-employment case. The hearing process tends to be more adversarial than an entitlement case and there is an implicit onus on the appellant to make a case. This is reinforced by the reverse onus of subs. 41(10) (see later). So, for example, in two cases the Tribunal noted the non-attendance of the employer in upholding the Reinstatement Officer finding of an employer breach.

(ii) The Nature of the Determination

Prior to January 1, 1998, the Board was required to make a determination that the worker was fit for regular or suitable work. With the move to "self-reliance", for cases in which the injury date is on or after January 1, 1998, the Board is no longer involved at this stage. For these cases, the onus is now on workers to:

- Notify the Board of any "material change in circumstance";
- Maintain contact with the employer "throughout the early and safe return to work (ESRTW) process"; and
- Notify the Board and the employer when they are able to perform their regular, or modified, employment.

See Bill 99 *Operational Policies*, 9.2.

Earlier Board policy on the date of determination raised the first of several disagreements between some early Tribunal decisions and the Re-employment Hearings Branch. With the change in Bill 99 and the removal of the Board from the determination process, these differences became moot.

(iii) The Nature of the Obligation

The Board consistently took the position that, once the threshold has been met, there is a general obligation on the employer. This position has also been adopted by subsequent Tribunal decisions. It should be noted, however, that according to at least two Reinstatement Officer decisions, there is not an *absolute* obligation. In two decisions, it was held that an employer could raise the same defences as those available in justifying a termination. It was held in both of these decisions that the Legislature could not have intended that an employer would be forced to go through the exercise of re-employing a worker for one day, then terminating the employment, so that it could avail itself of the defences available under subs. 41(10).

At least one Tribunal decision reached a similar conclusion and held that the "unconditional" obligation be tempered. In that case the worker did not file a workers' compensation claim until *after* he had been dismissed for poor work performance. The Board found that in not *re*-hiring the worker, the employer had breached its re-employment obligations. The Panel disagreed with an earlier Tribunal decision, suggesting that such an obligation might produce unreasonable or even absurd results. That Panel proposed that subs. 54(4) [now subs. 41(4)] should be read as obliging the employer within the context of the entire section and that subs. 54(10) [now subs. 41(10)] provides an employer relief from the reinstatement obligation.

Neither of these cases found that the employer had established such a defence and for that reason both employers were found to be in violation of their re-employment obligations. Therefore, it is not clear what the effect would be on a worker's subs. 41(13)(*b*) benefits, should it be found that an employer breached its s. 41 obligations, but such a breach was justified.

(iv) Other Remedies

Another remedy available to a worker is through the provisions of the *Occupational Health and Safety Act*, as administered by the Ontario Labour Relations Board (OLRB). One decision of the OLRB, for example, awarded a worker

$500 for mental stress. The worker had been injured on the job and had returned to work to find that the conditions that led to his injury still existed. On complaining about this fact, he was terminated. The medical evidence suggested that the major contributing factor to his stress condition arose from his compensable injury, and that condition had been recognized by the Board. However, the OLRB Panel majority found that the termination had aggravated his condition.

Although it is not clear from the decision whether this workplace met the threshold requirements of s. 54 [now s. 41], it is easily conceivable that the *Workers' Compensation Act* might also have provided a remedy. A claim of discrimination on the grounds of handicap might also have been pursued with the Ontario Human Rights Commission.

(b) The Duty to Accommodate

Subsection 41(6) provides:

> **41.** (6) The employer shall accommodate the work or the workplace for the worker to the extent that the accommodation does not cause the employer undue hardship.

The accommodation provision is closely modelled on the provisions of provincial and federal human rights legislation and labour arbitration law. When determining what would constitute "undue hardship" Board policy, Bill 99, *Operational Policies*, 9.6 specifically refers to the *Guidelines for Assessing Accommodation Requirements for Persons With Disabilities* published by the Ontario Human Rights Commission. Generally, these guidelines require that an employer will accommodate an injured worker — that is, provide him or her a job suitable for any disability — unless the "viability of the business enterprise" would be substantially affected. The policy provides that if the employer's expenses of accommodation reach a point of undue hardship,

> The Board may pay the remaining expenses if doing so allows the worker to return to employment within the worker's functional abilities, and restore the pre-injury earnings.

This convergence of human rights and workers' compensation requirements raises the potential for conflicting jurisdictions and findings of fact. This can be complicated even further by collective agreement rights and rights under the *Occupational Health and Safety Act* and even the *Employment Standards Act*.

The courts have had an opportunity to consider the duty to accommodate in various human rights provisions. In 1985, in the first Supreme Court of Canada decision dealing with "accommodation", it was held that an employer being required to accommodate a worker could raise as a defence the fact that the aspect of the job that breached the complainant's rights was a "bona fide occupational requirement" (BFOR) — also referred to as a "bona fide occupational qualification" (BFOQ). In essence, if an employer could establish that a rule was a BFOR, then the employer was not guilty of adverse impact discrimination. This defence was upheld in a second case, in which a human rights decision requiring that an employer accommodate a diabetic, was overturned.

The thrust of the case-law changed, however, with a 1990 Supreme Court decision. In this case, involving a complaint of discrimination on religious grounds, both a majority decision and concurring minority, limited the ability to rely on a BFOR defence. Essentially, the 1990 case narrowed the interpretation of what could be considered a BFOR defence from the broad interpretation given in the 1985 case.

These human rights cases all dealt with Acts that contained *statutory* BFOR language. There is no BFOR in subs. 41(6) which provides that an employer "shall accommodate ... to the extent that the accommodation does not cause the employer undue hardship". Board policy, however, as noted above, relies on the Ontario Human Rights Commission Guidelines, which include BFOR components.

At the Board, various policies detail:

- How to define "essential duties of a job", utilizing an analysis of what is called the "actual job outcome"; (Bill 99 *Operational Policies*, 9.3)
- What constitutes "alternative work comparable to the pre-injury job", by noting the duties performed, working conditions, skill and responsibility required, opportunities for advancement, whether the job is covered by the same collective agreement, etc.; (9.4)
- How "suitable employment" is to be determined, taking into account factors such as whether the worker has the necessary skills, is medically capable of performing the job and whether the worker is able to comply with occupational health and safety requirements; (9.5)
- The effect of an offer to re-employ at another geographic location, taking into account normal travel patterns with the employer. (9.4)

There have been only a few Tribunal decisions dealing with accommodation in a s. 41 context. In one decision, the Panel agreed with a Board worksite analyst that, with the provision of a chair, the worker would be able to do his job. It was further determined that the cost of providing a chair was not prohibitive and did not constitute a health and safety concern. In another Tribunal decision, the majority of the Panel rejected the argument that reinstating the worker to a "comparable" job would result in management-labour disputes. It also noted that the difference of salary — some $30,000 per year — was not likely to jeopardize the financial viability of the company which had some 1,000 workers. Still another Tribunal decision involved an accommodation that required having an apprentice assist the injured worker. When the apprentice left, and a second apprentice was hired, the Panel found that the second apprentice was not motivated and, therefore, the employer had not effectively accommodated the worker. There were other factors, however, that caused the Panel to find that the employer was not in breach of its obligations or, at worst, there was a technical breach.

(c) Rebutting the Presumption that a Termination within Six Months is a Violation of the Employer's Obligations

Under subs. 41(11) a worker may apply to the Board for a determination on whether his or her employer has complied with its re-employment obligations. The Board may also make such a determination on its own initiative. It should be stressed that this right to apply for a determination is *time limited*. Subsection 41(12) states that the Board is not required to consider such an application if it is not made within three months of the date of termination.

In a Tribunal decision in 1992, a worker was three days beyond the three-month limit, but the Panel accepted that the delay in having his compensation claim accepted exempted him from a strict enforcement of the time limit. The Panel in a 1995 Tribunal decision, despite finding on the merits that the employer had not breached its obligations, went on to note that the Board had no policy on subs. 54(12) [now subs. 41(12)]. The Board apparently took the position that these time limits should only be applied if a delay in the filing of a worker's application is materially prejudicial to the employer.

Subsection 41(10) reads:

> **41.** (10) If an employer re-employs a worker in accordance with this section and then terminates the employment within six months, the employer is presumed not to have fulfilled the employer's obligations under this section. The employer may rebut the presumption by showing that the termination of the worker's employment was not related to the injury.

In the first years of the re-employment provisions there were different approaches taken by the Board and the Tribunal in regard to what test an employer had to meet to rebut the presumption. The Board took the position that it could be rebutted on only two grounds: the employer had "just cause" related to the worker's conduct or performances of work duties, or the employment of the worker threatened the financial viability of the business.

The Tribunal, on the other hand, adopted a test that asked was there an "anti-injured worker animus in the termination"?

The wording in subs. 41(10) added the sentence "The employer may rebut the presumption by showing that the termination of the worker's employment was not related to the injury." This appears to adopt the Tribunal's approach and the Board policy, Bill 99 *Operational Policies*, 9.7, now provides that an employer is in breach of its obligations unless it can be established that

- the failure to re-employ or the termination was not caused, in any part, by the injury/disease or the claim for benefits under the insurance plan; or
- the nature of the termination does not discriminate against the worker.

(d) Employer Penalties and Worker Benefits

If an employer is found to be in contravention of its obligations, subs. 41(13) provides that the employer may be penalized and that the worker shall be compensated:

> **41.** (13) If the Board decides that the employer has not fulfilled the employer's obligations to the worker, the Board may,
>
> > (*a*)   levy a penalty on the employer not exceeding the amount of the worker's net average earnings for the year preceding the injury; and
> >
> > (*b*)   make payments to the worker for a maximum of one year as if the worker were entitled to payments under section 43 (loss of earnings).

(i) Employer Penalties

The Board originally maintained a stringent written policy with regard to employer penalties. That policy stated, in part:

> As a general rule, the Board levies the maximum penalty. However, the Board may reduce the amount of the penalty if, due to circumstances beyond the employer's control, the employer is unable to re-employ the worker ...
>
> The Board may also reduce a penalty if the employer agrees to re-employ the worker subsequent to a hearing at which it is determined that the employer failed to comply with its re-employment obligations.

In May 1995, the Board re-wrote its employer penalty policy to provide for greater flexibility in assessing penalties. It is no longer the general rule that a 100 per cent penalty is levied. Penalties may now be determined commensurate with the amount of time that the employer failed to meet its obligations. See Bill 99 *Operational Policies*, 9.8. The penalties imposed by the Board have varied considerably and it is worth a review of previous decisions.

(ii) Worker Benefits

In addition to the penalty provisions, subs. 41(13)(*b*) provides for the payment of benefits for up to one year, "as if the worker were entitled to compensation under section 43". To date, in most instances where a breach has been found to have occurred, the Board has provided full benefits up to the date of the Reinstatement Officer hearing and directed that, if the one-year period for benefits has not expired, further benefits should be determined by the Board's operating levels.

One Tribunal Panel suggested that these payments could be awarded retrospectively, "even for a period before the point at which the employer's obligation became manifest". In another case, the worker's refusal to work after 9 p.m. was considered by the Reinstatement Officer as unrelated to her compensable accident and the estimated hours that she could have worked after 9 p.m. were deducted in the calculation of her benefits. This decision was upheld by the Tribunal.

Another Tribunal decision considered the effect of severance pay on the payment of subs. 54(13)(*b*) benefits [now subs. 41(13)(*b*)]. In a majority decision it was held that these benefits were discretionary and intended to compensate for income lost because of an employer's breach of its re-employment obligations. That being the case, a severance package also met that need and subs. 54(13)(*b*) benefits were not payable during the period covered by the severance package. The relationship between worker benefits and ss. 37 [now s. 43] and 54 [now s. 41] is also discussed in another case where the Panel dealt with the worker's entitlement under both sections.

In a 1995 Tribunal decision, an agreement was reached between the worker and the accident employer prior to the hearing. The Panel accepted the settlement reached by the parties and allowed the employer's appeal, despite the apparent impediment presented by s. 18 [now s. 16] to such an arrangement.

(e) Collective Agreements

In determining a worker's re-employment rights, the Legislature noted that the return of a worker to modified duties might present a conflict in a workplace where a collective agreement established seniority rights. Therefore, the section provides that collective agreement rights should not be superseded by the Act, as follows:

> **41.** (15) If this section conflicts with a collective agreement that is binding upon the employer and if the employer's obligations under this section afford the worker greater re-employment terms than does the collective agreement, this section prevails over the collective agreement. However, this subsection does not operate to displace the seniority provisions of the collective agreement.

The Board will initially determine the worker's collective agreement status and if, in its view, the collective agreement offers greater rights, "the decision maker advises the worker to use the company's grievance procedure". Bill 99 *Operational Policies*, 9.9.

However, court decisions concerning provincial human rights provisions suggest that the requirement to accommodate may, under certain circumstances, take precedence over these provisions of a collective agreement. Of particular note is a case in which in the Supreme Court of Canada ruled that the provisions of a provincial human rights code took precedence over the provisions of the negotiated collective agreement. This case involved a worker who was found to have been the victim of adverse effect discrimination, discrimination that was not specifically directed at him, that was neutral on its face, but that had the effect of discriminating against a particular group — in this case, Seventh Day Adventists.

The Court found that the employer had an obligation to accommodate the worker's religious views, unless such an accommodation caused the employer "undue hardship". In addition, the worker's union also had a duty to accommodate the worker in two ways: (1) by refraining from negotiating collective agreements that contained provisions which might have an adverse effect; and (2) by not impeding "the reasonable efforts of an employer to accommodate".

This decision cited with approval a similar decision of the Ontario Divisional Court which held the worker's union had an equal obligation to accommodate the worker's religious beliefs. In that case, both the employer and the union were jointly and severally liable in the amount of $73,331.98, for wages lost as a result of the worker's dismissal.

These cases are significant because under the Ontario *Human Rights Code*, one of the prohibited grounds is handicap, including those resulting from compensable injuries. This raises the question as to the effect of subs. 54 (15) [now subs. 41(15)].

It would appear, on the face of it, that the direction of the Courts is that human rights code provisions can clearly over-ride provisions of collective agreements. The Court in one case noted that "private arrangements, whether by contract or collective agreement, must give way to the [Human Rights] statute". It remains to be seen whether the fact that seniority provisions are statutorily protected will have any effect. See M. Lynk and R. Ellis, "Unions and the Duty to Accommodate" (1992), 1:3 C.L.L.J. 238, for a critique of the relationship between human rights and labour relations. This whole issue of the journal deals with the duty to accommodate from a variety of perspectives.

In 1992, a tribunal held that the collective agreement subsections did not limit the obligation to re-employ to only bargaining unit jobs. This decision also held:

> It is our view that the intent of the *Workers' Compensation Act* reinstatement provisions is to ensure that the worker is returned, as far as is reasonably possible, to the position she would have been in had the accident not taken place. We are satisfied that that goal was met. In this case, it was not the worker's accident and disability, but the usual contingencies of the workplace and the effect of the collective agreement seniority provisions which resulted in the worker's demotions and lay-off.

This approach has been endorsed by the OLRB in a case in which it was ruled that returning injured workers could not "bump" more senior workers. This decision demonstrates the potential conflict of a trade union. In this case the union grieved the lay-off of the senior workers, taking a position contrary to that of their injured members.

Another complication arises out of the labour arbitration process sometimes being a parallel process that seeks to make findings of fact — and sometimes of law — arising out of the same events as those before a re-employment hearing. Two Tribunal decisions have dealt with situations in which the parties have had other labour relations disputes and have brought to the Tribunal global minutes of settlement. In each case, these minutes were accepted, although concern was expressed about the worker waiving benefits, contrary to s. 18 [now s. 16]. There were also concerns expressed about using the Tribunal as a discovery process for labour arbitration proceedings.

(f) Temporary/Contract Workers

The Board has a policy concerning the eligibility for workers on a temporary help agency's roster. In circumstances where a temporary worker has been injured, the return to comparable/suitable employment is judged to be a return to the "placement roster" for such employment. To date, there has been one Tribunal decision on point. That decision placed a restrictive interpretation on the Temporary and Contract workers policy, holding that it should be invoked only when an application of the statute would "be impossible or produce an absurd result".

CHAPTER 23

Employer Duties and Assessments

1. INTRODUCTION

A great number of issues relevant specifically to employers are dealt with in other chapters of this handbook. For example, see coverage (Chapter 5), accident reporting in the claims process (Chapter 11) and re-employment obligations (Chapter 22), *etc*.

This chapter discusses the employer's responsibility for providing information to the Board, making payment for the costs of coverage, ensuring that other employers make their payments to the Board and complying with other obligations to workers and to the Board.

2. REGISTERING WITH THE BOARD

Schedule 1 and Sch. 2 employers are required to register with the Board within ten days after becoming such an employer. Upon contacting the Board, employers are usually provided with a New Business Registration Kit that includes a guide for new employers.

Employers who are not mandatorily covered may apply for coverage and will be required to provide additional information regarding the coverage requested.

In addition to the obligation to register, Sch. 1 and Sch. 2 employers are also required to notify the Board within ten days if they cease to be a Sch. 1 or Sch. 2 employer or if they experience a material change in circumstances in connection with their obligations under the Act. Failure to notify is an offence that may be punishable by a fine and, in the case of individuals, imprisonment.

3. ELECTING COVERAGE FOR SOLE PROPRIETORS, EXECUTIVE OFFICERS, PARTNERS AND INDEPENDENT OPERATORS

A sole proprietor, partner in a partnership, independent operator, or executive officer of a corporation may apply to the Board to be deemed to be a worker under the Act. In the case of executive officers it is the corporation that actually makes the application to which the executive officer must join his or her consent. Applications must be in writing. The minimum period of coverage is three months.

Electing coverage can have a negative effect on an individual's ability to sue in case of workplace injury and on the ability to claim benefits under some private disability insurance plans. These negative effects, plus the cost of workers' compensation coverage, will often result in individuals being better off to select private insurance to provide protection against workplace injury.

The Board can, and does, place restrictions on accepting applications for personal coverage. These restrictions, many of which relate to the level of insured earnings that the Board will accept for coverage, are detailed in Board policies. For businesses in operation for less than one year, the Board sets the maximum covered earnings for a deemed worker at one-third of the annual maximum assessable earnings.

The Board may revoke its acceptance of an application if required premiums are not paid. The Board may also require payment of premiums in advance. In the case of injury, if payments are in arrears, the Board may recover the amount in arrears from the benefits payable.

Individuals who have elected coverage and then decided that they no longer wish coverage often end up in disputes with the Board about when coverage ended. According to Board policy, optional insurance continues until the Board receives a signed request to cancel it, the individual ceases to be associated with the business in an active way, the individual ceases to be eligible for coverage, or the Board terminates the insurance.

4. THE COST OF WORKERS' COMPENSATION COVERAGE

The cost of workers' compensation coverage is paid by the employer. It is an offence to demand a contribution from a worker for the cost of workers' compensation coverage. In addition to other penalties such as a fines or imprisonment, upon conviction, restitution may be ordered.

The cost of workers' compensation coverage for Sch. 2 employers with individual liability is directly driven by the cost of benefits in the claims for which the individual Sch. 2 employer is responsible. The Sch. 2 employer also pays a portion of the administrative costs of the Board. This is paid as a percentage of the employer's claims cost. The Board may also require a Sch. 2 employer to contribute to a reserve fund for Sch. 2 employers to relieve such employers from the costs associated with disasters or other circumstances.

The cost of workers' compensation coverage for Sch. 1 employers is largely determined by the assessment rate associated with the employer's rate group, the size of the employer's assessable payroll and the effect of the Board's experience rating programs. There are, in some instances, further adjustments based upon penalty assessments and other incentive programs.

(a) Assessment Rates

Assessment rates are expressed in dollars per $100 of payroll. This assessment rate is applied against the employer's assessable payroll to determine the size of the employer's assessment. The Board usually establishes and communicates its assessment rates on an annual basis.

The assessment rate applicable to a particular employer will depend upon the rate group in which the employer's operations belong. The classification of an employer within a rate group is based upon the end product or the business of the employer and not upon the production processes utilized by the employer. If the employer is conducting business within more than one industry, it may be possible that the employer might be included in more than one rate group. This will usually require a clear segregation of payroll between the two industries.

The assessment rate of a rate group is not appealable. The classification of an employer within a rate group, or groups, is appealable. Where an employer's rate group is changed, the Board may limit the retroactive benefit associated with a shift from a higher assessment rate group to a lower one.

To minimize workers' compensation assessments, employers may attempt to establish segregated payrolls to attract multiple classifications or they may contract out work or form associated companies to perform work that, on its own, attracts a lower assessment rate but is ancillary to the employer's primary business. Regulations under the Act provide the Board with the authority to limit, or eliminate, assessment rate savings that an employer might attempt to achieve through these types of reorganization.

The Board has developed an Employer Classification Manual to provide guidance on how classifications are supposed to take place.

(b) Assessable Payroll

Employers must report their assessable payroll periodically on a Premium Remittance form. Depending on the size of the employer, this reporting frequency might be monthly, quarterly, or annually. If the reporting is done monthly, at the end of the year the employer must do an additional reconciliation report (this is because there is a potential for under reporting of premiums with monthly reporting). Any employer who goes out of business within a year is also required to do a reconciliation report.

Assessable payroll is, essentially, the total pay received by workers of the employer eligible to receive workers' compensation payments, less any pay to individual workers that is in excess of the maximum insurable earnings ceiling. There are special rules for determining the assessable payroll associated with contractors who are considered to be workers of the employer.

The Board has developed a Premium Guide to provide instructions to employers regarding the completion of the Premium Remittance form and the Reconciliation form.

(c) Experience Rating

To encourage accident prevention, the Board has developed experience rating programs to create incentives for safety. There are currently three plans in effect.

Small employers with less than $1,000 per year in assessments may not be experience rated at all.

The Merit Adjusted Premium (MAP) program is directed at employers with between $1,000 and $25,000 per year in assessments. Discounts of up to 10 per cent of the employer's assessments and surcharges of up to 50 per cent of the employer's assessment (more in the case of fatal claims) are determined based upon the number of times in the last three years that the employer reported an injury that cost the Board more than $300.

The CAD-7 program is directed at employers in the construction industry and is based upon accident frequency and claims cost.

The NEER program is directed at non-construction employers with assessments in excess of $25,000 per year. The NEER program is also based upon accident frequency and claims cost.

Information can be obtained from the Board on the exact nature of the experience rating calculations under the MAP, CAD-7 and NEER programs. The MAP calculations are fairly straight forward. However, the CAD-7 and NEER calculations can be very complex.

(d) The Employer's Claims Cost Experience

Because the employer's claims cost history is utilized in the experience rating process (and in the penalty assessment process referred to below), many employers are very interested in the costs that the Board includes on the employer's claims cost record.

The Board is willing to remove charges from an employer's claims cost history if the employer can demonstrate that the charges were assigned to them in error, if the employer can obtain cost relief under the Board's Second Injury and Enhancement Fund (SIEF) policies, or if the employer can obtain a cost transfer to another Sch. 1 employer.

Second Injury and Enhancement Fund relief is granted when a pre-existing condition is responsible for increasing the duration of a disability or increasing the degree of residual disability following a compensable injury. Both physical and psychological disabilities are included. The pre-existing condition may or may not have been disabling prior to the compensable injury. SIEF relief lowers the employer's accident cost experience without reducing the benefits paid to the individual injured worker. However, depending upon the type of benefits in question, a pre-existing disability (rather than a condition) might reduce the worker's entitlement to benefits independently of SIEF considerations.

The first application of SIEF relief is likely to be cost relief at the 50 per cent level. However, on application by the employer the Board will apply the percentage figures as provided in Table 23-1.

Table 23-1
Percentages of Sief Relief Applicable

Pre-existing Condition	Minor Accident	Moderate Accident	Major Accident
Minor	50%	25%	0%
Moderate	75%	50%	25%
Major	90% to 100%	75%	50%

Source: Operational Policy Manual, Document No. D08-01-05.

According to this table, a minor accident is one that is expected to cause a non-disabling or minor disabling injury, a moderate accident is one that is expected to cause a disabling injury and a major accident is one that is expected to cause a serious disability with permanent disability a probability.

There may be a 100 per cent SIEF relief granted where there is a very strong relationship between the pre-existing condition and the accident itself, for instance, an accident caused by an epileptic seizure or by the wearing of an artificial appliance, or an accident occurring while the worker is involved in a rehabilitation program.

According to Board policy, with psychological conditions, the possibility of prior psychic trauma from life experience could be considered as evidence of vulnerability and could justify recommending relief to the employer, even in the absence of pre-existing psychological impairment.

(e) Cost Transfers

Where the Board is satisfied that the accident giving rise to the worker's injury was caused by the negligence of some other employer in Schedule 1 or that other employer's workers, the Board may direct that the benefits, or a portion of them, be charged against the accident cost record of the other employer. Once charged to the other employer, these costs will not appear on the accident employer's accident cost record.

(f) Incentive Programs

Under the Board's "Workwell" program additional assessments may be levied on employers who have not taken sufficient precautions to prevent accidents to workers, who have not provided safe working conditions, or who have not complied with first aid regulations. The Workwell program also provides for rebates for those employers demonstrating exemplary performance.

Workwell penalties are usually assessed where an employer who has been targeted for a Workwell evaluation does not, within a reasonable period of time, comply with a Board report indicating the need for improvements. Workwell penalties may be for amounts up to $100,000. An employer will, however, only be responsible for either an experience rating surcharge or the Workwell penalty, whichever is larger.

An additional incentive program offered by the Board is the Safe Communities Incentive Program (SCIP). The SCIP program has a geographic focus and relates to all employers within the targeted area who choose to participate. The program stresses training, partnership and evaluation in occupational health and safety matters. Through the achievement of cost reductions in the group as a whole, savings as defined by the Board are returned to the participating members in proportion to their share of workers' compensation premiums paid.

5. THE BOARD'S AUTHORITY TO INVESTIGATE AND ENFORCE THE REQUIREMENT TO PAY

If an employer incorrectly calculates the amount of premiums payable for a year and, as a result, pays an insufficient amount, the Board may fix the additional amount to be paid and, in addition, levy a penalty up to the size of the insufficient amount.

An employer who does not pay premiums when they become due shall pay the Board an additional percentage on the outstanding balance as the Board may require. In addition, the Board may require the employer to pay the Board the amount of the capitalized value (as determined by the Board) of the benefits payable in regard to any accident to the employer's workers during the period of default.

The Board may require security for payment of amounts that are, or may become, due, as long as the Board does so in accordance with policies it creates and complies with policies to govern this process.

The Board is also given extraordinary powers to set-off any money the Board may owe to a person, or to enforce any "debt" owing through a court application without appearance or through use of the municipal tax rolls.

The Board has the authority to examine the books and accounts of an employer and may investigate and make such inquiries as the Board considers necessary to ascertain the accuracy of statements given to the Board, the amount of the employer's payroll and whether the employer is a Sch. 1 or Sch. 2 employer.

In addition to other investigatory powers, the Board has the authority to enter into an employer's establishment to examine matters related to safety as well as related to determining the proportion in which the employer should be making payments under the Act.

Interference with the Board's investigatory authority is an offence.

6. LIABILITY FOR THE ASSESSMENTS OF CONTRACTORS

Unless the appropriate clearances from the Board are obtained, a person who retains a contractor or sub-contractor to execute work in an industry covered by the Act may be, subject to the right of reimbursement from the contractor or sub-contractor, liable to pay to the Board the workers' compensation premiums payable by the contractor or sub-contractor in regard to the work performed.

The owner of a premises, as defined under the *Construction Lien Act*, has a similar responsibility to ensure that workers' compensation premiums are paid by a Sch. 1 employer who is entitled to a lien under the *Construction Lien Act*. So too, a licensee under Part III of the *Crown Forest Sustainability Act, 1994* has responsibility for ensuring the payment of premiums by a person other than the licensee who harvests or uses forest resources for a designated purposes under that Act.

7. MISCELLANEOUS EMPLOYER OBLIGATIONS TO WORKERS

Employers are required to provide first aid appliances, including a first aid box, and services at a workplace. The requirements on what first aid appliances and services must be provided are set by regulation and vary according to the size of the employer. The Board produces a pamphlet explaining the requirements set by regulation.

The employer must maintain a notice board that includes the Board's poster, known as a Form 82, regarding the necessity of reporting all accidents and receiving first aid treatment. This Board must also display the valid first aid certificates of qualification of the trained workers on duty, an inspection card to record the date of the most recent inspection of the first aid box and the signature of the person making the inspection. The inspections must take place at least quarterly.

Records must be kept of all circumstances regarding an accident as described by the injured worker, the date and time of the accident, the names of witnesses, the nature and exact location of the injuries to the worker and the date, time and nature of each first aid treatment given.

At the time an injury occurs, if the worker needs transportation, the employer shall transport the worker to a hospital or to a physician located within a reasonable distance of the worker's home. The employer shall pay for the transportation.

8. OBJECTIONS

Employers are allowed to appeal most decisions regarding their obligations under the Act. However, there are some decisions, such as the setting of assessment rates, *etc.*, that are regarded as questions of general policy and are not appealable.

There is a limitation period of six months on making such objections to employer requirements. The exception to the six-month limitation is an objection concerning return to work or a labour market re-entry plan, which must be made within 30 days. Although a verbal objection might be effective, the Act requires a written objection. The Board has the authority to extend limitation periods to allow for objections "within such longer period as the Board may permit".

Outside of the ability to object within the time frames allowed, the Board retains the authority to reconsider any decision at any time.

Employers may obtain free legal advice from the Office of the Employer Advisor which is established pursuant to the Act within the Ministry of Labour.

Although the initial review of objections to employer assessment decisions may be slightly different from claims type objections in regard to the person or group of persons performing the review, the final level of appeal within the Board and then the appeal to the Workplace Safety and Insurance Appeals Tribunal are essentially similar to appeals regarding benefit matters.

CHAPTER 24

Medical Issues

1. INTRODUCTION

In addition to the income replacement aspect of workers' compensation, the Act provides for medical costs related to compensable disabilities. It is interesting that Meredith's draft Bill did not address the question of medical benefits, although, at the time, there was no health insurance to speak of (see Chapter 1, topic 2, The Meredith Report). During debate on the Bill, the opposition Liberals attempted to introduce an amendment providing that medical costs be covered. This amendment was due, in part, to a lobby from the medical profession who were concerned that their fees for treating injured workers might go unpaid. Although the amendment failed in 1914, it was soon adopted with the inclusion of a Medical Aid provision to the Act in 1917.

Health care benefits available through the workers' compensation system are discussed in Chapter 19. This chapter examines the Board's policies regarding medical issues, the right of employers to have injured workers examined by doctors chosen by the employer and, in general, the role of medicine in workers' compensation.

2. THE OUTSIDE PHYSICIAN'S ROLE

Subsection 33(1) provides that an injured worker "is entitled to such health care as may be necessary, appropriate and sufficient as a result of the injury and is entitled to make the initial choice of health professional practitioner". This choice is deemed to have been made when a worker seeks treatment from a particular physician. In circumstances in which a worker receives *emergency treatment* at the time of the accident — from a company doctor or the emergency ward of a hospital, for example — the Board would not consider that an "initial choice" until a follow-up visit is made. If the follow-up visit is to the company doctor, that doctor would then be considered the "physician of choice".

Once a physician of choice has been established, the Board will not accept a change without its approval. Board policy indicates, for example, that mere dissatisfaction with an attending physician's opinion is not necessarily sufficient grounds to approve a change in doctors. There was no new policy concerning these issues and it is presumed that Board's *Operational Policy Manual*, continues to prevail.

As is described elsewhere, the typical claim is established at the Board upon receipt of two documents — the Form 7, Report of Accident from the employer and the Form 8, Physician's First Report — usually filed by the first physician who attends the injured worker. Often Form 8 will not be filed by the worker's attending physician. In emergency situations, for example, the Form 8 may well be submitted by a hospital emergency ward staff member.

All doctors' reports regarding the worker are required to be submitted to the Board by virtue of subs. 37(1) of the Act. It is also this section that overrides the general prohibition against a doctor reporting to a third party, found in the regulations under the *Health Disciplines Act*. It is these reports, particularly in the early stages of a claim, upon which the Board will base its decisions on payment of benefits.

Subsection 33(2) provides that the Board shall pay for a worker's health care and subs. 33(3) gives the Board the authority to establish a fee schedule for this purpose.

Generally, the Board will not question a family doctor's diagnosis and prognosis in uncomplicated and/or short-term claims. If there is a clear accident history and the disability is compatible with the accident, the Board will generally leave treatment, and advice on a return to work date, to the family doctor's discretion. In short-term uncomplicated claims the injured worker and his or her doctor will, therefore, have minimal contact with the Board.

(a) Chiropractors

It should be noted that the worker has the choice of "health professional". Injured workers often seek treatment from a chiropractor. The Board will allow this, but the "treatment control" procedures tend to be a little more stringent than for a medical doctor. Where a worker is referred to a chiropractor, the Board's *Operational Policy Manual* indicates that, "initial treatment by a chiropractor is limited to a maximum of 12 weeks". Chiropractic treatment beyond that requires *pre*-authorization from the Board.

A more comprehensive explanation existed in the Board's former *Health Care Benefits Policy* and is worth noting:

> Control of the length of treatment by the Chiropractor or referral to a specialist will be an internal matter at the Board based upon these [chiropractic] reports ...
> ... recognizing that, in general terms, a large percentage of back disabilities are recovered within a six (6) week period irrespective of the type of treatment (or lack thereof), it is recommended that these claims [i.e., those involving Chiropractors] should be specifically reviewed at the end of six (6) weeks from the time of accident to determine future course of treatment. If chiropractic treatment is to be allowed after that date, it would be the responsibility of the Section Medical Advisor to establish an appropriate system of recall.

(b) Ongoing Treatment

In more serious claims, the doctor is required to submit ongoing "Physician's Progress Reports" to the Board. These reports, in part, ask the doctor's opinion on diagnosis, prognosis, whether complete recovery is expected, whether there are any medical restrictions on returning to regular or part-time work, whether the worker has been referred to a specialist and whether permanent restrictions are anticipated. At this stage the Board may seek further medical information through a referral to a specialist or an examination by a Board-employed doctor.

The outside physician may be called upon to perform a number of functions related to the compensation system. These functions include providing ongoing reports to the Board concerning the worker's medical status, giving opinions on the ability of patients to return to regular or modified work and responding to questions concerning causation.

Although the Board undertook a major training program for the roster of doctors undertaking non-economic loss assessments, many family doctors have received next to no training in this area. The result of this is that they may feel uncomfortable in corresponding with the Board on behalf of their patients. They will either defer to the authority of Board doctors or make sweeping statements in their patient's favour. Either response is not helpful to any party. Outside physicians will also often respond to requests for medical reports in the manner in which they have been trained; namely, by providing a description of the condition and the treatment being rendered. These reports will often omit the major question in many Board claims — causation, "Is the diagnosed disability compatible with the injury as described?"

(c) Causation

A legal approach to causation often differs markedly from a medical approach. In a workers' compensation system, which requires the "balance of probabilities" to establish entitlement, all that may be required is a finding that "more likely than not" a particular condition arose from a particular accident.

The medical profession, on the other hand, is trained to require a higher standard of proof in arriving at its conclusions. Hence, a doctor dealing with a Board patient may tend to be more conservative in his or her conclusions than the patient or representative would like. "It is possible ...", "cannot be ruled out ...", "may be related ...", *etc.*, are phrases that are often sprinkled throughout medical reports. These phrases may be compared with the opinions of Board doctors who are generally not so reticent in their opinions. Faced with a cautious "maybe" from an outside doctor and a definitive "no" from a Board doctor, it is not surprising that other personnel at the initial levels will opt for the latter medical opinion.

There are also situations in which the outside doctor, for a variety of reasons, makes a sweeping declaration in favour of the patient. This may result in a supportive medical opinion being discredited by its very enthusiasm. It is important that the doctor base his or her opinion on an accurate history, a solid understanding of the worker's job description and a knowledge of any previous, or coexisting, medical problems.

What is needed from the medical professional — both at the Board and outside — is as clear a description of the medical situation as can be provided. This will ideally include the reasoning behind a particular opinion. What scientific/ medical evidence drives the author of a report to reach one conclusion over another? If one explanation is "possible", is another one — or several — equally possible?

There is often a concern expressed on the part of employers, that some outside doctors tend to act as advocates for their patients. Medical professionals carelessly advocating for or against *a patient/claimant*, without scientific/ medical support, tend to act against everyone's interests in the long run. On the other hand, doctors dealing with workers, employers and the Board should not be afraid to advocate for or against a *scientific/medical proposition*, based upon their professional expertise and review of the literature, and such advocacy should explain the reasons behind their positions.

It is also the case that employers retain some doctors whose reports take an employer advocacy position. The same comments and cautions apply as those noted for workers' doctors.

(d) Disability, Impairment or Handicap?

In the 1989 Bill 162 amendments, the words "disability" and "impairment" were defined for the first time in the Act. The definitions were found in subs. 1(1) of the *Workers' Compensation Act* and read as follows:

> "disability", in relation to an injured worker, means the loss of earning capacity of the worker that results from an injury;
>
> . . .
>
> "impairment", in relation to an injured worker, means any physical or functional abnormality or loss including disfigurement which results from an injury and any psychological damage arising from the abnormality or loss.

Bill 99 eliminated the term "disability" and retained virtually the same definition of "impairment".

The semantics of workers' compensation can cause confusion among outside medical practitioners when the nature of what is being assessed is variously described as disability, impairment, handicap, etc. Each of these terms may appear interchangeable to the layperson, but each has a distinct and often separate meaning to the outside practitioner, the Board, the injured worker and the employer. This is particularly true since 1990 when the term permanent *impairment* replaced permanent *disability*.

(e) The Family Doctor's Role in Rehabilitation

Board staff have suggested that "outside doctors were a major cause of injured workers not returning to work", because of a "poor understanding of occupational medicine and the importance and benefits of early proactive medical rehabilitation in the profession". Despite this, the role of the family doctor still has a significant role in the workers' compensation system.

With regard to early and safe return to work (ESRTW), subs. 37(3) provides that the family doctor (or other health professional), "shall give the Board, the worker and the employer such information as may be prescribed concerning the worker's functional abilities".

In addition, the ESRTW elaborates on this by including the responsibility to:

- Identify the most appropriate treatment;
- Ensure the worker's timely access to treatment; and
- Ensure the possibility of return to work is discussed throughout treatment.

In many cases, it will be the family doctor who will be providing, at least initially, the front line opinion on whether a worker is medically able to do pre-employment duties or perform suitable other work or what accommodations to the work or the workplace are required. All of these require a knowledge on the doctor's part of exactly what the essential duties of the pre-injury employment entailed and what accommodations might be necessary. In addition, subjective considerations would be necessary on the doctor's part in determining what would constitute suitable or accommodated work.

If the worker becomes involved in a labour market re-entry programme, subs. 42(5)(*b*) notes that the plan shall be prepared in consultation with, among others, "the worker's health practitioners if the Board considers it necessary to do so".

(f) What to Ask

It is apparent that when there are medical disputes in a workers' compensation claim, the informed opinions of the attending family doctor and specialist(s) will often be extremely important. However, those opinions must be sought in light of the criteria required by the Board and the Tribunal; criteria that are often different than those asked of doctors for other purposes.

David Craig, one worker's representative, outlined in fairly extensive detail the procedure for soliciting information from the attending physicians. He recommends a "checklist" which should include:

1. a careful and objective outline of the relevant history and the medical issue in dispute;
2. enclosing any relevant medical reports from other sources;
3. asking for references from the medical literature, where appropriate;
4. asking for comment on any alternative explanations when, for example, there is a dispute concerning etiology;
5. ensuring that any special qualifications or special skills are included in the doctor's report;
6. stressing that what is being sought is evidence for a proceeding which deals with *probabilities*, not necessarily scientific *certainties*.

Finally, it is important to stress that what is being sought is a medical/scientific opinion on a medical/scientific question. There is often a tendency among doctors to want to express their *legal* opinions; that is, they will conclude that a condition is or is not compensable. A medical opinion is only one piece of evidence — although often the most critical — used to determine a claim. The claim will ultimately stand or fall on a legal and policy determination.

3. THE ROLE OF BOARD DOCTORS

One of the most contentious groups at the Board is the medical personnel. The Board has on staff a large number of doctors and other health professionals who provide advice at virtually every stage of a claim. Often that advice consists of a one- or two-sentence memo to the file, giving an opinion on whether the claim should be allowed (or continued) or not. Criticism of this function has come from a wide variety of sources.

Essentially, these criticisms centred on the medical opinions produced by the worker's or employer's physicians often being overridden in favour of a terse comment from a Board consultant or medical advisor. The scientific/medical basis for this comment was rarely given, so the aggrieved party was not in a position to develop a counter-argument in an appeal. Reliance on Board medical opinions also engendered an apprehension of bias in the minds of many parties.

The Board itself noted the criticism of its internal medical opinions in a 1988 report:

> Public criticism has raised fundamental concerns about the quality of medical opinions made by Board physicians and the manner of obtaining and assessing such opinions. Some groups have criticized the Board for showing a preference for internal medical opinions over those of external attending physicians, particularly when this preference results in adverse administrative decisions.

And it recommended,

> When the opinion of the Board physician is in conflict with that expressed by external attending physicians, the decision maker must decide how much weight should be given to the various opinions.

In a 1992 report it was recommended that,

> The Board must ensure that Board doctors use job descriptions and physical demands analyses in providing their medical opinions in the day-to-day management of claims.

In the past, the Board was also actively involved in medical assessment and rehabilitation through its Downsview Rehabilitation Centre in northwest Toronto. The assessment function is now carried out through regional evaluation centres, usually affiliated with local hospitals.

4. THE TRIBUNAL AND MEDICAL ISSUES

(a) General

The Tribunal has indicated in its decisions that it is interested in the *reasoning* of medical opinions. In dealing with issues involving conflicting medical opinions, the Tribunal has indicated that it prefers medical reports which outline the medical/scientific basis for a particular conclusion. In dealing with the adjudicative versus medical aspects of reports, the Tribunal has indicated that it expects a medical report to deal with *medical* issues.

It is apparent that the Tribunal has broadened the scope of inquiry into medical issues. As a result, in practical terms, there has been a broader discussion of the medical problems inherent in workers' compensation among workers, employers, their representatives and the medical community.

The Tribunal has refused to admit medical evidence that was obtained by an employer's representative without the worker's consent. This evidence was deemed to have been obtained in contravention of regulations under the *Health Disciplines Act*. Improperly obtained medical evidence has also been criticized, but accepted under particular circumstances.

(b) The Tribunal Panel of Medical Practitioners

The 1985 legislation establishing the Tribunal also authorized a roster of medical practitioners, appointed by Cabinet, to whom the Tribunal may submit medical disputes. The Tribunal has the authority to require a worker to submit to a medical examination. As of January 1, 1998, the Tribunal Chair could directly establish what is now known as a "list of health professionals".

The Tribunal roster or list, known as "assessors", are called upon from time to time to provide medical opinions concerning individual appeals. These opinions can be based on a full or partial physical examination of the worker or simply on a paper review of the existing medical reports. Subsection 134(5) limits an assessment to a doctor who has not treated or acted as a consultant in the treatment of the worker, or a member of the worker's family, in the past, and is not the partner of someone who has. The Tribunal has noted, however, that that does not preclude a panel from receiving a report, prepared for a party, from a roster doctor who was acting in a capacity other than under s. 134 (formerly s. 87).

It has also been noted that the assessment done pursuant to s. 134 is a process that is to be controlled by the Tribunal Panel and that the parties should not provide the assessor with information or seek clarification of information. Similarly, an assessment under s. 134 was to be done only at the panel's discretion, not automatically, at the request of a party. Finally, there have been at least three cases in which the worker refused to attend an assessor examination. In two of these cases, the Panels felt they could decide the issues on the existing evidence before them. The other case involved an employer appeal against a one-week period of benefits. The worker's refusal to attend was held to be a serious disregard of his obligations and the hearing was adjourned, although the employer's appeal was ultimately dismissed. In an addendum, the majority expressed a concern about the number of resources expended on a minor claim.

In addition to this case-by-case involvement, some assessors have written generic papers for the Tribunal concerning various areas of medicine, such as lumbar disc disease and chronic obstructive lung disease. These "discussion papers" are generally included in the Case Record material provided for an individual case and are also available in the Tribunal library.

The Tribunal has the power to order an examination by an assessor and there are negative consequences for a worker who fails to comply. Similar limitations protect possible conflicts of interest for health professionals. There is, however, one added clarification. Subsection 134(6) reads:

> (6) If the chair or a vice chair of the Appeals Tribunal determines that an issue on an appeal concerns the Board's decision on a health report or opinion, the chair or vice chair may require the worker to submit to an examination by a health professional (selected by the chair or vice chair) and the worker shall do so.

5. SECTION 23 — EMPLOYER-REQUESTED MEDICAL EXAMINATIONS

As of October 1, 1985, the Act provided for an employer's right to have a worker submit to a medical examination by a "medical practitioner selected, and paid for, by the employer". The history of s. 23 of the *Workers' Compensation Act* prior to that date indicates the difficulty that the courts, the Legislature and the Board have had in balancing the competing interests of a worker's right to privacy and an employer's right to information on the medical condition and restrictions of the employee.

(a) Employer Directed Medical Examinations for Post-1998 Injuries

Under Bill 99 an employer continues to have the right to order a medical examination. For injuries occurring on and after January 1, 1998, subs. 36(1) of the Schedule provides a requirement similar to s. 23 of the pre-1997 Act; that is, that an employer can require that a worker who "claims or is receiving benefits under the insurance plan shall submit to a health examination by a health professional selected and paid for by the employer". The worker continues to have the right to object.

The Board's Bill 99 *Operational Policies*, 16.2, indicates that it will *not* become involved in a dispute over an employer's request until three threshold conditions are met; that is:

1.   The issue involves a worker claiming or receiving benefits;
2.   The worker has refused to attend, or is objecting to the nature and extent of the employer requested examination; and,
3.   The accident employer has filed a request with the Board within 14 days of the worker's objection.

The Board's policy criteria for deciding on the necessity of an examination include consideration of whether such an examination would:

1.   assist the worker in an early and safe return to work;
2.   provide significant new information not already available to the employer through the usual file access provisions; or,
3.   clarify such matters as:
     • discrepancies in opinions between health professionals;
     • the nature of the injury;
     • work-relatedness;
     • the level of impairment;
     • the nature of the worker's physical precautions.

The Board's directions under s. 36 will be similar to those of the Tribunal under the pre-1997 Act; that is, direct the worker to attend the requested examination, find that the worker is not obliged to attend, or direct the employer to arrange an alternative examination. If the worker fails to attend such a directed examination the Board *will* determine whether there is reasonable cause, such as severe weather conditions, death in the family or serious illness. If no reasonable cause is found benefits are reduced or suspended.

It should be noted that there is no explicit authority to release a report on a s. 36 examination to the worker or to the Board. The policy does note:

> The examining health professional or the employer is encouraged to provide a copy of the health examination to the worker (or to the worker's health care practitioner) and/or to the Board.

Although there is no appeal to the Tribunal, a s. 36 decision is appealable within the Board's internal appeal system.

(b) The Transitional Provisions

The transition sections of Bill 99 pose a bit of a mystery concerning employer requested medical examinations. Subsection 123(2) of the Schedule clearly provides that, as of January 1, 1998, the Appeals Tribunal does not have jurisdiction to decide appeals under s. 36. Therefore, the Tribunal clearly has no jurisdiction to deal with any employer requested medical examination pursuant to an injury occurring after January 1, 1998.

Equally clear is that, under s. 23 of the pre-1997 Act, the Tribunal had *exclusive* jurisdiction to adjudicate employer requested medical examinations. Section 102 provides:

> **102.** The pre-1997 Act, as it is deemed to have been amended by this Part, continues to apply with respect to pre-1998 injuries.

"[T]his part", is Part IX of the Schedule and comprises sections 101–112. Therefore, the pre-1997 Act, *as amended by the sections in Part IX*, continue to apply. Section 112 provides that certain provisions of the pre-1997 Act are repealed, including the *general* jurisdiction of the Tribunal to hear appeals under the pre-1997 Act after January 1998. This jurisdiction is then replaced by subs. 112(3), which reads:

> **112.** (3) Sections 120 and 123, subsection 125(2), section 126 and subsections 174(1) to (5) of this Act apply, with necessary modifications, to pre-1998 injuries and to decisions of the Board rendered before January 1, 1998, but the time limits in section 120 and subsection 125(2) apply only from January 1, 1998.

Section 23 of the pre-1997 Act, however, is *not* repealed. And, under subs. 23(2), a worker may "apply to the Appeals Tribunal to hear and determine the matter and the Appeals Tribunal may set aside the requirement or order the worker to submit to and undergo a medical examination by a medical practitioner or make such further or other order as may be just".

Therefore, what final decision-making authority exists for an employer's request for a medical examination relating to a pre-1998 injury is not clear. The plainest reading results in an absurdity: the parties have a right to appeal to the Appeals Tribunal, but the Appeals Tribunal does not have the jurisdiction to hear and decide the appeal.

The Board, in a letter to the Tribunal's General Counsel, has taken the position that, effective January 1, 1998, the provisions of s. 36 of Bill 99 apply, no matter when the injury occurred. The previous s. 23 provisions "have been superseded and rendered inoperative by the new WSIA provisions". This position is so, it is argued, by virtue of the phrase "with necessary modifications" in subs. 112(3).

This matter is one of many remaining to be adjudicated.

(c) Employer Requested Medical Examinations for Pre-1998 Injuries

In the event that the transitional provisions do provide for the application of s. 23 of the pre-1997 Act to pre-1998 injuries, a review of Tribunal decisions is worthwhile.

Subsection 23(1) seems to provide, on a literal reading, an unbridled right for an employer to require a medical examination. Subsection (2) contemplates a worker objecting to such an examination and provides for an application to the Appeals Tribunal to resolve the matter. The legislation gives no hint about what a legitimate "objection" may be. The Appeals Tribunal developed criteria in its early decisions on the limits of a s. 23 examination and has discussed at some length the criteria to be used and the reasons for arriving at these criteria.

In a "Technical Appendix" to one Tribunal decision, a voluntary process was established by which the parties will be contacted by the Tribunal in an effort to informally mediate the dispute before the date set for hearing. To date, the Tribunal has found that this mediation has resulted in many potential s. 23 applications being resolved without the need for a formal hearing.

In setting these criteria there is clearly the influence of other legislation at work. The *Canadian Charter of Rights and Freedoms*, for example, was referred to several times in the debate leading to the 1985 amendments. Although no specific provision of the Charter was cited, presumably one of the concerns was s. 7, providing for "security of the person". An unwanted medical examination, it can be argued, represents a violation of the security of the person and, therefore, should be countenanced only in accordance with the "principles of fundamental justice".

On more substantive elements, Tribunal decisions have held that:

- An employer must establish "in all the circumstances, is the medical examination important to the achievement of a valid employer's workers' compensation goal?" A dissenting opinion in another case held that the test should be one in which it is demonstrated that the Board or Tribunal requires additional medical information to properly adjudicate the claim. The validity of the general test adopted by the Tribunal has been challenged by way of judicial review and upheld.
- As a general rule, an employer should have had access to a worker's Board file before applying under s. 23, although in one decision, an examination was ordered, without file access, where it was found that there was a lack of medical information in the Board file because of the passage of time.
- The provisions of s. 23 apply to workers and employers falling under the federal *Government Employees Compensation Act* and were not overridden by medical examination provisions in a collective agreement. The jurisdictional ruling in a number of similar decisions was upheld.
- A s. 23 application was premature, if brought during an appeal process at the Board.
- Section 23 examinations are limited to those carried out by a medical practitioner licensed under Part III of the *Health Disciplines Act*. In one case, for example, an employer's application was refused because it sought an examination by a doctor of psychology.
- While the worker may not have to attend an *employer*-selected doctor, the Tribunal may direct the selection of a doctor or other health professional. This is in keeping with the subs. 23(2) provision that the Tribunal may "make such further or other order as may be just".

One interesting situation was addressed by a Tribunal Panel. A worker had a sample of tissue removed from his lung during an operation. This sample had, apparently, never been subjected to a pathology test which, in the employer's opinion, might determine the presence of asbestos fibres. The "medical examination" request was therefore a request to examine already existing tissue samples from the worker, not the worker himself. The Panel did not have to directly address the question of whether this could be seen as a medical examination request, as it was found that the examination request failed for other reasons.

CHAPTER 25

The Appeals Procedure

1. OVERVIEW

Most decisions made by the Board are open to appeal by either the worker or the employer affected. This chapter examines the history and practice of appealing adverse Board decisions. Special circumstances involved in dealing with employer assessment appeals have been dealt with in Chapter 23. This chapter looks at other areas in which an injured worker or the worker's employer is unhappy with the initial decision of the Board.

(a) History

Prior to 1985, the question of appeals was addressed in the pre-1985 Act as follows:

> **79**. The Board shall determine its own practice and procedure in relation to applications, appeals and proceedings and may, subject to the approval of the Lieutenant Governor in Council, make rules governing such practice and procedure and the exercise of its powers in relation thereto and prescribe such forms as are considered advisable.

Later, in 1984, subs. (2) was added (s. 72(2)) to direct the Board to promptly communicate in writing its decisions with reasons. Further, the Board was declared exempt from the provisions of the *Statutory Powers Procedure Act* and given the general direction to make decisions based "upon the real merits and justice of the case" and was not "bound to follow strict legal precedent but shall give full opportunity for a hearing".

In 1980, Professor P.C. Weiler recommended that an independent Appeal Tribunal be established. This Tribunal came into being in 1985.

The 1967 McGillivray Royal Commission described the pre-1965 appeal process in three paragraphs. The process was a secretive one in which the parties had little input and "At no step of the former system was the rejected claimant formally advised of his rights of appeal."

As Table 25-1 shows, between 1977 and 1985 the appeal structure at the Board consisted of a three-tiered process. The initial stage — the Review Branch/Group — was composed of Claims Review, Rehabilitation Review and Medical Aid Review. Any one of these, as the names imply, served as an internal, paper review of initial decisions of these operating divisions. Claims would be forwarded for review upon an objection being voiced, although often they would be reviewed on the Board's own motion.

Table 25-1
Appeal Procedures in Workers' Compensation
1965 — Present

I. 1965-1975
1. The Review Committee
2. The Appeal Tribunal
3. The Appeal Board

II. 1975-1977
1. Claims Review Branch/Specialist
2. The Appeals Examiner Inquiry
3. The Appeal Board Hearing

III. 1977-1985
1. The Claims Review Branch/Review Specialist
2. The Appeals Adjudicator Hearing
3. The Appeal Board Hearing

IV. October 1, 1985 — October 2, 1995
1. Decision Review Branch
2. Hearing/Reinstatement Officer
3. Appeals Tribunal

V. October 2, 1995 — December 31, 1997

"Entitlement Stream"	"Mediation Stream"
1. Appeals Officer	1. Mediator/Reinstatement Officer
2. Appeals Tribunal	2. Appeals Tribunal

VI. January 1, 1998 — Current
1. Appeals Resolution Officer
2. Appeals Tribunal

An appeal from the decision of the CRB then lay with an Appeals Adjudicator. The Appeals Adjudicators were also long-term employees of the Board who had had considerable experience at the lower levels. The Appeals Adjudicator stage of the process in virtually all cases involved an oral hearing, in which both the worker and the employer were allowed to make submissions. As of October 1, 1985, the title "Appeals Adjudicator" was replaced with that of "Hearings Officer". In theory, an Appeals Adjudicator was allowed to make a positive decision in an appeal, without a hearing, based upon the file. This was, however, an extremely rare occurrence.

Finally, the Appeals Adjudicator decision could be appealed to a three-person panel of the Appeal Board. These panels were drawn from the Commissioners of the Board, many, if not most of whom, had no previous workers' compensation experience. The Commissioners were Cabinet appointments, some of whom were also Corporate Commissioners sitting on the Corporate Board. In some instances, the Board encouraged claimants to skip the Appeals Adjudicator stage and take adverse decisions dealing with policy matters in particular, directly to the Appeal Board. With the coming into force of Bill 101, in 1985, the Appeal Board was disbanded, and replaced by the Workers' Compensation Appeals Tribunal.

As of October 2, 1995, the Board introduced a new internal appeal structure intended to streamline an increasingly burdened appeal system. Excluding vocational rehabilitation, re-employment and non-economic loss appeals, incoming objections at the Board increased from 17,301 to 39,771 during the five-year period 1990-1994. During this same period, new claims declined significantly from 473,407 to 370,444.

During this same period, and beyond, there has been a huge increase of appeals to the Tribunal, from 1,534 appeals in 1990 to 11,054 in 1998.

2. THE APPEAL PROCESS WITHIN THE BOARD

(a) Overview

The Board has a long history of trying to remain isolated from the formal procedures of the courtroom, or even more formal administrative tribunals. The McGillivray Royal Commission commented, in 1967:

> I would be very much opposed to the appeal structure and procedures becoming overly formal or tending toward an adversary system with cross-examination and other features of such a system. I believe that this is also the view and policy of the Board. It is, of course, important that, while maintaining a degree of informality, the appeal hearings be conducted on some orderly, organized basis but I urge the Board to continue its efforts to see that in the process of developing an orderly procedure the hearings do not become formidable in the eyes of the workman so that he feels out of place in them or discouraged from presenting his case in person or by a non-legal representative.

So it was — and still is — that the workers' compensation appeals system attempted to walk the fine line between informality and due process; between making the average injured worker or small business manager feel comfortable in "having their say" and developing a jurisprudence of consistent and reasoned decisions in an area with a multitude of complex medical and legal pitfalls.

On the formal side, the appeal process is a hearing in which sworn, *vive voce* evidence is usually heard. Formerly, a court reporter recorded the proceedings and copies of transcripts were available to the parties free of charge, upon request. Although there is no strict burden of proof, the appellant usually goes first and presents his or her case.

On the informal side, strict rules of evidence do not apply and often second-hand, hearsay and written evidence is accepted. Presiding over a non-adversarial, inquiry system, the decision-maker will consider the evidence given and submissions made in light of the information already available on file, whether or not a "contrary" position has been taken at the hearing. In fact, it is not unheard of for a worker's appeal to be supported by his or her employer during a hearing. Such support, however, will not necessarily ensure a successful outcome of the appeal.

Prior to October 1995, a three-step process of internal appeal existed at the Board; the first two were generally paper reviews by the operating level and then by the Decision Review Branch. Following these paper reviews, there was an oral hearing before a Hearings/Appeals Officer or Reinstatement Officer. Each of these stages was intended to be independent of the other and, until the formal hearing process, there was little communication between the Board and the interested parties.

Between October 1995 and January 1998, the Board split its appeals process into two "streams": entitlement and mediation. Generally, the mediation stream dealt with:

- Section 54 re-employment cases;
- Section 7 employment benefits;
- Vocational rehabilitation decisions and benefit issues which might flow from such decisions;
- Objections to decisions about worker co-operation in medical rehabilitation programs; and
- Objections to future economic loss quantum decisions.

With the advent of Bill 99, the appeal system within the Board reverted to a single stream, although the new system is said by the Board to combine principles developed in both the previous streams. See the Workplace Safety and Insurance Board's *Appeals System: Principles and Procedures*, January 1998.

With the advent of re-employment provisions in 1990, the Board began to offer mediation services to assist workers and employers in arriving at mutually satisfactory re-employment accommodation. Since 1995, there is a general direction for the Board to provide mediation services and explicit directions under a number of specific circumstances.

Under Bill 99, mediation was explicitly provided in only one area; subs. 40(7) directed that the Board "attempt to resolve" a dispute through mediation concerning the "early and safe return to work" provisions. Otherwise, there is the general authority provided by s. 122 that "[t]he Board may provide mediation services in such circumstances as it considers appropriate".

There is also a similar brief, general authority for the Appeals Tribunal, in s. 130, to provide mediation services. In considering the mediation provisions, one should note s. 16 of the *Workplace Safety and Insurance Act, 1997* (the Act), which reads:

> **16.** An agreement between a worker and his or her employer to waive or to forego any benefit to which the worker or his or her survivors are or may become entitled under the insurance plan is void.

A similar provision is found at s. 18 of the *Workers' Compensation Act.*

A number of Tribunal decisions have considered this problem from a re-employment perspective.

(b) Evidence — the Board File

Apart from the testimony of the appellant, the most important evidence usually lies in the information already gathered by the Board in the initial adjudication stages. Prior to 1982 the Board file was unavailable to the appellant. To all parties requesting it, the Board supplied a "Summary of Information" which, as the name implies, summarized the material within the file.

Effective December 28, 1981 the Board reversed this policy of confidentiality and started to provide claimants and their employers with copies of virtually all information in their claim files.

The Board file is composed of a number of sections, separated by coloured pages. These sections include:

(1) *Internal memos and medical reports.*
  (a) All relevant phone conversations, recommendations from supervisors and some *Board* medical opinions are recorded in numbered Board memos. These appear, in chronological order at the top of this section, with the latest memo on top.
  (b) From Memo #1 to the bottom of the section are the medical reports from outside doctors and medical opinions and diagnoses from Board doctors. These include the various forms that the Board requires the attending physician to submit, as well as any relevant hospital records or special reports.

(2) *Correspondence.*
This section contains copies of all external, non-medical correspondence involved in the claim, and, somewhat oddly, copies of any Board Investigation Notes.

(3) *Rehabilitation Reports.*
If the injured worker was involved with the Board's former Vocational Rehabilitation Division, this section, containing Rehab reports, will also be present.

Claims registered since January 1990 have been "imaged"; that is, all information concerning the claim is electronically stored. Paper documents that arrive are scanned into this electronic file. Unfortunately, the start-up phase of this new technology has resulted in a number of problems. When hard copies of these imaged files are provided to parties, there have been problems with the quality of the copies and with the duplication or chronologically inaccurate numbering of memos.

(c) Subpoenas

Section 132 (1) of the Act provides the Board and the Tribunal with the power to summons witnesses. In practice, the Board does not utilize its subpoena power very frequently. When it does, it is most often at the request of an appellant who must satisfy the Board about why a subpoena is necessary. Summonses are more common at the Tribunal level, although still rare.

(d) The Appeals Resolution Officer

The main documentary evidence before an Appeals Resolution Officer (ARO) is the Board file. Board policy deals with the circumstances under which videotape evidence and hearsay evidence (other than the Board file) may be admitted. Generally, videotape evidence must be considered authentic, relevant and not prejudicial.

Using other decisions at the Appeals Officer level is more accepted than it once was. The Appeals Officer is expected to "consider", although not be bound by, other Board decisions. Tribunal decisions, being "made at the highest level of appeal" should also be considered. They are not, however, to be treated as precedents, "unless accepted by the Board". Board policy also notes that parties to a hearing may use decisions from other forums such as the Ontario Labour Relations Board and the Ontario Human Rights Commission. Again, such decisions will not be binding on the Appeals Officer. (09-01-08)

Board policy on the hearing process also deals with adjournments and postponements, witnesses and subpoenas and travel expenses to hearings. (09-02-02; 09-02-03; and 09-02-04, respectively).

Bill 99 provided a major change in the new statutory time limits on appeals in s. 120. Subsection 120(1)(*a*) provides that decisions concerning a labour market re-entry plan must be appealed within 30 days. Subsection (1)(*b*) provides a six-month limit for other decisions. In either case the Board may extend the time limit. These time limits apply to decisions made on or after January 1, 1998.

The Board issued a notice indicating that it expects to be notified of a party's *intention* to appeal within this six-month window. However, the party that chooses not to proceed immediately will receive a letter "explaining that the statutory time limit has been met and asking [the party] to confirm when [the party] want[s] to proceed". This notice does not indicate whether there is then any further time limit, within which the decision to proceed must be made.

The Board indicated that, in the early days of Bill 99, the operating levels would be expected to be involved in various forms of dispute resolution, including reconsiderations. If there continues to be a dispute, the party, or parties, move to the Appeals Branch ("AB") where they will be given three options:

1.   The "60-Day decision option", in which a decision is reached by an ARO, based on written evidence and submissions only;
2.   The "Review/Enquiry/Hearing option". This approach is expected to be the most common one and entails an ARO discussing the issues and determining the most appropriate method of resolving the disputes. Hearings are contemplated, but it is implied that they will be the exception.
3.   "Special ADR projects". These projects will be developed in areas where there are larger employers with unions. The example is given of a project involving Stelco and the United Steelworkers Union, Local 1005 and a "dedicated ARO". The ARO in these cases will act more as a facilitator. Again, how this process will interact with the s.16 prohibition on the waiving of benefits is unclear.

> A fundamental objective of the appeal system is to provide every opportunity to resolve cases without a formal hearing. In-person hearings can contribute significantly to delays and to an adversarial relationship developing between the workplace parties.

Workplace Safety and Insurance Board, "Appeal System: Principles and Procedures", WSIB, January 1998.

It is worth noting that the interests of a union local and an individual injured worker may not necessarily coincide and that this should be taken into account in these large scale mediation processes.

These options are intended to resolve disagreements promptly, by an ARO who is familiar with the particular industry and who will consider all the issues that may arise in resolving the dispute.

Section 121 of the Act provides that the Board may reconsider any decision. It has indicated that the exercise of this reconsideration power will occur where there is a "technical error" or substantial new evidence is submitted.

3. THE APPEALS TRIBUNAL

As of October 1, 1985 the final level of appeal on compensation matters was with the Workers' Compensation Appeals Tribunal (WCAT), a body created by Bill 101. The rationale for the creation of the Tribunal was described in the Tribunal's *First Report*:

> The appeals themselves were, in fact, heard and determined by the governing body of the WCB itself through panels of specially designated Commissioners. The fact that it was members of the governing body who heard and determined appeals is of particular interest with respect to cases involving issues concerning the meaning of the Act itself. In most cases, there would exist an established WCB view of the meaning of the Act. This view would be found in the Board's written directives and guidelines and, as well, in the unwritten, corporate conventional wisdom that would have evolved over the years. These directives and guidelines would have been approved either directly or indirectly by the Commissioners, and the corporate conventional wisdom

concerning the meaning of the Act would, of course, be part of the received wisdom amongst the Commissioners themselves.

In these circumstances, the Appeals Commissioners' sensitivity to interpretation issues would obviously have been influenced generally by an intrinsic, unconscious presumption of validity. The Appeals Commissioners' major focus was on factual and medical issues and on the determination of the outcomes which the Board's established views of the Act should produce. The compatibility of the established Board view of the Act with the wording of the Act was an issue that was not often on their active agenda.

The presence in the former appeals system of that unconscious, intrinsic presumption of validity with respect to the Board's view of the Act, and the absence in Ontario in workers' compensation matters of significant court review of interpretation issues, had the practical consequence of allowing the WCB to pursue its own common-sense view of what the Act meant, free, to a large extent, from effective challenge.

That independence was helpful in making practical sense of a complicated subject. That, presumably, is why it was there. It carried with it, however, the seeds and the appearance of arbitrariness, the eventual rejection of which, at a political level, was largely responsible for the adoption of the external appeals system.

The WCAT was continued by s. 173 of Bill 99 under the name Workplace Safety and Insurance Appeals Tribunal (WSIAT).

(a) Composition

The Tribunal is a tripartite body composed along the lines of the Ontario Labour Relations Board. Membership on the Tribunal is by Order-in-Council appointment and generally has been for a three-year, renewable term.

In addition to the Order-in-Council appointments, there are also staff members at the WSIAT included in three main areas: the Tribunal Counsel Office (TCO), Research and Publications and Administration and Support.

(b) Jurisdiction

For injuries on and after January 1, 1998, the Tribunal's jurisdiction is contained in s. 123 of the Act. For pre-1998 injuries the jurisdiction in the pre-1997 Act prevails, with some exceptions outlined below.

Basically, the Tribunal hears appeals from final decisions of the Board. Although in most cases this jurisdiction will be obvious, in many others the Tribunal has found that appellants are seeking a relief which does not meet the statutory direction of subs. 123 (1)(a), which requires that there be a "final decision" from the Board before the Tribunal may act. It is often, however, not always totally clear, on the face of the Board's final determination, what issues have been disposed of. The Tribunal has indicated it does not want to apply the jurisdictional restrictions in a mechanistic way and that all concerned seek to avoid a "ping pong" effect.

In addition to its function as an appellate body, subs. 123(1)(*c*) also gives the Tribunal originating jurisdiction in "such matters as are assigned". Such matters include s. 31 (formerly s. 17), The determination of a party's right to bring an action (see Chapter 10, Civil Actions) and ss. 57-59 (formerly s. 71), Adjudication in disputes involving a worker's refusal to allow an employer access to his or her claim file. The Tribunal also used to have jurisdiction over s. 23 (of the *Workers' Compensation Act*), Adjudication in disputes involving a worker's refusal to attend an employer requested medical exam. This jurisdiction is now repealed.

(c) Bill 99 Changes to Tribunal Jurisdiction

As noted, the pre-1997 Act continues to apply to pre-1998 injuries. The Tribunal's jurisdiction, however, is limited by s. 112 which repeals the structure and general jurisdiction found in the pre-1997 Act. In their place, the structure and general jurisdiction of Bill 99 apply. In particular, ss. 120, 123, 126 and subss. 174 (1) to (5) apply to both pre-1998 injuries and decisions and those that occur thereafter.

There are now also, for the first time in workers' compensation adjudication, time limits on appeal rights to the Tribunal. Section 125, a similar provision to s. 120, provides that an appeal from a (final) decision of the Board lies with the Tribunal "within six months after the decision or within such longer period as the tribunal may permit".

The Tribunal's initial review of the application of its s. 125 discretion was discussed in two decisions. In both the decisions the Panels noted that we were in the initial phase of the time limit era and suggested broad criteria to be applied in waiving the time limits.

Subsection 123(2) reduced some of the Tribunal's jurisdiction, providing that:

> ... the jurisdiction of the Appeals Tribunal under subsection (1) *does not include* the jurisdiction to hear and decide an appeal from decisions made under the following Parts or provisions:
>
> 1. Part II (injury and disease prevention).
> 2. Sections 26 to 30 (rights of action) and 36 (health examination). [As noted, jurisdiction for ss. 26 to 30 are granted directly by s. 31 (see Chapter 10). The Tribunal no longer has jurisdiction over medical examinations under s. 36.]
> 3. Section 60, subsections 62(1) to (3) and sections 64 and 65 (payment of benefits).
> 4. Subsections 81(1) to (6), 83(1) and (2) and section 85 (allocation of payments).
> 5. Part VIII (insurance fund).
> 6. Part XII (enforcement), other than decisions concerning whether security must be given under section 137 or whether a person is liable under subsection 146(2) to make payments.
>
> [Emphasis added.]

(d) Board Policy and the Tribunal

Subsection 126(1) provides that, "If there is an applicable Board policy with respect to the subject-matter of an appeal, the Appeals Tribunal shall apply it when making its decision." The Board is required to provide notice of which policy, "if any", applies to an appeal to the Tribunal.

There is a procedure for the Tribunal to notify the Board where it considers that a policy has not been provided. The Tribunal may also notify the Board if, in its view, the provided policy is not applicable or is inconsistent with, or not authorized by, the Act. At that point there is a statutory duty for the Board to reply to the Tribunal's concerns after hearing submissions from interested parties. At the end of this review process, "the Board shall issue a written direction, with reasons, to the tribunal that determines the issue raised in the tribunal's referral under subsection (4)".

At the time of this writing, the current Board practice is for its Legal Branch — not the Appeal Branch — to determine what the "applicable Board policy" is with regard to the particular decision under appeal.

The Board has now collected various policies together into "policy packages". The Tribunal is then notified of what policy package(s) apply in each case. It should be noted that this form letter does not list the actual topics of each package; rather, it notes that "A listing of the pertinent policies for each package has previously been forwarded to the Tribunal." The package numbers of that listing, however, have changed on numerous occasions and one should ensure that the cited policies are indeed the appropriate ones.

As of mid-1999, the formal mechanism of subs. 126(4) review has not yet been used and it is anticipated that such use will be limited. Rather, the Tribunal will request "clarification" or may simply find that there has been an "administrative error" where it is apparent to the Tribunal that such is the case.

Section 174 changed the structure of the Tribunal hearing. For all cases heard from January 1, 1998, the legislated preference will be for a single vice-chair — or the Tribunal chair — to hear appeals. Also, provisions now exist for the Tribunal Chair to appoint three-person Panels such as those who heard appeals prior to January 1998.

The Tribunal Chair has indicated that it would be "particularly useful" to exercise this discretion to appoint a three-person Panel in cases involving:

• Medical/scientific issues which have important workers' compensation implications;
• Novel legal interpretations;
• Significant credibility findings which may require a "jury-like" determination;
• "[A]ppeals in areas where tribunal caselaw is still developing...";
• Experiments in new hearing techniques; and
• Significant financial consequences for the system.

(e) Charter Issues

There have been a number of cases in which the Tribunal was asked to apply the *Canadian Charter of Rights and Freedoms*. Whether administrative tribunals are allowed to apply the *Charter* and whether they are required to, and in what way, are questions that obviously go far beyond workers' compensation matters. A series of Supreme Court of Canada decisions have ruled that administrative tribunals called upon to interpret law had "a duty to subject its enabling statute to *Charter* scrutiny".

In one case of interest the majority found that the Canadian Human Rights Commission was not mandated to determine questions of law. In concurring reasons by Chief Justice Antonio Lamer, he strongly argued that administrative tribunals do not have the authority to consider the constitutionality of their enabling legislation.

On the other hand, there is an equally strong dissenting opinion by McLachlin J., in which she argues that the *Charter* is not a "holy grail", but a document that "belongs to the people" and therefore:

> All law and law-makers that touch the people must conform to it. Tribunals and commissions charged with deciding legal issues are no exception. Many more citizens have their rights determined by these tribunals than by the courts. If the *Charter* is to be meaningful to ordinary people, then it must find its expression in the decisions of these tribunals.

In another Tribunal decision, the Supreme Court decisions on administrative tribunals and the *Charter* are reviewed and it is concluded that the Tribunal is the type of administrative tribunal that was called upon to interpret the law; the Tribunal is not a "court of competent jurisdiction", as contemplated by subs. 24(1) of the *Charter*; and, in the opinion of the Panel majority, it was still open to argue that, while the Tribunal had the jurisdiction to hear and decide *Charter* arguments, it also had the discretion to decline to hear them. In the particular case, in which an injured bank worker claimed that her *Charter* rights were abridged by the exclusion of banks from either Sch. 1 or Sch. 2, it was determined that the Tribunal did not have jurisdiction because this was not a question for which the Tribunal had a practical remedy; it was not simply a question of ignoring an exclusion and proceeding to adjudicate the case. It would have entailed a massive reorganization of a number of sections of the Act and Regulations, the total results of which were unknown.

As of this date, a number of other Tribunal decisions have considered the *Charter*, but none has upheld a challenge to the Act. The Supreme Court of Canada has now, in a split decision, also ruled that administrative tribunals may be "courts of competent jurisdiction", pursuant to subs. 24(1) "provided they have jurisdiction over the parties and the subject matter of the dispute and are empowered to make the orders sought". There is a strong dissenting opinion in which it is held that the significant differences between courts and tribunals require that the phrase "court of competent jurisdiction" apply only to a court in the traditional sense, and not to an administrative tribunal.

There has been only one Tribunal decision that has ruled on the merits of a *Charter* argument. In that decision it was held that the Board policy to recover an overpayment from a worker, who had been convicted of fraudulently obtaining benefits, was not "cruel and unusual treatment or punishment", as prohibited by s. 12 of the *Charter*.

The Supreme Court — including McLachlin J. who is the most sympathetic to administrative tribunal determination of *Charter* issues — has made it clear that the threshold required is that a tribunal be mandated to decide "questions of law". One might argue that the Appeals Tribunal is now statutorily prevented from determining questions of law, as s. 126 provides that the WSIAT shall apply "applicable Board policy with respect to the subject-matter of an appeal".

(f) WSIAT Procedures

As with the Board, subs. 131(2) empowers the Tribunal to "determine its own practice and procedure". Many of these practices are set out in a series of "Practice Directions" which are available through the Tribunal office. To date, the issues dealt with by these directions are illustrated in Table 25-2.

Table 25-2
Tribunal Practice Directions

Access to Workers' Files (1998), 44 W.S.I.A.T.R. 191
Determining the Tribunal's Right to Hear an Appeal of a Board Decision (1998), 44 W.S.I.A.T.R. 210
Transcripts of Board Hearings (1998), 44 W.S.I.A.T.R. 232
Applications for Leave to Appeal (1998), 44 W.S.I.A.T.R. 206
Post-hearing Procedure (1998), 44 W.S.I.A.T.R. 220
Applications Concerning the Right to Sue (1998), 44 W.S.I.A.T.R. 200
Reconsiderations (1998), 44 W.S.I.A.T.R. 221
Summonses (1998), 44 W.S.I.A.T.R. 230
Transcripts of Tribunal Hearings (1998), 44 W.S.I.A.T.R. 234
Inactive Files (1998), 44 W.S.I.A.T.R. 217
Fees and Expenses (1998), 44 W.S.I.A.T.R. 212

All practice directions are available at the Tribunal's web site: <http://wsiat.on.ca>.

The typical Tribunal appeal follows a somewhat different procedure than an appeal at the Board. Along with trying to balance informality and procedural fairness, the Tribunal is also faced with trying to balance an "appeal court" model with that of a totally *de novo* hearing. The result is a process that is somewhere between the two.

(i) The Tribunal Counsel Office

When the Tribunal started in 1985, it created the Tribunal Counsel Office (TCO), with the responsibility to review the information in the Board file, seek any further information which might be necessary for the determination of the issue, solicit input from the parties of record and prepare a "Case Record" to be forwarded to the parties. This Case Record is the major piece of documentary evidence at the hearing.

In the early years of the Tribunal, the TCO often attended hearings to make submissions on legal issues. That is now rare.

(g) Sections 57-59 — Access to Files

(i) To the Worker

As indicated above, the Board developed an access to files policy in late 1981. Bill 101 formalized most of that policy under the Act. Section 57 requires the Board to provide to a worker, upon request, a photocopy of his or her file when "there is an issue in dispute". Such access will also be provided to a worker's authorized representative.

This worker access is limited by subs. 47(4) which indicates that where "health or other information ... would be harmful to the worker to see", such information will not be provided. Instead, the information will be forwarded to either the worker's treating physician or his or her representative. This subsection flows from the original access policy of the Board which reserved the right to withhold, in particular, medical information unrelated to the claim. For example, if medical reports concerning a leg injury were to reveal a malignant tumour, and the worker was unaware of this, the Board felt that such information should not be made available through its files. This withholding of information is extremely rare.

(ii) To the Employer

Bill 99 provided a slightly different access regime for employers. Section 58 provides for non-appealable employer access to non-medical documents "about the claim as the Board considers to be relevant to the issue" or issues in dispute. Such information, where authorized, will also be given to the employer's representative, and the worker, or representative, shall be given the same documents.

The provision of *medical* information to the employer is addressed in s. 59. This section provides that the Board must notify the worker of any "report or opinion of a health care practitioner" that it intends to release to the employer. The worker (or claimant) may object to the disclosure of this information and the Board "shall consider the objection before deciding whether to disclose the report or opinion". The Board will then notify the parties of whether it plans to disclose the information, and the "worker, claimant or employer may appeal the Board's decision to the Appeals Tribunal and shall do so within 21 days" of this notice.

As with the pre-1997 Act, there is a requirement that employers not disclose any "health information" thus obtained. Section 150 provides that a violation of subs. 59(6) is an offence and subs. 158(1) provides that a person is liable, upon conviction, to a penalty of $25,000 and/or a jail term of up to six months, or if a "person is not an individual", to a $100,000 fine.

(iii) Access Issues

Most access appeals arise when a worker challenges an access decision of the Board without understanding that there are statutory access rights granted to employers. Inevitably, in these cases, the decision by the Board to grant access is upheld by the Tribunal. A number of substantive issues, however, have also arisen in Tribunal access decisions. These rulings include findings that the provisions of s. 71 supersede those in the *Freedom of Information and Protection of Privacy Act* and what constitutes "medical reports and opinions".

While the courts were to be left with the determination on a breach of the confidentiality in s. 71, one Tribunal decision should also be noted. In that case, the Board brought charges against an employer's representative, alleging a breach of subs. 71(8) (the access and confidentiality provisions under the pre-1997 *Workers' Compensation Act*) in that unedited information was provided to a consulting doctor. The case was dismissed because of a failure to identify that the offence occurred in Ontario. The majority of the Panel, however, found that there were enough concerns about how the report was obtained to lead it to the conclusion that the representative "knowingly and wilfully" obtained the report in violation of s. 71. The report was not admitted. A different result was found, however, in another Tribunal decision.

(h) The Tribunal Hearing Process

Recently, in response to a steady increase in its caseload, the Tribunal has adopted a variety of hearing processes, or streams. This section describes the "traditional" hearing process at the Tribunal.

(i) Pre-Hearing

The Tribunal compiles the Board file into a "Case Record" that is then sent to the "parties of record" (*e.g.*, the accident employer in a worker appeal) as well as any authorized representative(s). This material was formerly called a "Case Description" and included a brief narrative prepared by the TCO. The parties to the hearing, upon receipt of the Case Record, may add any further documents they consider relevant to the issue(s) in dispute through the TCO.

Routinely, in a worker appeal, the accident employer is notified of the appeal and invited to attend, whatever the issue. This notice arises from the direction of subs. 125(3).

A number of Tribunal decisions have considered the question of what constitutes a "party of record" and what rights such a party should have. In theory, the major criterion applied in the consideration of whether standing should be granted, is to ask whether the party seeking standing has an "interest" in the outcome of the matter. Given the explicitly bipartite nature of the Act, in practice the Tribunal has taken a very broad interpretation on the question of what constitutes interest and, therefore, whether standing should be granted.

In addition to this process, the TCO may do its own research into the case, including attaching relevant decisions made by the Tribunal, relevant decisions from other jurisdictions, medical literature on the issue, etc. All of this research is provided to the parties prior to the hearing. The TCO may also — on behalf of the Tribunal or at the request of one of the parties — issue subpoenas for witnesses who are considered necessary. As noted above, the Board is also required to notify the Tribunal of applicable policy.

Once all parties are satisfied with the material to be relied upon, a hearing date is set following consultation with the parties. Tribunal policy is that adjournments are not permitted except in exceptional circumstances.

The agreed upon material is then given to the Vice-Chair or Hearing Panel for review prior to the hearing. This Vice-Chair or Panel will have had no involvement in, nor knowledge of, the case prior to receiving this material. It will also have *only* the material agreed upon (*i.e.*, the entire Board file will not have been reviewed). Correspondence with the parties also indicates that any further material may not be considered by the Vice-Chair or Panel unless it is submitted three weeks prior to the hearing date.

(ii) The Hearing

At the hearing the following people will typically be present:

- The appellant;
- The other "party of record" (the employer or worker);
- Their representatives;
- The vice-chair or panel;
- The TCO counsel (he or she normally does not participate in the actual hearing unless there is a complex legal/policy issue involved).

The hearing is not subject to the *Statutory Powers Procedures Act*. The usual order of presentation (appellant first) is generally followed. Opportunity is given to the other party, the TCO (if present) and the Hearing Panel or Vice-Chair, to clarify the information given through "cross-questioning". However, an attempt is made not to be bound by strict rules of evidence, and intimidating or badgering cross-examination is not permitted.

Often, it will be determined that further information is required before a decision can be made. This is usually medical information from doctors who have already treated the worker. Sometimes the Vice-Chair/Hearing Panel will seek its own medical assessment, often through a doctor appointed pursuant to s. 134. In those cases in which further information is sought, the parties are given the opportunity to make post-hearing submissions on the evidence that is generated.

Once the evidence is in, and the arguments heard, the Vice-Chair/Hearing Panel will reserve its decision in all but exceptional cases. A numbered, written decision, with reasons, will then be sent to all participants. The decision will not mention the worker, the employer or any witnesses by name, except in right to sue cases.

(i) The Alternative Hearing Streams

With the increase in appeals, the Tribunal has tried a number of different hearing approaches in an attempt to expedite the appeal process. It is likely that those modified approaches will continue. Modified approaches may include:

* A fact-finding, mediation approach undertaken by members of the TCO, in conjunction with the parties. The resolution may be subject to Panel/Vice-Chair approval;
* Much earlier intervention by a Panel/Vice-Chair to rule on procedural or jurisdictional issues and to direct the gathering of further evidence, either by the TCO, or by the parties themselves;
* A variety of other approaches under the heading of alternate dispute resolution (ADR).

4. POST-APPEAL OPTIONS

The Appeals Tribunal represents the final authority in determining matters related to most areas of workers' compensation. Subsection 123(4) of the Act indicates that, "An action or decision of the Appeals Tribunal under this Act is final and is not open to question or review in a court".

Despite these words, which similarly applied to the Board before the institution of the Tribunal, there are a number of avenues nominally open to a dissatisfied appellant. It should be stressed that *all* these options carry a higher burden of proof and/or are extremely time-consuming.

(a) Office of the Ombudsman

At one time, workers' compensation problems were regularly at or near the top of the provincial Ombudsman's list. A complaint to the Ombudsman will be accepted only after the appropriate appeal processes have been exhausted. The Office of the Ombudsman will investigate the complaint by reviewing all the documentary information on file and often obtaining further information, particularly medical information.

The Ombudsman's office uses a number of criteria to determine whether it will support a complaint. In most cases, the test used is whether the complained-about decision was "reasonable".

Following the investigation, the Ombudsman will indicate whether he or she believes that the claimant's complaint about the decision is justified or not. If it is felt that the complaint is not justified, no further action will be taken. If the complaint is upheld, the Board or Tribunal will consider the recommendations of the Ombudsman, but are not in any way bound to implement them.

Even if the Ombudsman upheld a complaint, there was no guarantee that the decision would be reversed. Most cases that were supported by the Ombudsman, but still denied by the Board, were included in the Ombudsman's Annual Report, which was discussed by a Legislative Committee, entailing yet more delays. The Committee voted on the Ombudsman's recommendations and, by practice, the Board would then implement a Committee vote. To date, no Tribunal decision has gone as far as this Committee.

(b) Application to Reconsider

Section 129 of the Act provides the Tribunal can "reconsider its decision and may confirm, amend or revoke it".

The Tribunal has a two-step process for determining whether a decision should be reconsidered. The first step — the threshold question — is to determine whether the party seeking the reconsideration has raised persuasive reasons for *re-opening* the case. If so, the other party, if any, is asked to make submissions on whether the original decision itself should be *reconsidered*. Most applications fail at the threshold stage where, "The onus is on the applicant to persuade the [reconsideration] panel [or Vice-Chair] that it is advisable to reconsider the decision."

If a party is successful in meeting the threshold test, then the second stage involves a hearing on the merits of the case, either by the reconsideration panel/vice-chair, or by a new panel/vice-chair. It is possible that only one part of a decision may be reconsidered, rather than rehearing the whole case.

(c) Judicial Review

Judicial review of workers' compensation is definitely not as bleak a prospect as a strict reading of the privative clause may suggest. It should be stressed, however, that the restrictions are not nearly as superficial as many, who would look to the courts, would like.

A number of grounds, upon which the courts have proved sympathetic to judicially reviewing workers' compensation decisions, have developed over the years. These grounds include:

(1)   A denial of natural justice.
(2)   A decision that incorporates a "patently unreasonable" interpretation of a statutory direction.
(3)   A decision in which the decision-makers have "asked themselves the wrong question".

On all these grounds, however, the courts have generally set a fairly rigid test of error before they have intervened.

The Supreme Court of Canada has reaffirmed the position against judicial intervention in the decisions of administrative tribunals. In one case, a decision of the Quebec equivalent of the WSIAT had been overturned by the Quebec Court of Appeal on the grounds of resolving a conflict in statutory interpretation between the C.A.L.P. and the Quebec Labour Court. The Supreme Court held that when a decision is made within a tribunal's jurisdiction and is not patently unreasonable, the principles of curial deference should prevail even if there are conflicting interpretations. The Court noted, "a lack of unanimity is the price to pay for the decision-making freedom and independence given to these tribunals".

In another right to sue case, the court noted:

> It was within the exclusive jurisdiction of the Board [and now the Tribunal] to determine whether or not the applicant's right of action and right to recover damages is barred by the provisions of the *Workers' Compensation Act* ... The decision of the Board is not so patently unreasonable as to constitute a jurisdictional error.

Similarly, in another case, Finlayson J.A. indicated:

> ... I believe that the interpretations of the definition of "accident" made by the Appeal Boards in both cases is within the range of possible interpretations of "accident" and I am not persuaded that their interpretations of s. 1(1)(a) are so patently unreasonable that their construction cannot be rationally supported.

As of early 1996, some four dozen applications for judicial review of tribunal decisions had been decided. In every case, the court refused to interfere with the original Tribunal decision. In four of these cases, leave to appeal to the Ontario Court of Appeal was sought and denied. In one case, the Court of Appeal did grant leave, but refused to interfere. Leave to appeal this decision to the Supreme Court of Canada was dismissed.

(d) Section 93 of the Pre-1997 Act

While, technically, s. 93 was not intended to represent an appeal stage in any way, it provided the Board, in circumstances in which it considered a particular decision "turns upon an interpretation of the policy and general law of [the] Act", with the opportunity to review the decision and "direct the Appeals Tribunal to reconsider the matter in light of the determination of the [WCB] board of directors". The Board invoked s. 93 on two occasions.

In one decision review, the Board of Directors considered the Tribunal's interpretation of the word "accident" in s. 1, the general entitlement provision in subs. 4(1) and the presumption clause at subs. 4(3). The majority finding was that the Tribunal had incorrectly interpreted the term "accident". However, in the particular case, the majority Board of Directors did not "direct the Appeals Tribunal to reconsider", on the grounds that it was the first time that the section had been used and the worker had already suffered a lengthy and emotional procedure. At the same time the employer was relieved of any costs.

In another review a total of 25 Tribunal decisions were considered. These decisions dealt with chronic pain and the date from which chronic pain benefits should be payable.

The reconsideration Panel in another decision denied the Board of Directors' direction to reconsider. The Panel accepted that, in most instances, a Board of Directors' direction to reconsider required the Tribunal to do so. It was not necessary to meet a threshold test in the same way as in a typical reconsideration. (See earlier topic (b), Application to Reconsider.) It was still necessary, however, for the Board to meet some preliminary requirements, which were far less stringent.

All of the s. 93 chronic pain cases have now been finally disposed of by the Tribunal, and not one of these cases has resulted in a revocation of the original decision. Rather, it was determined in these cases that the original complaint was primarily organic in nature, not primarily chronic pain; the disability was a mixed organic and non-organic one, although without chronic pain; there had been no direction in the original decision to pay benefits prior to March 1986; the review decisions had been rendered without reasons and the limitation of benefits was contrary to the real merits and justice of the case; the original decision was based on psychotraumatic disability, not chronic pain; it was the Board that had erred in granting permanent partial disability benefits retroactive to 1983, in contravention of its policy; the worker was suffering from fibromyalgia, not chronic pain; and even if there was a difference between the Board and the Tribunal, which was arguable, that difference arose *after* the original appeal was heard.

Presumably, as a result of this ponderous process and because of the s. 126 direction to apply Board policy, the Board's authority to review Tribunal decisions was repealed.

Appendix 1

Glossary of initials, short forms and acronyms commonly used in workers' compensation context.

AA	- Appeals Adjudicator
AB	- Appeal Board
ACOCD	- Advisory Committee on Occupational Chest Diseases
AD	- Accident Date
ADL	- Activities of Daily Living
AE	- Accident Employer
AMA	- American Medical Association
_AO	- _____ Area Office; *e.g.,* Windsor Area Office
ARO	- Appeals Resolution Officer
BARC	- Back Assessment and Rehabilitation Clinic (at DRC)
CA	- Claims Adjudicator
CCU; CCU-D; CCU-I	- Complex Case Unit; Diseases/Injuries
CD	- Case Description
CJST	- Creative Job-Search Techniques
CLT	- Claimant
CPD	- Chronic Pain Disability/Disorder
C.P.P.	- Canada Pension Plan
CR	- Case Record
CRB	- Claims Review Branch
CW	- Caseworker (Vocational Rehabilitation)
D1	- Initial FEL Determination
DRB	- Decision Review Branch
DRC	- Downsview Rehabilitation Centre (formerly H&RC)
DRS	- Decision Review Services
DSM-III-R	- *Diagnostic and Statistical Manual of Mental Disorders* (3rd ed., revised)
ESL	- English as a Second Language
ESRTW	- Early and Safe Return to Work
FAE	- Functional Abilities Evaluation
FEL	- Future Economic Loss
FIRM	- Field Investigation Referral Memo (Form 630)
FLA	- Family Law Act
Form 6	- Worker's Report of Accident
Form 7	- Employer's Report of Accident
Form 8	- Physician's First Report
Form 26	- Physician's Progress Report

Form 42	- Worker's Progress Report
GECA	- Government Employees' Compensation Act
GVRA	- General Vocational Rehabilitation Assessment
HO	- Hearings Officer
H&RC	- Hospital & Rehabilitation Centre
I.A.V.G.O.	- Industrial Accident Victims Group of Ontario
ICD-9	- International Classification of Diseases (9th rev.)
ID and Reg	- Identification and Registration Section
IDC	- Inter-Divisional Communication
ID&D	- Industrial Disease and Dependants
IDSP	- Industrial Disease Standards Panel
IE; IW	- Injured Employee; Injured Worker
ISU	- Integrated Service Unit
LMR	- Labour Market Re-entry
LO	- Layoff/Laid off
LOE	- Loss of Earnings
LT	- Lost Time
LW	- Light Work
MMR	- Maximum Medical Recovery/Rehabilitation
MR	- Medical Rehabilitation
MVA	- Motor Vehicle Accident
NEL	- Non-Economic Loss
NFA	- No Further Action
NLT	- No Lost Time
NOC	- National Occupational Classification
OAS	- Old Age Security
OCDRC	- Occupational Chest Disease Review Committee
ODP	- Occupational Disease Panel
OEA	- Office of the Employer Adviser
OHSA	- Occupational Health and Safety Act
O.P.M.	- Operational Policy Manual
OWA	- Office of the Worker Adviser
PA	- Pensions Adjudicator
p.d.	- Permanent Disability
PI	- Permanent Impairment
PMA	- Pensions Medical Adviser
PPD	- Permanent Partial Disability
PSEM	- Psychological Social Evaluation Module (at DRC)
Q.P.P.	- Quebec Pension Plan
R1	- First FEL Review
R2	- Second FEL Review
RB	- Reinstatement Branch
RC	- Rehabilitation Counsellor/Caseworker
RCA	- Royal Commission on Asbestos

REC	- Regional Evaluation Centre
REO	- Reopen (claim)
RFE	- Ready for Employment (DRC discharge diagnosis)
RMA	- Regional Medical Officer
RO	- Regional Office
RTLW	- Return to Light Work
RTM	- Round Trip Memo
RTW	- Return to Work
SEB	- Suitable Employment or Business
SIEF	- Second Injury Enhancement Fund
SMA	- Section Medical Adviser
SPAD	- Strategic Policy and Analysis Division (of WCB)
SRAP	- Special Rehabilitation Assistance Programme
TA	- Technical Adviser
TC	- Team Co-ordinator
TCO	- Tribunal Counsel Office
TOJ	- Training-on-the-Job
TP	- Temporary Partial (Disability)
TS	- Temporary Supplement
t.t.	- Temporary Total Disability
U.I.	- Unemployment Insurance
UMA	- Unit Medical Adviser
VR	- Vocational Rehabilitation
VRS	- Vocational Rehabilitation Services
WBS	- Workers' Benefits System
WCAT	- Workers' Compensation Appeals Tribunal
WCB	- Workers' Compensation Board
WLS	- Wage Loss Supplement
WSIA	- Workplace Safety and Insurance Act
WSIAT	- Workplace Safety and Insurance Appeals Tribunal
WSIB	- Workplace Safety and Insurance Board

Appendix 2

Some common medical abbreviations used in workers' compensation cases. Space does not permit an explanation of the medical significance of these terms. Reference should be made to medical texts.

For other medical abbreviations, see M.F. Delong, *Medical Acronyms & Abbreviations* (Oradell, New Jersey; Medical Economics Company Inc., 1985); C.M. Logan and M.K. Rice, *Logan's Medical and Scientific Abbreviations* (Philadelphia: J.B. Lippincott Company, 1987).

AFDE	- Asbestos Fibre Dust Effect
BP	- Blood Pressure
CNS	- Central Nervous System
C/O	- Complain (s); (ed); (ing) Of
COLD	- Chronic Obstructive Lung Disease
COPD	- Chronic Obstructive Pulmonary Disease
CT; CAT	- Computerized (Axial) Tomography
Dx	- Diagnosis
EEG	- Electroencephalogram
EMG	- Electromyogram
FEV	- Forced expiratory volume
FEV_1	- Forced expiratory volume in one second
Hx	- History
,	- Left
MMPI	- Minnesota Multiphasic Personality Inventory
OT	- Occupational Therapy
ppm	- Parts per million
PT	- Physiotherapy
Px	- Prognosis
q.i.d.	- 4 times daily (Latin abbreviation)
quotid	- Daily (Latin abbreviation)
2	- Right
ROM	- Range of motion
Rx	- Prescription
SLR	- Straight leg raising
SOB	- Shortness of breath
SRAP	- Special Rehabilitation Assistance Program
STEL	- Short Term Exposure Limit
TLV	- Threshold Limit Value
Tx	- Treatment
WBC	- White blood count
WFL	- Within Functional Limits

Index